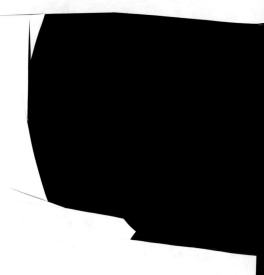

BLACKS IN THE AMERICAN WEST

The involvement of blacks at every point in the exploration, history, and ongoing life of the American West remains a little-known story. The books—both fiction and nonfiction—in this series aim to preserve these stories and to celebrate the achievement and culture of early African American westerners.

Henry O. Flipper

AS A CADET

THE COLORED CADET

AT

WEST POINT.

AUTOBIOGRAPHY

OF

LIEUT. HENRY OSSIAN FLIPPER,

U. S. A.,

FIRST GRADUATE OF COLOR FROM THE
U. S. MILITARY ACADEMY.

Introduction to the Bison Books Edition
by Quintard Taylor Jr.

UNIVERSITY OF NEBRASKA PRESS
LINCOLN AND LONDON

Library of Congress Cataloging-in-Publication Data
Flipper, Henry Ossian, 1856–1940.
The colored cadet at West Point / autobiography of Henry
Ossian Flipper.
p. cm.
Originally published: New York: Homer Lee & Co., 1978.
ISBN 0-8032-6890-4 (pbk.: alk. paper)
1. United States Military Academy.   2. Flipper, Henry
Ossian, 1856–1940.   3. Military cadets—New York (State)—
West Point—Biography.   I. Title.
U410.P1F6   1998
355'.0071'173—dc21
[B]
98-30001   CIP

Originally published in 1878 by Homer Lee & Co., New York.
Reprinted from the 1991 edition by Ayer Company, Publish-
ers, Inc., Salem NH. This Bison Books edition follows the
original in beginning chapter 1 on arabic page 7; no material
has been omitted.

INTRODUCTION

Quintard Taylor

Henry Ossian Flipper (1856–1940) emerged as one of the late-nineteenth-century West's most remarkable individuals. He considered his life's primary achievements to be his distinction as the first African American graduate of West Point and his subsequent four years as a cavalry officer. Following his court-martial and dismissal from the U.S. Army in 1882 for "conduct unbecoming an officer and a gentleman," Flipper spent over half a century in a vain attempt to restore his name and honor. Yet Flipper's postmilitary years, which were all but ignored in many accounts of his life, are equally exceptional and reflect a level of achievement that would have been impossible had he remained in the U.S. Army. The list of his accomplishments, many of them firsts for an African American, is impressive by any standard and period. During his postarmy years Flipper was a surveyor, cartographer, civil and mining engineer, interpreter, translator, historian, inventor, newspaper editor, special agent for the Justice Department, deputy U.S. mineral surveyor, aide to the Senate Committee on Foreign Relations, and consultant to the secretary of the interior, as well as executive for various mining and oil companies. His work carried him to northern Mexico, Venezuela, and Spain and ensured the success of some of the nation's first multinational corporations. Flipper's enormous talents allowed him to confront and surmount numerous barriers in an era when American racism was palpably apparent.[1]

Flipper, however, was no racial crusader and thus did

not generate the support or acclaim from much of the African American leadership that accompanied those of far more modest accomplishments. This was partly because Flipper's postmilitary achievements in the Southwest and northern Mexico were generally unknown or unacknowledged by the newspapers of the era. But Flipper remained estranged from the national black intelligentsia because he refused to transform his personal difficulties into a racial *cause celebre*. Indeed, in the beliefs he espoused, Flipper would easily be considered a neoconservative in some circles. Taking exception to a call for Congress to pass legislation to end racial discrimination at West Point, for example, Flipper declared, "I disdainfully [reject] the idea of such protection. If my manhood cannot stand without a government prop, then let it fall. If I am to stand on any other ground than the one white cadets stand upon, then I don't want the cadetship."[2]

Flipper's legacy was nonetheless ensured by his own actions. In 1878, one year after his graduation from the U.S. Military Academy, he published *The Colored Cadet at West Point*, which is herein reprinted. *The Colored Cadet* is, according to one historian, "one of the earliest authentic black autobiographies in American literary history and remains the most detailed chronicle of cadet education, customs, social life, and race relations at West Point during the 1870s."[3] Thirty-eight years later Flipper wrote a second autobiography, titled *Black Frontiersman: The Memoirs of Henry O. Flipper*, which covered the period after his graduation from West Point. These two works give contemporary readers enormous insight into this articulate, gifted, but troubled figure who never found complete acceptance in either the Euro-American or African American worlds.

Henry Ossian Flipper, the oldest of five sons, was born on March 21, 1856, in Thomasville, Georgia, to slave parents, Isabella Buckhalter and Festus Flipper. Until 1859

Isabella and her children belonged to Rev. Reuben H. Lucky, a Methodist minister, while Festus was the property of Ephraim Graham Ponder, a local slave-dealer and Thomasville city alderman. Thomasville was typical of many pre–Civil War Deep South communities. With 1,500 people, it was the prosperous county seat of Thomas County and the rural hub of large plantations and small farms, which produced cotton, corn, wheat, sugar cane, and tobacco. In 1860, four years after Flipper's birth, Thomas County had 4,522 whites and 6,244 slaves. Four hundred slaveowners resided in the county but only three owned more than a hundred slaves. Later, during the Civil War, Thomas County was the site of the notorious Andersonville Prison, where thousands of Union prisoners of war were incarcerated.[4]

Festus Flipper Sr. was born in 1832 in Guinea Station, Virginia, near Washington DC. The date of his arrival in Georgia is unknown but by the 1850s he was the property of James Ponder, who then sold Flipper to his nephew, Ephraim, for $1,180. Festus returned to Virginia frequently with the Ponders and was serving as an apprentice to a carriage repairer when Henry was born in 1856. Far less is known about Flipper's mother, Isabella Buckhalter. She was a native of Georgia who was described by her son as a mulatto with possible German ancestry. Despite his servile status, Festus Flipper, like other Ponder skilled slaves, was permitted to earn an income during his free time, working as a shoemaker and carriage repairman. "Mr. Ponder would have absolutely nothing to do with their business other than to protect them," recalled Henry Flipper years later. "These bonded people were virtually free. They acquired and accumulated wealth, lived happily and needed but two things to make them like other human beings . . . absolute freedom and education." Festus Flipper never gained freedom or education but with his personal savings he loaned Ephraim Ponder the money to purchase Isabella and their two children, Henry and Joseph, so that the Flippers could be united and accompany Ponder and his other slaves to the new family home in Atlanta.[5]

Following the outbreak of the Civil War in 1861 the fate of the Flipper family changed dramatically. The fortunes of marriage, however, affected their prospects as much as the fortunes of war. Shortly before moving to Atlanta, Ephraim Ponder married Ellen B. Gregory. "Beautiful, accomplished, wealthy," and fourteen years his junior, she took little interest in their life together. Henry Flipper called her the "dissolute" mistress of the Ponder household. Rumors of infidelity immediately surrounded Ellen Ponder and in October 1861 Ephraim filed for divorce. The couple separated at once, although the divorce proceedings continued for nearly a decade. Ephraim returned to Thomasville while Ellen remained in Atlanta with most of the Ponder slaves. Ellen retained possession of the slaves, but neither she nor Ephraim could sell them without the other's consent. Mrs. Ponder took scant interest in the slaves, allowing them to develop their varied business interests in Atlanta without interference. Moreover, in 1864, in blatant violation of Georgia law, she allowed one of her slave mechanics, John F. Quarles, to teach the younger slave children to read and write. Quarles, with only a rudimentary education, nonetheless opened a night school in the same workshop where he labored as a wheelwright during the day. Here, eight-year-old Henry Flipper gained his first exposure to reading, writing, and calculation, ironically by reading a Confederate reprint of Webster's *Blueback Speller*.[6]

By 1864 Sherman's army captured Atlanta, prelude to its fateful march to the sea that signaled the impending collapse of the Confederacy. As Federal forces approached Atlanta, Ellen Ponder and the slaves fled to Macon, Georgia. Sometime in December 1864 the Flipper family gained its freedom and by the following spring returned to a devastated Atlanta now occupied by the Second Massachusetts Infantry. Soldiers from the regiment assisted the family in moving into one of the few houses left standing. The Flippers soon found work with Union troops. Establishing a business out of their Decatur Street home, Isabella cooked for army officers while Festus repaired boots and shoes. As Union forces abandoned the city to returning civilians, Isabella operated out of her house one of the few restaurants in Atlanta. Compared with many of Atlanta's whites and most of the ex-slaves pouring into the city, the Flipper family was well off. They were part of a proud African American petite bourgeoisie emerging in the postwar city. One of their impoverished neighbors, the widow of a former Confederate captain, was hired to tutor the Flipper boys. She instructed the children, according to Henry, with remarkable condescension and for a small remuneration. Although he was ten when he learned to read and write, Flipper was already far ahead of most Georgia ex-slave children in education. By one estimate only 5,000 of the 462,000 Georgia slaves could read and write on the eve of the Civil War. Henry and his younger brother, Joseph Simeon, became part of that slowly growing minority.[7]

The Flippers' opportunities for learning soon increased due to the rising economic fortunes of their parents. Both Henry and Joseph took advantage of the early Reconstruction-era efforts to provide education for the ex-slaves. The boys excelled at the New England–sponsored American Missionary Society college for black youth in Atlanta, soon to be known as Atlanta University. There Flipper was taught by ex-slaves and northern white educational missionaries, the most prominent of whom was Edmund Asa Ware, a New England Congregational minister, Yale graduate, and guiding force behind the creation of Atlanta University. Joseph Simeon Flipper graduated from Atlanta University and eventually served as a director of a black-owned bank, president of Atlanta's Morris Brown College from 1904 to 1908, and bishop of the African Methodist Episcopal (A.M.E.) Church. Two of the younger Flipper sons, also exposed to postwar educational opportunities, prospered as well. Carl Flipper became a professor at Savannah State College and Emory became a physician. Festus Jr. followed his father's occupation and became a bootmaker in Savannah. Henry pursued a different course. In 1873, while a college freshman at Atlanta University, he received his appointment to West Point.[8]

Henry Flipper dated his interest in the U.S. Military Academy to the fall of 1872, when he overheard a conversation in his father's carriage workshop about a white cadet then at West Point who would soon graduate. Flipper decided to apply for the vacancy, motivated by his contact with Union soldiers and Northern abolitionist teachers in Atlanta as well as by his family's belief that education was the key to economic success. Flipper may have also realized that a military education was tuition-free and that cadets earned a stipend of forty-one dollars per month.[9]

Nineteenth-century appointments to West Point were subject to a curious combination of merit and political influence. Given the politics of Georgia at the time, only a Republican congressman would advance an African American candidate for consideration. The congressman representing Atlanta, James Crawford Freeman, a native of Griffin, Georgia, and a pre–Civil War Unionist who had opposed secession, seemed likely to make such an appointment. After the war Freeman had joined the newly formed state Republican Party and in 1872 was elected to Congress with heavy black support. Nonetheless, when Flipper wrote Freeman about his desire to attend West Point, the congressman was initially cool. "You are a stranger to me. . . . Give me assurance that you are worthy and well qualified and I will recommend you." In subsequent correspondence Freeman informed Flipper of the academy's various strict entrance requirements. "If . . . you think you can undergo the examination without doubt, I will nominate you. But I do not want my nominee to fail to get in."[10]

Meanwhile Freeman selected several men to examine Flipper's physical condition and mental ability. The congressman also gathered testimonials from Flipper's teachers, including Edmund Asa Ware, and from Dr. Thomas Powell, the family physician, before deciding to support Flipper's candidacy. On April 21, 1873, Powell examined Flipper and certified him as meeting the academy's physical requirements. Powell also administered an academic examination and declared Flipper, in the terminology of the time, "proficient." Upon satisfying himself about Flipper's motives and qualifications, the congressman six days later nominated the young man to Secretary of War William W. Belknap, who confirmed the appointment.[11]

Flipper was determined to enter the academy. He refused a five-thousand-dollar bribe from a white Atlantan attempting to gain admission to West Point for his own son. But Flipper was also well aware of the adamant opposition of white Democratic political leaders who were again politically ascendant in the state. He was prepared for an onslaught of negative press publicity, which soon came, and even refused to allow an Atlanta newspaper to publish a photograph with a biographical profile, fearing "some evil might befall me while passing through Georgia en route to West Point if too great a knowledge of me should precede me." Flipper's fears were hardly unfounded. In 1867 white ex-Confederate soldiers attacked a prosperous African American settlement on the outskirts of Atlanta, pillaging homes and stores. Festus Flipper was among those seized and severely beaten. Although understandably cautious, Flipper remained undaunted by the opposition to his appointment. "I have a due proportion of stubbornness in me, I believe, as all of the Negro race are said to have, and my [opponents] might as well have advised an angel to rebel as to have counseled me to resign and not go."[12] Flipper would need that stubborn courage to survive the challenges he would confront at the nation's oldest military service academy.

The U.S. Military Academy at West Point, New York, was created in 1802 to train officers to lead soldiers on the battlefield. However, the academy's initial academic focus provided for training in engineering. The philosophical and pedagogical underpinnings of the academy were established by Gen. Sylvanus Thayer, a West Point mathematics professor who was appointed superintendent in 1812. By the time of Flipper's arrival in 1873, the academy had developed a curriculum that emphasized French, Spanish, geology, chemistry, engineering, philosophy, and law, overlying basic instruction in military drill and tactics. Moreover, school policy after 1812 discouraged faculty from lecturing. Instead, each day students went to the instructor's desk, received assigned problems, recited their answers, and received evaluations. Thus a cadet's education was a combination of extensive memorization and applied knowledge.[13]

From the academy's founding, Congressional critics argued it was elitist, expensive, and superfluous in a democratic society. They repeatedly urged elimination of the institution and the transfer of its officer training responsibilities to state institutions. West Point fell under additional disfavor when large numbers of its graduates quickly joined the Confederacy after the outbreak of the Civil War. The academy survived the war but it would soon be tested by a new challenge, the admission of African Americans, including ex-slaves, who would presumably upon graduation be welcomed as "officers and gentlemen" by the all-white officer corps of the U.S. Army.[14]

Academy defenders such as Maj. Gen. John Schofield, the superintendent of West Point immediately after Flipper's years there, insisted the school could never become the propagandist of political, religious, or social theories of social equality. The institution reflected, he asserted, the prevailing social sentiment and practices of the nation. Social recognition of black cadets, he warned, could not be forced upon white cadets by official action. While Schofield insisted that the academy could not deny admission to qualified black nominees, he registered his reservations in the 1880 annual report on the institution. "To send to West Point for four years competition a young man who was born in slavery is to assume that half a generation has been sufficient to raise a colored man to the social, moral, and intellectual level which the average white man has reached in several hundred years. As well might the common farm horse be entered in a four mile race against the best blood inherited from a long line of English racers."[15]

Despite such attitudes African Americans did attempt to enter West Point. In the years between 1870 and 1887 twenty-seven African Americans were nominated for appointment to the academy. Twelve of this group passed the rigorous academic and physical examinations for admission, but only three black cadets—Flipper, John Hanks Alexander, and Charles Young—graduated and were commissioned as U.S. Army second lieutenants. Four African Americans preceded Flipper as cadets at West Point. All were eventually rejected upon presenting themselves at the academy or were dismissed after their arrival. By the time Flipper arrived in May 1873 only James Webster Smith remained. A native of Columbia, South Carolina, Smith was the first African American to enter West Point. He immediately encountered discrimination. During his first days at the academy he was refused a meal at the government-owned Rose Hotel frequented by cadets. Later, when white cadets taunted and hazed him, Smith responded by physically retaliating and reporting his harassment to the press, actions that intensified his ostracism and torment.[16]

Seventeen-year-old Flipper officially became a cadet on July 1, 1873, after passing a series of on-campus academic and physical examinations. Easily passing the academic examination that eliminated most black or white nominees, Flipper demonstrated a command of math and the rules of grammar and an extensive knowledge of U.S. and world geography and history. Flipper, who stood six feet, one inch tall and weighed 170 pounds, passed the rigid physical examination designed to eliminate candidates with infectious diseases, chronic illnesses, and minor deformities. However, like James Webster Smith, Flipper experienced harassment from the day he entered the academy. During his first day he was jeered by many of the cadets standing at their windows as he walked from the adjutant's office to his barracks. Flipper, who later roomed with Smith, received a letter upon his arrival from the South Carolina cadet imploring him to avoid the problems the older cadet had encountered. "It was a sad letter," Flipper recalled. "I don't think any thing has so affected me or influenced my conduct at West Point as its melancholy tone."[17]

Flipper and Smith eventually became friends and they were soon joined by another African American cadet, John Washington Williams of Virginia. Like Flipper, Williams did well on his preliminary examinations. However, on the semiannual reexamination six months later Williams was found deficient. Although Flipper tutored him, the cadet failed a subsequent examination and was dismissed. In June 1874 Smith failed one of his examinations and was also dismissed. Thus, one year after his arrival, Flipper became the sole black cadet at West Point. He continued to hold that distinction until August 23, 1876, when Johnson C. Whittaker of South Carolina was admitted. The difficulties of those cadets impressed upon Flipper both a rededication to succeed and the conclusion that his conduct in the face of insult mattered as much in his ability to succeed at West Point as his academic and physical capabilities.[18]

Flipper soon became the object of curiosity both on and

off the campus. His West Point autobiography recalled how he ignored giggling girls who often pointed out the "colored cadet." But Flipper's national audience could not be as easily dismissed. Flipper's presence at West Point insured him national notoriety. Much of the Northern press considered him a symbol simultaneously of racial progress and of the undermining of the elitism so long characteristic of West Point. Apparently few Northern editors knew of Flipper's disdain for his social inferiors. The Southern press heaped scorn and ridicule upon "the experiment," often delighting in exposing his treatment at the academy as evidence of Northern hypocrisy on race.[19]

Flipper was temperamentally suited to the U.S. Military Academy, with its emphasis on hierarchy, social class, and the code of gentlemanly honor. Like most of his fellow cadets, he believed himself intellectually superior to most Americans of the era, regardless of their racial background. He held in contempt impoverished, poorly educated Euro-Americans, whom he saw as the repositories of most racial prejudice. But he scorned equally African Americans who he believed were not prepared for social equality because of their low educational and cultural attainments. "Social equality . . . must be the natural . . . outgrowth of a similarity of instincts and qualities in those between whom it exists," he wrote in *The Colored Cadet*. While granting the existence of racial prejudice, Flipper quickly noted that "in the great majority of instances it is the mental and moral condition" of African Americans that prompted discrimination. "Little or no education, little moral refinement, and all their repulsive consequences will never be accepted as equals of education, intellectual or moral." Flipper then declared, "I have this right to social equality for I and those to whom I claim to be equal, are similarly educated." As one biographer has aptly noted, at West Point and through the remainder of his life, Flipper exhibited the manners of a Southern military aristocrat.[20]

Flipper's disdain extended to other cadets. Of his fellow African American cadets, he had little to say publicly. Privately he felt that those who preceded him had failed due to academic deficiencies and, equally, to their inability to accept the hazing and harassment they faced. He defended hazing, declaring, "It would simply be impossible to mold and polish the amalgamation at West Point without it." The African American press and black leaders criticized Flipper for abandoning his former roommate, James Webster Smith. Clearly subject to unfair treatment, Smith remembered the admonition of his father, Israel Smith, an ex-slave, a veteran of Sherman's army, and a Columbia, South Carolina, alderman, "Do not let them run you away, for then they will say the nigger won't do. Show your spunk and let them see that you will fight." Yet Flipper believed Smith brought much of the harassment upon himself by his belligerent attitude. After a physical altercation with another cadet, Smith was expelled from the academy upon the orders of President Ulysses S. Grant. When reporters asked Flipper's comments, he replied, "Of Smith, I prefer to say nothing." Later he privately wrote, "To stoop to retaliation is not compatible with true dignity, nor is vindictiveness manly." With his public abandonment of a fellow African American cadet whom he once considered a friend, Flipper earned the lifelong enmity of a significant segment of African American leaders.[21]

Flipper's feelings about the white cadets were more complex. He incorrectly assumed that the white cadets who shunned or ridiculed him were from working-class backgrounds, thus ratifying his own social prejudices. Yet given his belief in the privileges of rank, Flipper rarely challenged their actions if they were upperclassmen. Resisting the temptation to retaliate as other black cadets, notably James Webster Smith, had done and relying on the academy's ability to transform brawlers into gentlemen, Flipper fervently believed his quietude in the face of insults would eventually overcome their prejudices against him. "We must force others to treat us as we wish, by giving them such an example of meekness and of good conduct as will at least shame them into a like treatment of us. This is the safer and surer method of revenge."[22]

Regardless of his response, Flipper was sensitive to slights and was particularly hurt when they came publicly from fellow cadets who privately professed their admiration for him. Although appalled at their "want of backbone," Flipper invariably accepted their explanation that they could not act otherwise toward him for fear of being ostracized by racist cadets. Flipper, however, immediately responded to challenges to his rank privileges. When he was forced to march at the rear of a line behind lowerclassmen or move to another chapel pew following the objections of cadets of lower standing, he quickly brought these slights to academy authorities and was usually upheld in his protest. Ironically it was both his superiors (the faculty) and his inferiors (the servants) for whom Flipper had the kindest praise. In a comment intended to deflect the often reported remark that Flipper "never heard anything but the sound of his own voice," he betrayed his ambivalence about his isolation. "I always had somebody to talk to every single day I was at the Academy. Why, I was the happiest man in the institution, except when I'd get brooding over my loneliness."[23]

That loneliness emerged palpably through his writing. "I had not from October 1875 till May 1876 spoken to a female of any age . . . so absolute was my isolation." Since West Point operated on a year-long curriculum, he never visited Atlanta during his four years at the academy. However, Flipper was also never invited to a holiday dinner at the home of another cadet. Only once, during his senior year, did he venture to Philadelphia to celebrate the Centennial with a group of fellow cadets. Nor was he included in the usual revelry at nearby taverns or at the weekly dances. As someone who neither smoked nor drank, Flipper could easily dismiss his exclusion from the forays into the surrounding local taverns. He could not so easily dismiss other snubs. "A blow I may resist or ignore. In either case I soon forget it. But a sneer, a shrug of the shoulder mean more. Either is a blow at my sensitiveness, my inner feelings . . . which cannot be altogether forgotten. It is a sting that burns long and fiercely."[24]

On June 14, 1877, Flipper graduated from the U.S. Military Academy at West Point, fiftieth in a class of seventy-six, and assumed the rank of second lieutenant, U.S. Army. His classmates included Charles Gatewood, who would, a decade later, become famous for his role in the capture of the Apache Indian leader Geronimo; Wilbur Wilder, second in command of the 1916 Pershing Punitive Expedition in pursuit of Pancho Villa; John Bigelow, son of New York's secretary of state, who eventually became superintendent of Yosemite National Park in 1904; and Benjamin Butler, son of the prominent Civil War general, who became the postwar governor of Massachusetts.[25]

During the outdoor graduation ceremony, the graduates, their families, and friends heard from a number of speakers including Secretary of War James G. Blaine, Civil War hero Maj. Gen. Winfield S. Hancock, and Professor C. O. Thompson, president of the Board of Visitors. Flipper noted the applause that greeted him when he stepped forward to receive his degree, remarking that finally his classmates had acknowledged his presence. Later, in describing the congratulations he received from those who before had snubbed him, he wrote, "Oh how happy I was! I prized these good words of the cadets above all others. They knew me thoroughly. They meant what they said, and I felt I was in some sense deserving of all I received from them by way of congratulation. . . . All signs of ostracism were gone. All felt I was worthy of some regard, and did not fail to extend it to me."[26]

Flipper's success at West Point remained, in his view, his

singular achievement. That achievement soon made him a person of considerable fame in the national African American community. Flipper, as one historian has written, "was regarded—and regarded himself—as having in trust the reputation and, to an extent, the future prospects of the coloured races." His aloofness from the problems of other black cadets as well as from the national debate over African American citizenship rights in the Reconstruction era were temporarily forgotten as the West Point graduate was feted by prominent black leaders upon his triumphant return to Atlanta. Charles Redmond Douglass, son of abolitionist Frederick Douglass, sponsored a reception for Flipper in New York that was attended by two hundred people, including Rev. and Mrs. Henry Highland Garnett. Resplendent in a full dress-blue uniform with a heavy yellow horsehair plume over his cavalry helmet and a saber at his waist, the still shy Flipper refused to give a speech, protesting that he had been trained as a soldier rather than an orator. But by the time he reached Atlanta in July 1877, Flipper's oratorical skills had improved considerably, and for the next few weeks he was the most eagerly sought lecturer in the Georgia state capital.[27]

The August 11, 1877, reception in his honor at Atlanta's African Methodist Episcopal Church was typical of such engagements. Guests were charged twenty-five cents to see the first black West Point graduate, a price many were willing to pay since there was a standing-room-only crowd that included many prominent local African American residents, several white instructors at local schools and Atlanta University, and an assistant U.S. attorney. The reception entertainment included songs, readings, orations, and children's performances as well as a lecture by Rev. Joseph Flipper. Lieutenant Flipper was introduced by J. O. Wimbish, a leading local African American politician. The notoriety extended to Flipper excited anger and jealousy among Atlanta's conservative white establishment. "He talks at the reception and makes of himself an ass," declared the *Atlanta Constitution* bitterly in its report on the event, "the anomalous creature on exhibition—he shows the cloven foot."[28]

True to the Victorian standards of the day, Flipper recorded little about his personal life. One rare exception was his announced engagement in 1876 to Anna White, a woman he met four years earlier while both were students at Atlanta University. Anna broke off the engagement on the advice of Rev. Joseph Flipper, who warned that "Henry was not the marrying kind." Anna White's parents were also concerned that a marriage to a young army officer soon to be transferred to the West would produce a life of hardship and deprivation for their daughter. The couple's affection for each other remained, however, for the rest of their lives, and forty-one years later they renewed their engagement.[29]

On leave from June 15, 1877, to January 1, 1878, awaiting orders from the War Department, Lieutenant Flipper was assigned to Company A of the Tenth U.S. Cavalry, one of four all-black regiments. The Tenth Cavalry, organized in 1866 under Civil War hero Gen. Benjamin Grierson, famous for his six-hundred-mile, sixteen-day Union cavalry raid through Mississippi in April 1863, had by the late 1870s compiled a decade-long record of outstanding service in the U.S. Southwest.[30]

In December 1877 Flipper was ordered to Fort Sill, Oklahoma Territory, his first assignment with the Tenth Cavalry. Traveling by stagecoach, Flipper arrived at the outpost, nestled on a plateau at the foot of the Wichita Mountains, on New Year's Day, 1878. Flipper was assigned to "A" Troop, commanded by Irish-born Capt. Nicholas Nolan. Less than a month after his arrival, Flipper served with Nolan on a court-martial board. Flipper also served as "acting captain" of "G" troop for four months. In the fall Flipper was sent to the Wichita Indian Agency to inspect and receive cattle for the Indians. Here he encountered civilian prejudice for the first time when local cowboys complained that a "nigger officer" was there to inspect their cattle and moreover had received the only room in the local hotel. During his year at Fort Sill, Flipper supervised the building of a road from the Red River to Gainesville, Texas, directed the construction of telegraph lines throughout the region, and distributed food to Comanche and Kiowa Indians at a temporary camp in the Texas Panhandle. Later, while back at Fort Sill on temporary assignment in 1879, Flipper constructed a ditch that drained a series of nearby shallow ponds to reduce the breeding ground of malaria-carrying mosquitoes. The drainage system, now known as Flipper's Ditch, continues to control floodwaters and erosion in the Fort Sill area.[31]

Soon after Flipper arrived at Fort Sill, Captain Nolan married an Irish immigrant thirty years his junior, Annie Dwyer, and brought her and her younger sister Mollie to the Oklahoma Territory outpost. Flipper and Mollie Dwyer soon became friends and riding partners, the beginning of a platonic relationship that the young black officer claimed was the source of his subsequent problems with his fellow officers. Surprisingly, the public interracial friendship of a black officer and a white single woman did not immediately cause alarm. Flipper, after all, was invited to board with the Nolans and Mollie, which gave him the opportunity to become familiar with one of the few eligible young ladies at the post. Moreover, unlike his years at West Point, at Fort Sill Flipper was always included in post social affairs—picnics, parties, and miliary balls. In one particularly revealing episode at his second post, Fort Elliott, Flipper, who had declined his associates' party invitation and retired to his quarters, was awakened by an officer from the all-white Twenty-third Infantry, Lt. J. A. Maney, and his wife, who demanded he accompany them to the social affair. After persuading him to get dressed, Mrs. Maney insisted that he dance every square dance with her and the other women all night.[32]

Fort Elliott, an isolated outpost in the Texas Panhandle,

allowed Flipper for the first time to hone many of the skills that would support him during his postmilitary career. His first assignment required him to survey and map the sprawling military reservation. Soon afterward he was given responsibility for investigating an ammunition theft. Flipper led a five-man patrol to Tascosa, New Mexico Territory, where he discovered that the post's quartermaster sergeant was selling stolen ammunition to local cowboys. Flipper's investigation led to the sergeant's arrest, court-martial, and three-year prison sentence at Fort Leavenworth, Kansas. During the winter of 1879 Flipper supervised the construction of a telegraph line from Fort Elliott to Fort Supply, Oklahoma Territory.[33]

The next assignment, at Fort Concho in May 1880, in a more populated region of West Texas, introduced the young army officer to the cauldron of the state's racial politics. The U.S. War Department assigned most soldiers to western frontier defense outposts. While all-white regiments expected to be rotated between the frontier and more populated areas east of the Mississippi River, African American regiments remained on the frontier. The War Department rationalized that decision by arguing that African Americans' presence in eastern states, and particularly in the South, would prompt racial violence. "However senseless and unreasonable it may be regarded," wrote Gen. Christopher C. Auger, commander of the Department of the South in 1879, ". . . a strong prejudice exists at the South against colored troops."[34]

Texas, however, the only state that experienced both Reconstruction-era violence and frontier warfare, was a particular problem for African American soldiers. They epitomized the hated occupation of the state, generating the animosity of white civilians that lasted decades. In 1866, following the killing of two African American privates by the deputy town marshal of Jefferson, Texas, Gen. Phil Sheridan, military commander of Union forces in the Southwest, took no action, concluding that "the trial of a white man for the murder of a freedman in Texas would be a farce." Although African American soldiers comprised nearly half of the federal garrison in Texas during the entire Reconstruction era, the racial prejudices of white Texans forced them, by 1869, to be assigned to the West Texas frontier rather than eastern Texas, where anti-black violence reigned.[35]

Two episodes at San Angelo, Texas, near Fort Concho, a decade later suggest the situation Flipper was about to enter. In 1878 white cowboys and buffalo hunters in a San Angelo saloon humiliated a black sergeant by removing his stripes. Angry troopers from Fort Concho stormed the saloon in retaliation and in the subsequent gunfight killed one of the hunters. Nine troopers were indicted for murder and one, William Mace, was condemned to death. But when sheepherder Tom McCarthy killed unarmed Tenth Cavalry private William Watkins in a San Angelo saloon in 1881, he was indicted for murder, transferred to Austin for trial, and promptly acquitted. After repeated confrontations with civilians, the soldiers of the Tenth Cavalry issued an anonymous warning, "We, the soldiers of the U.S. Army do hereby warn the first and last time all citizens and cowboys, etc., of San Angelo and vicinity to recognize our right of way as just and peaceable men. If we do not receive justice and fair play, which we must have, some one will suffer—if not the guilty then the innocent. It has gone too far, justice or death."[36]

Civilian-soldier tension, however, was secondary to the more immediate problem confronting Flipper's troop upon its arrival at Fort Concho—the capture of a band of Mescalero Apaches under a brilliant leader, Victorio. Vowing he would die before submitting to confinement on the Fort Stanton Reservation in New Mexico Territory, the Mescalero chief led a desperate group of one hundred Apaches in a year-long attempt to gain freedom and sanctuary along the Rio Grande border region. Within two weeks of Victorio's flight from Fort Stanton in 1879, his followers' confrontations with civilians and with military pursuers resulted in seventeen deaths, including eight troopers of the all-black Ninth Cavalry. Victorio's initial success prompted the War Department to deploy virtually all of the cavalry in West Texas, New Mexico, and Arizona to apprehend his band.[37]

Flipper's Tenth Cavalry troop joined in the pursuit of Victorio over twelve hundred miles across West Texas and New Mexico. When informed that the Apaches had crossed the Rio Grande, Flipper rode ninety-eight miles in twenty-two hours to bring the information to Colonel Grierson at Eagle Springs, Texas. Upon reaching Grierson's headquarters, the young officer presented his message and collapsed upon the ground. His dedication to duty generated a lasting impression on Grierson, who remained a supporter of Flipper through his court-martial. On July 30 Flipper came under hostile fire, for the only time in his brief Army career, when buffalo soldiers and Victorio's warriors engaged in a five-hour battle. Flipper presided over the funeral of three of his troopers killed in battle. The Victorio campaign ended on October 14, 1880, when the Apache leader and most of his followers were killed at Tres Castillos by Mexican troops.[38]

Flipper and his men were now ordered to a new post, Fort Davis, Texas. Partly in recognition of his battlefield accomplishments, post commander Maj. Napoleon Bonaparte McLaughlen immediately assigned Flipper to be Fort Davis's quartermaster and commissary agent. As quartermaster he was responsible for all military property and for the hiring of civilians for post jobs. As commissary agent he controlled the sale of military rations and a variety of foodstuffs to officers, enlisted men, and civilians near the fort. With these combined duties, the twenty-four-year-old officer assumed supply responsibility for the entire Fort Davis military reservation—food, clothing, housing, water, fuel, transportation, and equipment for both soldiers and their animals. Although he had no training for the enormous bureaucratic paperwork required of the two positions, Flipper discharged his duties to the satisfaction of his commanding officer. Unfortunately for Flipper, Major McLaughlen would be replaced on March 11, 1881, by a new commanding officer, Lt. Col. William Rufus Shafter.[39]

Flipper's social life also became more troubled after reassignment to Fort Davis. He continued his good relationship with Captain Nolan, who had designated him as post adjutant—the ranking officer on his staff at Fort Elliott. As a persecuted Irishman, Nolan once remarked he shared a bond of suffering with "the oppressed Negro race." Other officers, however, grew notably cool to Flipper. Years later Flipper concluded that his ongoing relationship with Mollie Dwyer was the reason. Although they continued their horseback rides through the countryside, Flipper now found a rival for Mollie's attention in fellow officer Lt. Charles Nordstrom. In order to win her favor, Nordstrom purchased a luxurious riding buggy. Impressed with the gesture, Mollie ended her rides with Flipper. Writing bitterly in his memoirs, Flipper disparaged Nordstrom as an uneducated Swede from Maine, a product of the Civil War army who "hated me and gradually won Miss Dwyer from her horseback rides with me." Dwyer married Nordstrom after Flipper was dismissed from the Army. The bitter rivalry between Flipper and Nordstrom, who shared quarters but did not speak to each other, divided the Fort's officer corps as well. On New Years Day, 1881, Flipper received only one guest in his quarters, Lt. Wade Hampton, the nephew of the Confederate Civil War hero and post-Reconstruction governor of South Carolina. Given the growing concern over the extended breach of racial etiquette by Dwyer and Flipper, not surprisingly, most officers sided with Nordstrom. Also not surprisingly, Flipper became increasingly convinced that his professional difficulties, culminating in his court-martial, grew from his personal rivalries.[40]

Lieutenant Colonel Shafter, who inherited the command at Fort Davis, was well known in army circles as "notoriously coarse, profane, and harsh with his junior officers." A former commander of the all-black Twenty-fourth Infantry Regiment, by the time of his arrival at Davis he led the all-white First Infantry. Shafter's opinion of Flipper when he arrived at Fort Davis is unknown. However, in 1875 he relieved Nicholas Nolan of his command and attempted to bring court-martial charges against him until Colonel Grierson intervened.[41]

Soon after he arrived Shafter allowed Flipper to continue as post quartermaster but promised to relieve him of commissary responsibilities as soon as he had an officer to replace him. For the next two months Flipper's performance was exemplary. He collected weekly accounts and presented them to the post commander for verification and approval before the funds were forwarded to Maj. M. L. Small, the commissary officer of the Department of Texas, headquartered at San Antonio. When Small announced in May 1881 that he would be on a one-month leave of absence, Flipper decided, unwisely as subsequent developments would illustrate, to store the collected funds in a locked trunk in his quarters. Later Flipper would adamantly claim, and Shafter would emphatically deny, that the commanding officer ordered him to store the funds in his private quarters rather than in the quartermaster's vault. Inexplicably, Shafter ceased conducting his weekly fund examination from May 28 to July 8, 1881, and allowed Flipper to keep the funds in his apartment.[42]

Flipper held the funds in a trunk he shared with his servant, Lucy Smith. He compounded that error, however, by carelessly leaving checks and cash lying around his apartment and by extending loans and credit to some of his enlisted men and to Fort Davis business owners. When Colonel Shafter ordered Flipper to prepare an audit of the commissary fund, the second lieutenant discovered a discrepancy of $1,440 in what should have been a $4,000 accounts receivable balance. Wishing to "avoid giving [Shafter] any knowledge of my embarrassment," Flipper wrote a personal check for the missing money drawn upon the San Antonio National Bank, although he had no account there at the time. He then falsely indicated in his ledger that the funds had been transmitted to the commissary office in San Antonio. When Major Small telegraphed Fort Davis that no funds had been received, Colonel Shafter relieved Flipper of his duties as commissary officer on August 11. Two days later Shafter order Lieutenants Louis Wilhelmi and Frank H. Edmunds to search Flipper's apartment and upon finding anything suspicious, arrest him. Confident of his innocence and that all funds except the $1,440 would be located in his apartment, Flipper accompanied the officers to his quarters and cooperated fully with the search. When their search turned up only $1,717 in cash, checks, and coins, the discrepancy now totaled $2,074. Shafter relayed the search results to Army headquarters in San Antonio, concluding tersely, "Flipper has stolen."[43]

Flipper was arrested, charged with embezzlement, and confined to a sweltering six-and-one-half- by four-and-one-half-foot cell in the post guard house. This humiliation of a junior officer incited indignation across the United States. In Washington both Secretary of War Robert Todd Lincoln and General of the Army William Tecumseh Sherman concluded that racial prejudice accounted for Flipper's extraordinary treatment. Sherman telegraphed Brig. Gen. Christopher C. Auger, commander of the Department of Texas, saying, "Both the Secretary of War and the General of the Army require that this officer must have the same treatment as if he were white." Auger in turn ordered Shafter to "arrange for [Flipper's] security by providing a place other than the guard house."[44]

Meanwhile Shafter and his officers continued to search

for the missing funds, the colonel increasingly focusing his attention on Lucy Smith, Flipper's servant. Persuaded by the discovery of personal clothing of the officer and his servant in the same trunk, Shafter concluded that Lucy was Flipper's mistress and confidant in a scheme to steal government funds. He interrogated her on August 15 and had her bodily searched by another female servant in a nearby room. This inspection revealed $2,800 in Lucy's clothing, including Flipper's $1,440 check in her blouse. Unconvinced by her claim that she was hiding the money from a dishonest associate, Shafter arrested her for theft of government property and set her to the county jail in Presidio.[45]

On September 3, Gen. C. C. Augur signed Special Order #108, which created a court to hear evidence against Flipper. Two charges were leveled: embezzlement of $3,791 between July 8 and August 13, 1881, and "conduct unbecoming an officer and gentleman." The trial of 2d Lt. Henry Ossian Flipper began on September 17, 1881, in the post chapel, which had been converted into a courtroom. Upon entering the building Flipper surely pondered his rapid reversal of fortune. Three months earlier he had served as judge advocate of a general court-martial at Fort Davis. The court panel then included four fellow officers, Captains Kinzie Bates and Charles Viele and Lieutenants Frank Edmunds and Louis Wilhelmi, all of whom would now testify against Flipper in his own court-martial. Proceedings were postponed, however, for nearly two months, first because weather problems delayed the arrival of the prosecutor, Capt. John W. Clous, a German-born officer of the Twenty-fourth Infantry who also served as judge advocate of the Department of Texas, and second to give Flipper time to raise money to hire legal counsel. His urgent appeals for financial assistance to prominent African Americans in New York, Boston, Philadelphia, and Washington DC were unsuccessful. Moreover, no civilian lawyer would accept the case for less than $1,000. "Depressed [and] helpless, Flipper resigned himself to fight yet another battle in his life alone."[46]

Flipper's prospects soon improved. Civilian friends near Fort Davis raised $1,700 in twenty-four hours and eventually repaid all of the missing money before the court-martial began, thus lessening the pressure for conviction on the embezzlement charge. Fort Davis merchant J. B. Shields, who contributed $50, claimed, "plenty of other citizens [would] have contributed, but it happened at a very dull time, when very few except the storekeepers had any money. . . . I liked the man and tried to help him if I could." On November 1, 1881, Col. Benjamin Grierson wrote to the court-martial panel, attesting to Flipper's bravery and integrity. Grierson declared that despite his arrest, Flipper's "character and standing as an officer and gentleman was beyond reproach" and added that his opinion was shared by fellow officers Gen. J. W. Davidson (Flipper's commander at Fort Sill) and Capt. Nicholas Nolan. Flipper also received a last-minute offer of legal counsel from Capt. Merritt Barber, an attorney assigned to the Sixteenth Infantry. Barber defended Flipper without pay since Army regulations prohibited military lawyers from charging for their work. Convinced of Flipper's innocence, Barber offered an inspired defense of the young lieutenant.[47]

On November 1, 1881, the first testimony was entered in a trial the nation would eagerly follow. The government set out to prove Flipper's intent to embezzle funds. Its case was difficult from the outset since it had to present persuasive evidence that Flipper converted to his own use or destroyed missing checks. Through the thirty-day trial Judge Advocate Clous failed to prove that Flipper had stolen the money. Defense attorney Barber easily undermined the credibility of Clous's principal witnesses, Colonel Shafter and Lieutenant Wilhelmi, showing the former to be derelict in his supervisory responsibilities over the commissary account and the latter to hold a personal animus against the accused. Lucy Smith's testimony, which both sides hoped would bolster their case, was inconclusive. Smith portrayed herself as a naive, dim, easily intimidated servant, playing to the stereotypes of the era. In doing so, she succeeded in removing herself from culpability.[48]

If the government had difficulty proving that Flipper knowingly embezzled funds from the commissary account, defense attorney Barber failed to discredit the second charge, engaging in conduct "unbecoming an officer and gentleman." The charge, taken from the Sixty-first Article of War, could result in an officer's dismissal from the service. Certainly Flipper's carelessness and "gross neglect of duty" in monitoring the commissary funds could be considered proof of the second charge. But more serious was his intentional misrepresentation to his commanding officer. Flipper assured Colonel Shafter on August 10 that he had followed Shafter's order to send the commissary funds to San Antonio, "well knowing the same to be false," and his check for $1,440 on a nonexistent bank account in San Antoino was "fraudulent and intended to deceive" his commanding officer. As one skeptical historian wrote, Flipper was not, as he claimed years later, the victim of a "cunning trap" or "nefarious scheme." Instead he "lost his [commission]—almost tossed it away—by his own youthful follies, aggravated to a fatal degree by his own repeated errors of judgement."[49]

After deliberating for several hours the court-martial panel found Lieutenant Flipper innocent of embezzlement but guilty of "conduct unbecoming an officer and gentleman" and sentenced him to be dismissed from the service. As was standard in such cases, the verdict was reviewed by the judge advocate of the army, the secretary of war, and finally the president. Acknowledging the severity of the charges, Judge Advocate General David G. Swaim nonetheless recommended a reprimand rather than dismissal to Secretary of War Robert Todd Lincoln, who in turn passed the recommendation forward, without comment, to President Chester A. Arthur. The president responded on June 14, "The sentence in the foregoing case of Second Lieut. Henry O. Flipper 10th Regiment of U.S. Cavalry, is hereby confirmed." Sixteen days later, on June 30, 1882, Flipper was dismissed from the U.S. Army.[50]

Humiliated and dishonored, Flipper moved to El Paso, where he found a job as a clerk in a steam laundry. Yet in 1883 Flipper embarked on the first of a series of professional opportunities that would earn him a permanent place in the history of the American Southwest. That fall he joined a former Confederate officer, A. O. Wingo, in Chihuahua, Mexico, as a surveyor for American mining companies holding Mexican lands. In 1886, when the surveying job ended, he remained in Chihuahua compiling maps of northern Mexico for a Mexican banking firm, Banco Minero. Later that year Flipper was named chief engineer for the Sonora Land Company of Chicago, and in 1887 he opened a civil and mining engineer office in Nogales, Arizona Territory. A Flagstaff newspaper, the *Arizona Champion*, commented on the thirty-one-year-old former army officer's "distinguished arrival" in Nogales, a border town of fifteen hundred people. While there Flipper soon became a confidant of two prominent local residents, Jesse Grant, son of President Ulysses Grant, and *Nogales Sunday Herald* publisher J. J. Chatham, who left him in charge of the paper for six months. Flipper thus was the first African American to edit and publish a newspaper for a Euro-American community. Afterward he returned to the more familiar field of mine engineering, working as chief engineer for the Altar Land and Colonization Company in Nogales from 1890 to 1892. However, it was his role in the Nogales de Elias land grant controversy in 1892–93 that earned him the admiration of his neighbors.[51]

In 1892, when the residents of Nogales were informed that the United States was going to formally recognize legally documented Mexican land grants, three lawyer-speculators, Santiago Ainsa, George Hill Howard, and Rochester Ford, claimed that the Nogales de Elias grant, which they controlled, included the entire town of Nogales and the surrounding countryside. Several Nogales residents hired Flipper to ascertain if the grant was legitimate and covered the property they thought they legally owned. From documents in Mexican archives Flipper determined that the Elias grant not only failed to encompass their community but ended one mile south of the U.S.-Mexican border. Supported by Flipper's data, the landowners filed the Los Nogales de Elias case in the Court of Private Land Claims in Tucson on August 15, 1892.[52]

Testifying in the case, Flipper dismissed a fraudulent survey marker monument. "I don't think it is a monument at all," he declared, "I don't think it ever was." Flipper then noted that he had found another just twenty steps to the northeast. "They are recent monuments beyond any question," he concluded. "I never saw any monuments like that anywhere in Mexico." In December 1893 the case was settled in favor of the citizens of Nogales, allowing them to retain control of their property. Flipper was hailed a local hero, having saved over seven hundred thousand acres from falling into the hands of speculators, and feted at a town banquet. The December 17 *Nogales Sunday Herald* announced, "Lieut. Flipper rendered Nogales people excellent service," while rival newspaper the *Oasis* proclaimed, "Long live Flipper."[53]

His crucial role in the Elias case and his familiarity with Spanish and Mexican land and mining laws brought Flipper to the attention of U.S. Attorney Matthew G. Reynolds, who in 1893 hired him as a special agent with the Court of Private Land Claims formed by the U.S. Justice Department. The court was created by Congress in 1891 to determine the titleholders of a large number of

Spanish and Mexican land grants in Arizona and New Mexico. For the next eight years Flipper researched the Mexican archives, translated thousands of documents, surveyed land grants throughout southern Arizona, and prepared court materials. In the course of this work he translated and arranged, and the Justice Department published, a collection of Spanish and Mexican laws dating from the sixteenth century to 1853. U.S. Attorney Reynolds, in his final report, praised the former army officer: "During the seven years Mr. Flipper was connected with this office, his fidelity, integrity and magnificent ability were subjected to tests which few men ever encountered in life. How well they were met can be attested by the records of the Court of Private Land Claims and the Supreme Court of the United States." [54] In 1898 Flipper accompanied Reynolds to Washington DC to assist him in arguing cases before the U.S. Supreme Court. During this period he also worked as deputy U.S. mineral surveyor for Arizona and New Mexico.

It was during the Nogales years that Flipper first exercised yet another of his myriad talents, becoming an amateur historian. His knowledge of Spanish, his various assignments as researcher and translator in Mexico, and his intellectual curiosity combined to propel Flipper's interest in southwestern and Mexican history and folklore. His first scholarly article, *Did a Negro Discover Arizona and New Mexico?* appeared as a privately printed monograph in 1896. Based on primary research, Flipper's account presented the first English translation of Pedro de Castañeda's account of the 1539 Marcos de Niza expedition from Mexico City to what is now Arizona and New Mexico. Flipper, consequently, became the earliest scholar to claim that the African-born slave Esteban, while serving as an advanced scout for the de Niza expedition, became the first non-Indian to enter the U.S. Southwest. "There is no possible doubt," he wrote, "that the Negro Stephen [Esteban] was the first foreigner to tred upon what are now the Territories of Arizona and New Mexico. To him belongs the honor of having discovered them." While conducting research on the region, Flipper noted the presence of other persons of African descent among the early Spanish explorers. His study concluded that "there were Negroes in Florida, Texas, Arizona, New Mexico, and Kansas nearly a century before the Anglo Saxon set foot upon the North American continent."[55]

Flipper continued to write southwestern history for the next two decades. His "Early History of El Paso," published in 1914 in *Old Santa Fe*, illustrates his extensive use of Mexican and Spanish documents to reconstruct the history of the first European settlers of the region. Ever conscious of the historian's ongoing responsibility to locate additional documentary sources, Flipper concluded his article with these words: "The writer is constantly looking for other links in the chain and confidently hopes to fill the gaps. . . . It is slow work but exceedingly interesting."[56]

Flipper also contributed to southwestern folklore, writing extensively about the lost silver mine of Tayopa in northern Mexico. In perhaps one of the strangest episodes of his career, mining magnates William Randolph Hearst and William Cornell Greene, convinced that he was the investigator most likely to find Tayopa, sent Flipper to the Archivo General de las Indias in Seville, Spain, in 1911 to research the location of the fabled mine. The archives yielded unsatisfactory results, prompting Flipper to conclude, "The only definite thing that all my researches in Spain netted was a traveling direction."[57]

In 1901 Flipper returned to Mexico, where President William Gibbs McAdoo of the Balvanera Mining Company hired him as resident engineer for company mines in western Chihuahua. McAdoo sold Balvanera four years later and entered politics, eventually becoming U.S. secretary of the treasury in the Woodrow Wilson administration and later U.S. senator from California. Balvanera's new owner,

"Colonel" William Cornell Greene, incorporated it into his Green-Gold Company, a vast copper-, gold-, and silver-mining empire on both sides of the U.S.-Mexican border. Flipper remained Greene's employee and soon met the individual who would eventually become his principal mentor, company vice president Albert Bacon Fall. The New York–based Sierra Mining Company purchased Greene's firm in 1908 and Flipper remained with the new firm as resident engineer. Nonetheless, he and Fall continued their friendship. In March 1912, two years after the Mexican Revolution began, Flipper and other U.S. citizens were evacuated to El Paso. Upon his arrival Flipper wrote Albert Fall, wishing him success in his campaign to become one of New Mexico's first U.S. senators. Fall, a Republican, won the seat in November, providing Flipper his most powerful voice in his ongoing campaign to clear his name and record.[58]

From 1912 to 1919 Flipper, working from the Sierra Mining Company's El Paso office, dispatched information from Mexican mine caretakers to company headquarters in Chicago. Flipper also apprised Senator Fall of the political situation in Mexico. Flipper's dispatches illustrated his support of conservative, pro–foreign investment leaders such as the then recently deposed Mexican dictator Porfirio Díaz and his successor Victoriano Huerta. But Flipper's politics also flowed from his own long-standing prejudice against people with little formal education. Like the mineworkers he supervised, most Mexicans were illiterate and thus, according to Flipper, incapable of self-government. In a 1913 letter to Fall he wrote: "We know the Mexicans are barbarous; we have not just now learned it nor did it require the assassination of [Francisco] Madero to convince us of it. It is not a new development in their character but simply another manifestation of it." Flipper had no sympathy for the revolutionary leaders, such as Emiliano Zapata or Venustiano Carranza, who called for sweeping political and economic reform. Instead, urging the restoration of dictatorship, he anticipated that as soon as the government was powerful enough to "chop off heads without scruple" the Mexicans would settle down to peaceable pursuits. Thus Flipper was understandably shocked when in 1914 he learned of an article in the *Boston Advertiser* describing him as a military advisor to revolutionary leader Francisco (Pancho) Villa. Elsewhere Flipper had characterized Villa as a "proven bandit, rapist, looter murderer and assassin" and implored the U.S. government to recognize his political opponent, Huerta. The articles claiming his sympathy with Villa continued into 1915 and 1916, prompting Flipper to write a rebuttal from El Paso in 1915 and to send angry letters and threaten libel suits against editors who continued to run such stories.[59]

Throughout his postmilitary career Flipper attempted to gain vindication for what he considered his unfair dismissal from the U.S. Army. In 1898, after unsuccessfully attempting to enlist Booker T. Washington's aid, he met Barney M. McKay, a former Ninth Cavalry sergeant who persuaded Wisconsin congressman Michael Griffin to introduce the first of a series of bills designed to restore Flipper to the military's roster. McKay, Flipper recalled, "held interviews with Congressmen, took me to call on Congressmen" to plead his case. When Griffin's bill died in committee, McKay convinced Maryland congressman George A. Pearre and Kansas senator Lucien Baker to introduce legislation into their respective chambers, again with each measure failing to emerge from committee. Congressmen from New Mexico and Ohio introduced subsequent bills, which met the same fate. Meanwhile Flipper returned to Washington once a year between 1898 and 1901, continuing his crusade to obtain restoration to duty at the rank he would have attained had he remained in the Army.[60]

In 1919 Senator Fall summoned Flipper to Washington to serve as translator and interpreter for his subcommittee of the Senate Committee on Foreign Relations, then investigating political affairs in postrevolutionary Mexico. Flipper served Fall in that capacity until 1921. After Warren G. Harding was elected president, he appointed Fall as U.S. interior secretary on March 5, 1921. On the same day Fall hired Flipper as his special assistant in the Alaska Engineering Commission. Officially Flipper's job was to oversee the locating, building, and operating of Alaska railroads. In fact sixty-five-year-old Flipper used the position to exploit what seemed to him the last opportunity to clear his name. Flipper prepared and printed his own fifty-one-page statement seeking to be restored to the rank of second lieutenant and placed on the retirement list. While Flipper's legal counsel was former Minnesota senator Moses Clapp, Washington senator Miles Poindexter introduced another bill on Flipper's behalf. When the Committee on Legal Affairs voted to postpone his bill, Flipper appealed to his closest Washington friend, Albert Fall. "My whole soul is in this matter as you know," he wrote to Fall on August 29, 1922, requesting that the interior secretary discuss his case with the president. Fall in turn pleaded Flipper's case in an emotional letter to Senator J. W. Wadsworth, chair of the Military Affairs Committee. Fall, however, was soon embroiled in the Teapot Dome political scandal and resigned from Harding's cabinet in disgrace on March 4, 1923. He later was convicted for conspiracy and bribery and sentenced to a one-hundred-thousand-dollar fine and a year's imprisonment. Although Flipper was not implicated in the scandal, he resigned the same day as his political mentor. Massachusetts senator Henry Cabot Lodge vowed to reintroduce the bill the following year, but by then Flipper was working in Venezuela.[61]

Flipper's Venezuelan years began when William F. Buckley Sr., a friend of former interior secretary Fall, formed New

York–based Pantepec Oil Company in 1923 to help develop the nation's oil resources. Flipper's background with U.S. firms in northern Mexico and his familiarity with the Spanish language and laws led Buckley to hire him as a consultant. Flipper moved to Caracas and soon became a confidant of wealthy, well-connected Venezuelan businessmen called *gomecistas* because of their ties with the country's dictator, Juan Vicente Gómez. For the next seven years Flipper acquired oil concession leases throughout Venezuela. By 1927 Pantepec, largely through his efforts, controlled over three million acres of Venezuelan oil lands. One 1926 transaction was typical of Flipper's activities. Pedro Augusto Chacin, a *gomecista*, acquired from Sinforoso de Armas a 28,923-hectare concession known as Las Bombitas for $108,460. Soon afterward Flipper arranged for its purchase by Pantepec for $180,770. He then sold the concession to California Petroleum Corporation for $375,000. Such deals, while immediately lucrative for Pantepec, nonetheless helped generate the overspeculation in oil concessions and oil stocks that eventually fueled the stock market crash of 1929. As a salaried employee with few shares of stock, Flipper never personally profited from the numerous concessions deals he arranged for Pantepec. Nonetheless, Flipper lost his job when Buckley's firm became one of the first casualties of the crash. One year later his meager Pantepec stock shares were liquidated for $318.[62]

In the summer of 1930, seventy-four-year-old Flipper sailed to New York. Virtually penniless, he subsisted on the support of friends in New York and Washington DC before returning home to Atlanta in 1931 for the first time in fifty-four years. Once in Atlanta he would never work professionally again. Flipper moved into the home of his brother, A.M.E. bishop Joseph Flipper, and assumed the persona of retired army officer, in effect becoming in private what the federal government refused to grant him in public. His family and friends addressed him as "Lieutenant" and he exhibited the proper soldierly bearing, dressing almost daily in a white shirt and steel-gray suit with a vest and tie. Flipper rose promptly at 5:30 A.M. for a 7:00 A.M. breakfast and then moved to his brother's study to answer correspondence from the West, Mexico, and South America and to write others almost daily. "He busied himself," according to historian Steve Wilson, "like a man working against time, seeking to set straight the charges that had been levied against him, [and] attempting to answer the questions surrounding his actions in the West."[63]

Flipper did, however, allow himself one distraction, his relationship with Anna White. The two had been engaged briefly in 1877 just before his first cavalry assignment in Indian Territory. Anna White in the interim married Augustus Shaw of Brunswick, Georgia, and after his death in 1914, returned to Atlanta. Four years later Flipper and Shaw resumed their correspondence and were engaged. During Flipper's service in Washington DC in the early 1920s, Anna White Shaw visited her fiancé. While in Venezuela Flipper sent Shaw a diamond ring. Although they discussed her relocating in Venezuela with Flipper, she was responsible for two grandchildren and feared his salary at Pantepec would not adequately support all of them. When Flipper returned to Atlanta in 1931, he and Anna White Shaw lived only a block apart but rarely visited each other.[64]

His only other relationships with women were far more fleeting than his affair with Anna White Shaw. On September 10, 1891, in Nogales, Flipper entered into a common-law marriage with Luisa Montoya, a woman of Mexican descent. The two were prevented from marrying officially because of Arizona Territory's miscegenation law. The relationship with Montoya lasted seven months, after which Flipper declared in a letter to his brothers, "I shall certainly not marry any one I have ever seen out here. . . . I have never seen any . . . woman out this way, colored, white or Mexican, that I would give a fin for as a wife. All the nice girls are back east where you are." Flipper also maintained a platonic relationship with a Mrs. Brown, an African American woman from Augusta, Georgia. His 1916 memoirs that became *Black Frontiersman* were written expressly for her.[65]

On the morning of May 3, 1940, when Flipper failed to appear for breakfast, Winnie Braswell, the family cook, went to his room, rang his doorbell, and received no answer. Upon investigating she discovered his body. Flipper had nearly completed dressing for the day when he suffered a fatal heart attack and fell across his bed. He died at the age of eighty-four. His brother, Bishop Joseph Flipper, handled the funeral arrangements, including the preparation of the death certificate. In the space for "Usual Occupation" Bishop Flipper wrote, "Retired Army Officer." Flipper's remains were entombed in an unmarked grave in Atlanta's Southview Cemetery, near his brother's home. Although Flipper's graduation from West Point had been reported by dozens of newspapers across the nation, only the *New York Herald* and two Atlanta African American papers noted his passing. Dr. Thomas Flanagan, editor of the *Atlanta Daily World*, one of the two local newspapers, lamented that the lieutenant "died unwept, unhonored, unsung."[66]

The Flanagan assessment, however, was not the end of the Flipper saga. Four decades after his death, his supporters, led by Georgia schoolteacher Ray MacColl, persuaded the U.S. Army to begin a lengthy review of Flipper's court-martial proceedings. In December 1976 the Department of the Army granted Flipper an honorable discharge dated June 30, 1882. Ceremonies were held at Atlanta University and the U.S. Military Academy, where a bust of Flipper was unveiled. Moreover, the Military Academy created a memorial scholarship in Flipper's honor, to be granted to "the cadet who demonstrated the highest qualities of leadership, self-discipline, and perseverance in the face of unusual difficulties." Lt. William Davis, a 1976 graduate of the Air Force Academy and a great-grand-nephew of Flipper, presented the first scholarship on June 7, 1977. The following February Flipper's remains were exhumed from the unmarked, unkept grave in Atlanta and removed to a full military burial in Old Magnolia Cemetery in his hometown of Thomasville, Georgia. There he was eulogized by Veterans' Administration official H. Minton Francis, the first twentieth-century African American graduate of West Point, before five hundred observers. Flipper had now returned home, to a site within two blocks of the slave quarters that were his birthplace 121 years earlier.[67]

Before his own collapse into disgrace Secretary of the Interior Albert Fall wrote Senator James W. Wadsworth Jr., chairman of the U.S. Senate Military Affairs Committee, urging that his friend and associate of twenty years be reinstated to the military. His words, while specifically addressing Flipper's removal from service in 1882, nonetheless summarize the lifelong dilemma of this exceptional figure. "His life is a most pathetic one," wrote Fall. "By education, by experience and because of his natural high intellectual characteristics, he can find no pleasure in association with many of his own race, and because of his color he was and is precluded in this country from enjoying the society of those whom he would be mentally and otherwise best fitted to associate with."[68] Flipper's boundless optimism and his extraordinary professional accomplishments would have precluded his agreeing with Fall's conclusion that his life was "pathetic." Yet Flipper's life reflects the paradox of a society pledged to egalitarianism but self-evidently conscious of class and status hierarchies. The first African American graduate of West Point was clearly constrained by his race, as evidenced by his tenure at the academy and his abbreviated career as a

U.S. Army officer in Oklahoma Territory and Texas. Nonetheless, his superior intellect and able talents and his presence on the southwestern frontier allowed him to transcend many of the standard color-determined restrictions of the era. Ultimately Henry Ossian Flipper's successes and his failures remind us of the complexities, contradictions, and ironies of race in the late nineteenth and early twentieth centuries.

PUBLISHED MONOGRAPHS AND TRANSLATIONS BY HENRY O. FLIPPER

Black Frontiersman: The Memoirs of Henry O. Flipper. Edited by Theodore D. Harris. Fort Worth: Texas Christian University, 1997.

The Colored Cadet at West Point: Autobiography of Lieut. Henry Ossian Flipper, U.S.A., First Graduate of Color from the U.S. Military Academy. New York: H. Lee, 1878. Reprint, New York: Arno Press, 1969.

Did a Negro Discover Arizona and New Mexico? Nogales, Arizona Territory: privately printed, 1896.

Translations

Law Governing Hydrocarbons and Other Combustible Minerals of the Republic of Venezuela. New York: Evening Post Job Printing Office, 1922.

Mining Laws of the United States and Mexico and the Law of Federal Property Tax on Mines with Regulation Thereunder and Other Laws Relating Thereto. Nogales, Arizona Territory: P. Aguire Press, 1892.

(with Matthew G. Reynolds) *Spanish and Mexican Land Laws: New Spain and New Mexico*. St. Louis MO: Buxton & Skinner Stationery Company, 1895.

(with Will Tipton) *Official Report on the Condition of the Archives or Records of the Titles to Land Grants in Arizona*. n.p., n.d.

NOTES

1. For a synopsis of Flipper's accomplishments and career see Steve Wilson, "A Black Lieutenant in the Ranks," *American History Illustrated* 18:8 (December 1983): 31–39. There is an impressive array of scholarship on Henry Ossian Flipper but to date, surprisingly, no book-length biography by a professional historian. The literature on Flipper is anchored by his two autobiographies, *The Colored Cadet at West Point: Autobiography of Lieut. Henry Ossian Flipper* (New York: Homer Lee & Co, 1878), and *Black Frontiersman: The Memoirs of Henry O. Flipper*, ed. Theodore D. Harris (Fort Worth: Texas Christian University Press, 1997). The monographs on Flipper include Jane Eppinga, *Henry Ossian Flipper: West Point's First Black Graduate* (Plano TX: Republic of Texas Press, 1996) and Lowell D. Black and Sara H. Black, *An Officer and A Gentleman: The Military Career of Lieutenant Henry O. Flipper* (Dayton OH: Lora Company, 1985). The court-martial of Flipper has generated a number of monographs including Charles M. Robinson III, *The Court-Martial of Lieutenant Henry Flipper*, Southwestern Studies, No. 100 (El Paso: University of Texas at El Paso, 1994); Barry C. Johnson, *Flipper's Dismissal: The Ruin of Lt. Henry O. Flipper, USA, First Colored Graduate of West Point* (London: privately printed, 1980); and James C. Cage and James M. Day, *The Court-Martial of Henry Ossian Flipper: West Point's First Black Graduate* (El Paso: El Paso Corral of Westerners, 1981). Bruce J. Dinges, "The Court-Martial of Lieutenant Henry O. Flipper: An Example of Black-White Relationships in the Army," *The American West* 9:1 (January 1972): 12–17, 59–61; Wilson, "A Black Lieutenant in the Ranks"; and Jane Eppinga, "Henry O. Flipper in the Court of Private Land Claims: The Arizona Career of West Point's First Black Graduate," *Journal of Arizona History* 36:1 (spring 1995): 33–54 are among the significant articles on Flipper's life. Also of interest is Theodore Delano Harris, "Henry Ossian Flipper: The First Negro Graduate of West Point," (Ph.D. diss., University of Minnesota, 1971). For historical background on black westerners see Quintard Taylor, *In Search of the Racial Frontier: African Americans in the American West, 1528–1990* (New York: W. W. Norton, 1998) and Bruce A. Glasrud, *African Americans in the*

West: A Bibliography of Secondary Sources (Alpine TX: Center for Big Bend Studies, 1997).

2. The quotation appears in Flipper, *Colored Cadet*, pp. 137–38. For background on Flipper's racial and social views see Harris, "Henry Ossian Flipper," chap. 6.

3. Theodore Harris in Flipper, *Black Frontiersman*, p. 4.

4. See Eppinga, *Henry Ossian Flipper*, pp. 1–2, and Brenda K. East, "Henry Ossian Flipper: Lieutenant of the Buffalo Soldiers," *Persimmon Hill* 23:2 (summer 1995): 68–69.

5. The Flipper quote appears in Robinson, *Court-Martial of Lieutenant Henry Flipper*, p. 1. See also Donald R. McClung, "Second Lieutenant Henry O. Flipper: A Negro Officer on the West Texas Frontier," *West Texas Historical Association Year Book* 47 (1971): 20–21.

6. See Eppinga, *Henry Ossian Flipper*, pp. 7–9. After the Civil War Quarles continued his own education, eventually migrating to Pennsylvania to attend Wilmington College. He graduated with a law degree in 1870 and became the first African American admitted to the Georgia bar. Later he was appointed by President Rutherford Hayes to serve as U.S. consul in Malaga, Spain.

7. See Flipper, *Colored Cadet*, p. 12, and Clarence A. Bacote, *The Story of Atlanta University: A Century of Service, 1865–1965* (Atlanta: Atlanta University Press, 1965), p. vii.

8. See Flipper, *Black Frontiersman*, p. 4, and McClung, "Second Lieutenant Henry O. Flipper," p. 21. For a discussion of Edmund Asa Ware and the founding of Atlanta University, see Bacote, *Story of Atlanta University*, chap. 1.

9. See Flipper, *Colored Cadet*, pp. 17, 22.

10. Quoted in Flipper, *Colored Cadet*, pp. 18, 19.

11. See Eppinga, *Henry Ossian Flipper*, pp. 17–20, and Robinson, *Court-Martial of Lieutenant Henry Flipper*, p. 3.

12. Both quotes appear in Flipper, *Colored Cadet*, p. 27. See also Wilson, "A Black Lieutenant in the Ranks," p. 32.

13. See Stephen E. Ambrose, *Duty, Honor, Country: A History of West Point* (Baltimore: Johns Hopkins Press, 1966), pp. 22–37, 58–105, and James L. Morrison Jr., *The Best School in the World: West Point, the Pre–Civil War Years, 1833–1866* (Kent OH: Kent State University Press, 1986), chap. 6–7.

14. See George L. Andrews, "West Point and the Colored

Cadets," *International Review* 9:5 (November 1880): 477; Ambrose, *Duty, Honor, Country*, pp. 112–20, 167–90; and Morrison, *Best School in the World*, chap. 9–10.

15. The quotation appears in Jack D. Foner, *Blacks and the Military in American History* (New York: Praeger, 1971), p. 65. For an example of the nineteenth-century defense of West Point racial practices see Andrews, "West Point and the Colored Cadets," pp. 479–85. See also Eppinga, *Henry Ossian Flipper*, pp. 22, 26.

16. On James Webster Smith and other early black cadets see Wesley A. Brown, "Eleven Men of West Point," *Negro History Bulletin* 19:7 (April 1956): 148–57. See also Eppinga, *Henry Ossian Flipper*, pp. 23–24; Robinson, *Court-Martial of Lieutenant Henry Flipper*, p. 3; and Ambrose, *Duty, Honor, Country*, pp. 231–37.

17. Quoted in Flipper, *Colored Cadet*, p. 37n.

18. See Robinson, *Court-Martial of Lieutenant Henry Flipper*, pp. 3–4. Johnson C. Whittaker was also dismissed from the academy, in 1880. For an account of his experiences at West Point see John F. Marszalek Jr., *Court-Martial: A Black Man in America* (New York: Charles Scribner's Sons, 1972).

19. See Dinges, "The Court-Martial of Lieutenant Henry O. Flipper," pp. 12–13.

20. The quotations appear in Flipper, *Colored Cadet*, pp. 179, 181. See also Eppinga, *Henry Ossian Flipper*, p. 26, and Harris, "Henry Ossian Flipper," chap. 6.

21. The first quotation appears in Flipper, *Colored Cadet*, p. 61. On Flipper's assessment of the Smith incident see pp. 288–317. The three quotations on Smith appear on pp. 316, 164, and 161. After his expulsion James Webster Smith served as commandant of cadets at the South Carolina Agricultural Institute at Orangeburg until his death in November 1876. In 1997, 123 years after being forced out of West Point, Smith received a posthumous officer's commission after the intercession of Senator Strom Thurmond and Congressman John Spratt of South Carolina. See *Portland Oregonian*, September 23, 1997, p. A-9. See also Ezra J. Warner, "A Black Man in the Long Grey Line," *American History Illustrated* 4:9 (January 1970): 32–33.

22. See Flipper, *Colored Cadet*, p. 170. Apparently Flipper's compliance earned him respect in some circles. George L.

Andrews, a popular West Point instructor, writing three years after his graduation, declared that Flipper "conducted himself in a straight-forward self-respecting manner neither cringing nor meeting trouble more than half way. He never obtruded himself on others." Because of that posture, Andrews concluded that "the story of the colored cadets might have been quite different if Flipper had been the first instead of Smith." See Andrews, "West Point and the Colored Cadets," pp. 484, 480, respectively.

23. Flipper, *Colored Cadet*, pp. 249–50.

24. Flipper, *Colored Cadet*, pp. 106–7, 135–36.

25. Eppinga, *Henry Ossian Flipper*, p. 44.

26. Flipper, *Colored Cadet*, p. 244. Although he was the first African American West Point graduate, in 1877, Flipper was eventually followed by two others in the nineteenth century. John Hanks Alexander (1887) and Charles Young (1889) served in Western outposts with the four black regiments, as did the chaplains Allen Allensworth, Henry Plummer, George Prioleau, Theopolis Gould Steward, and William Anderson. See Taylor, *In Search of the Racial Frontier*, p. 168.

27. The quotation appears in Johnson, *Flipper's Dismissal*, p. 6. See also Flipper, *Colored Cadet*, p. 258, and Eppinga, *Henry Ossian Flipper*, pp. 49–51.

28. Quoted in Eppinga, *Henry Ossian Flipper*, p. 51.

29. Eppinga, *Henry Ossian Flipper*, p. 51.

30. See William H. Leckie, *The Buffalo Soldiers: A Narrative of the Negro Cavalry in the West* (Norman: University of Oklahoma Press, 1967), pp. 7–8, chap. 2–3; and William H. Leckie and Shirley A. Leckie, *Unlikely Warriors: General Benjamin H. Grierson and His Family* (Norman: University of Oklahoma Press, 1984), chap. 6.

31. Flipper's Ditch was designated a National Historic Landmark in 1977. See Flipper, *Black Frontiersman*, p. 5, and Eppinga, *Henry Ossian Flipper*, pp. 56–58, 63–64.

32. See Flipper, *Black Frontiersman*, p. 31.

33. See Flipper, *Black Frontiersman*, p. 28, and Black and Black, *An Officer and a Gentleman*, pp. 87–89.

34. Arlen L. Fowler, *The Black Infantry in the West, 1869–1891* (Norman: University of Oklahoma Press, 1996), p. 48.

35. The Sheridan quote appears in William L. Richter, *The*

Army in Texas During Reconstruction, 1865–1870 (College Station: Texas A&M University Press, 1987), p. 32.

36. Quoted in Leckie, *Buffalo Soldiers*, pp. 235–36. For background on tension between buffalo soldiers and civilians throughout the West see Taylor, *In Search of the Racial Frontier*, pp. 172–81.

37. See Leckie, *Buffalo Soldiers*, chap. 8.

38. See Flipper, *Black Frontiersman*, p. 34; Eppinga, *Henry Ossian Flipper*, pp. 66–67; and Leckie and Leckie, *Unlikely Warriors*, pp. 261–62.

39. By the time he reached Fort Davis, Col. William R. Shafter had acquired considerable experience with African American soldiers. During the Civil War he recruited and led the all-black Seventeenth Infantry. In 1866 he was given the command of the newly organized Forty-first U.S. Infantry, which by 1869 was consolidated with the all-black Thirty-eighth Infantry to become the Twenty-fourth Infantry. Although he and Flipper became bitter antagonists, Shafter "vociferously defended his black soldiers when he believed they were not being treated properly." See Paul H. Carlson, *"Pecos Bill": A Military Biography of William R. Shafter* (College Station: Texas A&M University Press, 1989), chap. 3, 5. The quotation appears on page 197. See also Eppinga, *Henry Ossian Flipper*, pp. 68–71.

40. The Nolan quote appears in Eppinga, *Henry Ossian Flipper*, p. 62, while Flipper's comments appear in Flipper, *Black Frontiersman*, p. 37.

41. Black and Black, *An Officer and a Gentleman*, p. 106.

42. See Johnson, *Flipper's Dismissal*, pp. 12–13; Robinson, *Court-Martial of Lieutenant Henry Flipper*, pp. 14–16; and Black and Black, *An Officer and a Gentleman*, pp. 111–12.

43. The first quote appears in Eppinga, *Henry Ossian Flipper*, p. 122, the second is in Robinson, *Court-Martial of Lieutenant Henry Flipper*, p. 18. See also Carlson, *Pecos Bill*, pp. 124–25, and Johnson, *Flipper's Dismissal*, pp. 31–35.

44. Robinson, *Court-Martial of Lieutenant Henry Flipper*, p. 18. See also Black and Black, *An Officer and a Gentleman*, pp. 112–19.

45. See Black and Black, *An Officer and a Gentleman*, pp. 122–23; Robinson, *Court-Martial of Lieutenant Henry Flipper*, p. 17; and Johnson, *Flipper's Dismissal*, pp. 18–19, 35–38.

46. Quoted in Dinges, "The Court-Martial of Lieutenant Henry O. Flipper," pp. 16–17. See also Eppinga, *Henry Ossian Flipper*, p. 70. Flipper's alienation from the national black intelligentsia continued throughout his life. In 1898 he was stranded at a Washington DC dinner party hosted by Mary Church Terrell and her husband, Judge Robert H. Terrell. Mrs. Paul Lawrence Dunbar was also present. After discussing women's suffrage, the Terrells and Mrs. Dunbar abruptly announced that they were going to church and he was not invited to join them. See Flipper, *Black Frontiersman*, pp. 59, 61.

47. The quotations appear in Robinson, *Court-Martial of Lieutenant Henry Flipper*, pp. 72, 81–82. On Grierson's support of Flipper see Leckie and Leckie, *Unlikely Warriors*, pp. 274–75.

48. British historian Barry C. Johnson concluded that Lucy Smith was probably the person responsible for the missing funds. See *Flipper's Dismissal*, pp. 123–24. See also Robinson, *Court-Martial of Lieutenant Henry Flipper*, chap. 4–8, 11, and Black and Black, *An Officer and a Gentleman*, pp. 130–39.

49. The first and second quotations appear in Robinson, *Court-Martial of Lieutenant Henry Flipper*, pp. 20, 21. See also chapter 11. The third quotation is from Johnson, *Flipper's Dismissal*, p. 124.

50. Robinson, *Court-Martial of Lieutenant Henry Flipper*, p. 99. See also Carlson, *Pecos Bill*, pp. 126–27, and Dinges, "The Court-Martial of Lieutenant Henry O. Flipper," pp. 59–60. For an assessment of the review of the court-martial by Judge Advocate Swaim, Secretary of War Lincoln, and President Arthur, see Johnson, *Flipper's Dismissal*, pp. 83–88.

51. See Eppinga, "Henry O. Flipper in the Court of Private Land Claims," pp. 33–34, and Wilson, "A Black Lieutenant," p. 36.

52. See Eppinga, "Henry O. Flipper in the Court of Private Land Claims," pp. 34–41.

53. Eppinga, "Henry O. Flipper in the Court of Private Land Claims," p. 40, 41. For additional background on the Nogales de Elias grant see Richard Wells Bradfute, *The Court of Private Land Claims: The Adjudication of Spanish and Mexican Land Grant Titles, 1891–1904* (Albuquerque: University of New Mexico Press, 1975), pp. 163–65. See also Sara Dunlop Jackson's introduction to Flipper, *Colored Cadet* (reprint, Salem NH: Ayer,

1986), pp. vi–ix. Flipper's work as a surveyor was not universally admired. In 1898 he resisted a bribery attempt by Alabama senator J. T. Morgan on behalf of Dr. Edward B. Perrin, who claimed ownership of a Mexican land grant of 123,000 acres. With Flipper's testimony the claim was reduced to 33,000 acres. Two years later Flipper conducted a survey of cattleman and former Cochise County sheriff John Slaughter's ranch, San Bernardino, reducing its acreage from 13,000 to 2,300 acres. See Eppinga, *Henry Ossian Flipper*, pp. 165–67, and Warner, "A Black Man in the Long Grey Line," pp. 35–37.

54. Quoted in Bradfute, *The Court of Private Land Claims*, p. 66. See also pp. 64–66, 70, 80, and Eppinga, "Henry O. Flipper in the Court of Private Land Claims," pp. 34–41.

55. Both quotations appear in "Did A Negro Discover Arizona and New Mexico?" reprinted in Flipper, *Black Frontiersman*, p. 92. The entire monograph appears as chapter 3. For a contemporary account of Esteban and of other early Spanish-speaking persons of African descent in the Southwest see Taylor, *In Search of the Racial Frontier*, pp. 27–37.

56. Quoted in "Early History of El Paso," *Old Santa Fe: A Magazine of History, Archaeology, Genealogy and Biography* (July 1914): 88–95, quote on p. 95.

57. Quoted in J. Frank Dobie, *Apache Gold and Yaqui Silver* (Boston: Little, Brown, 1939), p. 206. See also pp. 203–9.

58. Eppinga, *Henry Ossian Flipper*, pp. 172–73, 177–79.

59. Eppinga, *Henry Ossian Flipper*, pp. 187, 190. For a full background discussion of the origins of the Flipper-Villa connection and the text of his letters of protest see Flipper, *Black Frontiersman*, pp. 93–104.

60. See Eppinga, *Henry Ossian Flipper*, pp. 221–30; Wilson, "A Black Lieutenant in the Ranks," p. 37; and Johnson, *Flipper's Dismissal*, pp. 92–110.

61 Wilson, "A Black Lieutenant in the Ranks," pp. 37–38.

62. For a discussion of Flipper's activities in Venezuela see B. S. McBeth, *Juan Vicente Gómez and the Oil Companies in Venezuela, 1908–1935* (Cambridge: Cambridge University Press, 1983), pp. 72–76, and Eppinga, *Henry Ossian Flipper*, pp. 205–15.

63. See Wilson, "Black Lieutenant in the Ranks," pp. 31, 39. The quotation appears on p. 31.

64. See Eppinga, *Henry Ossian Flipper*, pp. 205, 214.

65. Eppinga, *Henry Ossian Flipper*, p. 170. For a discussion of Mrs. Brown see Flipper, *Black Frontiersman*, pp. 13, 17. Since in Arizona persons of Mexican ancestry were classified as white, Luisa Montoya was legally barred from marrying Flipper. See Roger D. Hardaway, "Unlawful Love: A History of Arizona's Miscegenation Law," *Journal of Arizona History* 27:4 (winter 1986): 377–90.

66. Quoted in Warner, "A Black Man in a Long Grey Line," p. 38. See also W. E. B. DuBois, "Henry O. Flipper," *Phylon* 1:3 (3rd quarter): 288.

67. Wilson, "A Black Lieutenant in the Ranks," p. 39.

68. Quoted in Johnson, *Flipper's Dismissal*, pp. 104–5. The entire Fall letter appears here.

TO

𝔖𝔥𝔢 𝔣𝔞𝔠𝔲𝔩𝔱𝔶 𝔬𝔣 𝔄𝔱𝔩𝔞𝔫𝔱𝔞 𝔘𝔫𝔦𝔟𝔢𝔯𝔰𝔦𝔱𝔶, 𝔄𝔱𝔩𝔞𝔫𝔱𝔞, 𝔊𝔞.,

AND TO

THE PRESIDENT IN PARTICULAR,

TO WHOSE CAREFUL

MENTAL AND MORAL TRAINING OF MYSELF IS DUE ALL

MY SUCCESS AT THE MILITARY ACADEMY

AT WEST POINT, N. Y.,

I AFFECTIONATELY DEDICATE THIS VOLUME,

AS IN SOME SORT

A TOKEN OF THAT HEARTFELT GRATITUDE WHICH

I SO DEEPLY FEEL, BUT CAN SO

POORLY EXPRESS.

CONTENTS.

PREFACE.

THE following pages were written by request. They claim to give an accurate and impartial narrative of my four years' life while a cadet at West Point, as well as a general idea of the institution there. They are almost an exact transcription of notes taken at various times during those four years. Any inconsistencies, real or apparent, in my opinions or in the impressions made upon me, are due to the fact that they were made at different times at a place where the feelings of all were constantly undergoing material change.

They do not pretend to merit. Neither are they written for the purpose of criticising the Military Academy or those in any way connected with it.

My "notes" have been seen and read. If I please those who requested me to publish them I shall be content, as I have no other object in putting them before the public.

H. O. F.

FORT SILL, INDIAN TER., 1878.

THE COLORED CADET

WEST POINT.

CHAPTER I.

RETROSPECT.

HENRY OSSIAN FLIPPER, the eldest of five brothers, and the subject of this narrative, was born in Thomasville, Thomas County, Georgia, on the 21st day of March, 1856. He and his mother were the property (?) of Rev. Reuben H. Lucky, a Methodist minister of that place. His father, Festus Flipper, by trade a shoemaker and carriage-trimmer, was owned by Ephraim G. Ponder, a successful and influential slave-dealer.

In 1859 Mr. Ponder, having retired from business, returned to Georgia from Virginia with a number of mechanics, all slaves, and among whom was the father of young Flipper. He established a number of manufactories in Atlanta, then a growing inland town of Georgia. He married about this time a beautiful, accomplished, and wealthy lady. "*Flipper*," as he was generally called, had married before this, and had been taken back alone to his native

Virginia to serve an apprenticeship under a carriage-
trimmer. This served, Mr. Ponder joined his wife
in Thomasville, bringing with him, as stated, a number of mechanics.

All were soon ready for transportation to Atlanta
except "Flipper." As he and his wife were each
the property (?) of different persons, there was, under
the circumstances, every probability of a separation.
This, of course, would be to them most displeasing.
Accordingly an application was made to Mr. Ponder
to purchase the wife and son. This he was, he said,
unable to do. He had, at an enormous expense,
procured and fitted up a home, and his coffers were
nearly, if not quite, empty. Husband and wife then
appealed to Mr. Lucky. He, too, was averse to parting them, but could not, at the great price asked for
him, purchase the husband. He was willing, however, to sell the wife. An agreement was finally
made by which the husband paid from his own
pocket the purchase-money of his own wife and
child, this sum to be returned to him by Mr. Ponder
whenever convenient. The joy of the wife can be
conceived. It can not be expressed.

In due time all arrived at Atlanta, where Mr.
Ponder had purchased about twenty-five acres of
land and had erected thereon, at great expense, a
superb mansion for his own family, a number of substantial frame dwellings for his slaves, and three
large buildings for manufacturing purposes.

Of sixty-five slaves nearly all of the men were
mechanics. All of them except the necessary household servants, a gardener, and a coachman, were permitted to hire their own time. Mr. Ponder would

have absolutely nothing to do with their business other than to protect them. So that if any one wanted any article of their manufacture they contracted with the workman and paid him his own price. These bond people were therefore virtually free. They acquired and accumulated wealth, lived happily, and needed but two other things to make them like other human beings, viz., absolute freedom and education. But

> " God moves in a mysterious way
> His wonders to perform."

And through that very mysteriousness this people was destined to attain to the higher enjoyment of life. The country, trembling under the agitation of the slave question, was steadily seeking a condition of equilibrium which could be stable only in the complete downfall of slavery. Unknown to them, yet existing, the great question of the day was gradually being solved ; and in its solution was working out the salvation of an enslaved people. Well did that noblest of women, Mrs. Julia Ward Howe, sing a few years after :

> " Mine eyes have seen the glory of the coming of the Lord ;
> He is tramping out the vintage where the grapes of wrath are stored ;
> He hath loosed the fateful lightning of his terrible swift sword ;
> This truth is marching on.

> " I have seen him in the watch-fires of a hundred circling camps ;
> They have builded him an altar in the evening dews and damps ;
> I can read his righteous sentence by the dim and flaring lamps ;
> His day is marching on.

> " I have read a fiery gospel, writ in burnished rows of steel ;
> ' As ye deal with my contemners, so with you my grace shall deal ;
> Let the Hero, born of woman, crush the serpent with his heel,
> Since God is marching on.'

" He hath sounded forth the trumpet that shall never call retreat ;
 He is sifting out the hearts of men before his judgment-seat ;
 Oh ! be swift my soul to answer him ! be jubilant my feet !
  Our God is marching on.
" In the beauty of the lilies, Christ was born across the sea,
 With a glory in his bosom that transfigures you and me ;
 As he died to make men holy, let us die to make men free,
  While God is marching on."

Another influence was as steadily tending to the same end. Its object was to educate, to elevate intellectually, and then to let the power thus acquired act.

The mistress of this fortunate household, far from discharging the duties and functions of her station, left them unnoticed, and devoted her whole attention to illegitimate pleasures. The outraged husband appointed a guardian and returned broken-hearted to the bosom of his own family, and devoted himself till death to agricultural pursuits.

The nature of the marriage contract prevented the selling of any of the property without the mutual consent of husband and wife. No such consent was ever asked for by either. No one was, therefore, in that state of affairs, afraid of being sold away from his or her relatives, although their mistress frequently threatened so to sell them. " *I'll send you to Red River*," was a common menace of hers, but perfectly harmless, for all knew, as well as she did, that it was impossible to carry it into execution.

In this condition of affairs the " servants" were even more contented than ever. They hired their time, as usual, and paid their wages to their mistress, whose only thought or care was to remember when it became due, and then to receive it.

The guardian, an influential stockholder in several railroads, and who resided in another city, made periodical visits to inspect and do whatever was necessary to a proper discharge of his duties.

Circumstances being highly favorable, one of the mechanics, who had acquired the rudiments of an education, applied to this dissolute mistress for permission to teach the children of her " servants." She readily consented, and, accordingly, a night-school was opened in the very woodshop in which he worked by day.   Here young Flipper was initiated into the first of the three mysterious R's, viz., "*reading 'riting and 'rithmetic.*" Here, in 1864, at eight years of age, his education began. And the first book he ever studied—I dare say ever saw—was a confederate reprint of Webster's " *Blue-back Speller.*" His then tutor has since graduated at Westminster College in Pennsylvania, and is, at the time of this writing, United States Consul at Malaga, Spain, having served in the same capacity for four years at Port Mahon, Spain.

But alas ! even this happy arrangement was destined to be disturbed. This dissolute mistress and her slaves, with all valuable movable property, were compelled to flee before Sherman's victorious arms. Macon, a city just one hundred and three miles south-east of Atlanta, became the new home of the Flippers. A spacious dwelling was secured in West Macon. In a part of this was stored away Mrs. Ponder's plate and furniture, under the guardianship of Flipper, who with his family occupied the rest of the house. Here all was safe. The terrible fate of Atlanta was not extended to Macon. The

only cause of alarm was Wilson, who approached
the city from the east, and, having thrown in a few
shells, withdrew without doing further damage or
being molested. Every body was frightened, and it
was deemed advisable to transfer Mrs. Ponder's effects to Fort Valley, a small place farther south.
However, before this could be done, it became indisputably known that Wilson had withdrawn.

After an uneventful stay—other than this incident just related—of nine months in Macon, the
office of custodian was resigned, and although yet a
slave, as far as he knew, and without permission
from any one, Flipper returned to Atlanta with
his wife and two sons, Henry, the elder, and Joseph,
the younger. This was in the spring of 1865.
Atlanta was in ruins, and it appeared a dreary place
indeed to start anew on the unfinished journey of
life. Every thing was not destroyed, however. A
few houses remained. One of these was occupied.
The people were rapidly returning, and the railroads
from Atlanta were rapidly being rebuilt.

During all this time the education of the young
Flippers had been necessarily neglected. In the early
spring of 1865, the family of an ex-rebel captain became neighbors of the Flippers, now well to do, and
were soon on the most friendly terms with them. With
remarkable condescension the wife of this ex-rebel
offered to instruct Henry and Joseph for a small remuneration. The offer was readily and gladly accepted, and the education of the two, so long neglected, was taken up again. This private school of
only two pupils existed but a short time. The
American Missionary Association having opened bet-

ter schools, the Flippers were, in March, 1866, transferred to them. They attended school there till in 1867 the famous Storrs' School was opened under the control of the American Missionary Association, when they went there. In 1869, the Atlanta University having been opened under the same auspices, they entered there. At the time of receiving his appointment Henry was a member of the freshman class of the collegiate department. His class graduated there in June, 1876, just one year before he did at West Point.

The following article from a Thomasville paper, published in June, 1874, will give further information concerning his early life :

" ' It is not generally known that Atlanta has a negro cadet at the United States National Military Academy at West Point. This cadet is a mulatto boy named Flipper. He is about twenty years old, a stoutish fellow, weighing perhaps one hundred and fifty pounds, and a smart, bright, intelligent boy. His father is a shoemaker, and gave him the euphonious name of Henry Ossian Flipper.

" ' Flipper has been at the great soldier factory of the nation for a year. He was recommended there by our late Congressman from the Fifth District, the Hon. J. C. Freeman. Flipper has made a right booming student. In a class of ninety-nine he stood about the middle, and triumphantly passed his examination, and has risen from the fourth to the third class without difficulty.

" ' The only two colored boys at the Academy were the famous Smith and the Atlanta Flipper. It is thought that Smith at the last examination failed. If so, Atlanta will have the distinguished honor of having the sole African representative at West Point.

" ' Flipper has had the privilege of eating at the same table with the poor white trash ; but Smith and Flipper bunked together in the same room alone, without white companions.

" ' It is an astonishing fact that, socially, the boys from the Northern and Western States will have nothing to do with these colored brothers. Flipper and Smith were socially ostracized. Not even the Massachusetts boys will associate with them. Smith has been a little rebellious, and attempted to thrust himself on the white boys ; but the sensible Flipper accepted the situation, and proudly refused to intrude himself on the white boys.

" ' The feeling of ostracism is so strong that a white boy who dared to recognize a colored cadet would be himself ostracized by the other white cubs, even of radical extraction. '

" We copy the above from the Atlanta *Herald* of last week, for the purpose of remarking that among colored men we know of none more honorable or more deserving than Flipper, the father of the colored West Point student of that name.   Flipper lived for many years in Thomasville as the servant of Mr. E. G. Ponder—was the best bootmaker we ever knew, and his character and deportment were ever those of a sensible, unassuming, gentlemanly white man.   Flipper possessed the confidence and respect of his master and all who knew him.   His wife, the mother of young Flipper, was Isabella, a servant in the family of Rev. R. H. Lucky, of Thomasville, and bore a character equal to that of her husband.   Young Flipper was baptized in his infancy by the venerable Bishop Early.   From these antecedents we should as soon expect young Flipper to make his mark as any other colored youth in the country."

(*From the Louisville Ledger.*)

" It is just possible that some of our readers may not know who Flipper is.   For their benefit we make haste to explain that Flipper is the solitary colored cadet now at West Point.   He is in the third class, and stands forty-six in the class, which numbers eighty-five members.   This is a very fair standing, and Flipper's friends declare that he is getting along finely in his studies, and that he is quite up to the standard of the average West Point student.   Nevertheless they intimate that he will never graduate.   Flipper, they say, may get as far as the first class, but there he will be ' slaughtered. '

" A correspondent of the New York *Times* takes issue with this opinion.   He says there are many ' old heads ' who believe Flipper will graduate with honor, and he thinks so too.   The grounds for his belief, as he gives them, are that the officers are gentlemen, and so are the professors ; that they believe merit should be rewarded wherever found ; and that they all speak well of Flipper, who is a hard student, as his position in his class proves.   From this correspondent we learn that Flipper is from Georgia ; that he has a light, coffee-colored complexion, and that he 'minds his business and does not intrude his company upon the other cadets,' though why this should be put down in the list of his merits it is not easy to understand, since, if he graduates, as this writer believes he will, he will have the right to associate on terms of perfect equality with the other cadets, and may in time come to command some of them. We are afraid there is some little muddle of inconsistency in the brain of the *Times*' correspondent.

"The Chicago *Tribune* seems to find it difficult to come to any conclusion concerning Flipper's chances for graduating. It says : 'It is freely asserted that Flipper will never be allowed to graduate ; that the prejudice of the regular army instructors against the colored race is insurmountable, and that they will drive away from the Academy by persecution of some petty sort any colored boy who may obtain admittance there. The story does not seem to have any substantial basis ; still, it possesses considerable vitality.'

"We don't profess to understand exactly what sort of a story that is which has 'considerable vitality' without any substantial basis, and can only conclude that the *darkness of the subject* has engendered a little confusion in the mind of the *Tribune* as well as in that of the writer of the *Times*. But the *Tribune* acquires more confidence as it warms in the discussion, and it assures us finally that 'there is, of course, no doubt that some colored boys are capable of receiving a military education ; and eventually the presence of colored officers in the regular army must be an accepted fact.' Well, we don't know about that 'accepted fact.' The white man is mighty uncertain, and the nigger won't do to trust to, in view of which truths it would be unwise to bet too high on the 'colored officers,' for some years to come at least.

"But let not Flipper wring his flippers in despair, notwithstanding. Let him think of Smith, and take heart of hope. Smith was another colored cadet who was sent to West Point from South Carolina. Smith mastered readin', 'ritin', and 'rithmetic, but chemistry mastered Smith.* They gave him three trials, but it was to no purpose ; so they had to change his base and send him back to South Carolina. But what of that ? They've just made him inspector of militia in South Carolina, with the rank of brigadier-general. How long

* Cadet Smith failed in Natural and Experimental Philosophy. In Chemistry he was up to the average. He was never appointed Inspector-General of South Carolina. He was Commandant of Cadets in the South Carolina Agricultural Institute at Orangeburg, S. C., which position he held till his death November 29th, 1876.

might he have remained in the army before he would have become 'General Smith?' Why, even Fred Grant's only a lieutenant-colonel. Smith evidently has reason to congratulate himself upon being 'plucked;' and so the young gentleman from Georgia, with the 'light, coffee-colored complexion,' if he meets with a similar misfortune, may console himself with the hope that to him also in his extremity will be extended from some source a helping flipper."

CHAPTER II.

HAVING given in the previous chapter a brief account of myself—dropping now, by permission, the third person—prior to my appointment, I shall here give in full what led me to seek that appointment, and how I obtained it. It was while sitting "in his father's quiet shoeshop on Decatur Street"—as a local paper had it—that I overheard a conversation concerning the then cadet from my own district. In the course of the conversation I learned that this cadet was to graduate the following June ; and that therefore a vacancy would occur. This was in the autumn of 1872, and before the election. It occurred to me that I might fill that vacancy, and I accordingly determined to make an endeavor to do so, provided the Republican nominee for Congress should be elected. He was elected. I applied for and obtained the appointment. In 1865 or 1866—I do not now remember which : perhaps it was even later than either—it was suggested to my father to send me to West Point. He was unwilling to do so, and, not knowing very much about the place, was reluctant to make any inquiries. I was then of course too young for admission, being only ten or twelve years old ; and knowing nothing of the place myself, I did not care to venture the attempt to become a cadet.

At the time I obtained the appointment I had quite forgotten this early recommendation of my father's friend ; indeed, I did not recall it until I began compiling my manuscript.

The suggestion given me by the conversation above mentioned was at once acted upon, and decision made in a very short time ; and so fully was I determined, so absolutely was my mind set on West Point, that I persisted in my desire even to getting the appointment, staying at the Academy four years, and finally graduating. The following communications will explain how I got the appointment.*

Reply No. 1

GRIFFIN, January 23, 1873.

MR. H. O. FLIPPER.

DEAR SIR : Your letter of the 21st, asking me, as member-elect to Congress from this State, to appoint you cadet to West Point, was received this morning. You are a stranger to me, and before I can comply with your request you must get your teacher, Mr. James L. Dunning, P.M., Colonel H. P. Fanorr, and other Republicans to indorse for you. Give me assurance you are worthy and well qualified and I will recommend you.

Yours respectfully,
J. C. FREEMAN.

Reply No. 2.

GRIFFIN, March 22, 1873.

MR. H. O. FLIPPER.

DEAR SIR : On my arrival from Washington I found your letter of the 19th. I have received an invitation from the War Department to appoint, or nominate, a legally qualified cadet to the United States Military Academy from my district.

---

* It has been impossible for the author to obtain copies of his own letters to the Hon. Congressman who appointed him, which is to be regretted. The replies are inserted in such order that they will readily suggest the tenor of the first communications.

As you were the first applicant, I am disposed to give you the first chance ; but the requirements are rigid and strict, and I think you had best come down and see them. If after reading them you think you can undergo the examination without doubt, I will nominate you. But I do not want my nominee to fail to get in.

Yours very respectfully,

J. C. FREEMAN.

Reply No. 3.

GRIFFIN, GA., March 26, 1873.

MR. H. O. FLIPPER.

DEAR SIR : Your letter of the 24th to hand, and contents noted. While your education may be sufficient, it requires many other qualifications—such as age, height, form, etc.; soundness of lungs, limbs, etc. I will send you up the requirements, if you desire them, and call upon three competent gentlemen to examine you, if you desire it. Let me hear from you again on the subject.

Yours respectfully,

J. C. FREEMAN.

Reply No. 4.

GRIFFIN, March 28, 1873.

MR. H. O. FLIPPER.

DEAR SIR : Yours of 26th at hand I have concluded to send the paper sent me to J. A. Holtzclaw, of Atlanta, present Collector of Internal Revenue. You can call on him and examine for yourself. If you then think you can pass, I will designate three men to examine you, and if they pronounce you up to the requirements I will appoint you.

Yours truly,

J. C. FREEMAN.

Reply No. 5.

GRIFFIN, April 5, 1873.

MR. H. O. FLIPPER.

DEAR SIR : The board of examiners pronounce you qualified to enter the Military Academy at West Point. You will oblige me by sending me your given name in full, also your age to a month, and the length of time you have lived in the Fifth District, or in or near Atlanta. I will appoint you, and send on the papers to the Secretary of War, who will notify you of the same. From his letter to me you will have to be at West Point by the 25th day of May, 1873.

Yours respectfully,

J. C. FREEMAN.

P.S.—You can send letter to me without a stamp.

Reply No. 6.

GRIFFIN, April 17, 1873.

MR. HENRY O. FLIPPER.

DEAR SIR : I this day inclose you papers from the War Department. You can carefully read and then make up your mind whether you accept the position assigned you. If you should sign up, direct and forward to proper authorities, Washington, D. C. If you do not accept, return the paper to my address, Griffin, Ga.

I am yours very respectfully,

J. C. FREEMAN.

The papers, three in number, referred to in the above letter, are the following :

WAR DEPARTMENT, }
WASHINGTON, April 11, 1873. }

SIR : You are hereby informed that the President has *conditionally* selected you for appointment as a Cadet of the United States Military Academy at West Point.

Should you desire the appointment, you will report in person to the Superintendent of the Academy between the 20th and 25th days of May, 1873, when, if found on due examination to possess the qualifications required by law and set forth in the circular hereunto appended, you will be admitted, with pay from July 1st, 1873, to serve until the following January, at which time you will be examined before the Academic Board of the Academy. Should the result of this examination be favorable, and the reports of your personal, military, and moral deportment be satisfactory, your warrant of appointment, to be dated July 1st, 1873, will be delivered to you ; but should the result of your examination, or your conduct reports. be unfavorable, you will be discharged from the military service, unless otherwise recommended, for special reasons, by the Academic Board, but will receive an allowance for travelling expenses to your home.

Your attention is particularly directed to the accompanying circular, and it is to be distinctly understood that this notification confers upon you no right to enter the Military Academy unless your qualifications agree fully with its requirements, and unless you report for examination within the time specified.

You are requested to immediately inform the Department of your acceptance or declination of the contemplated appointment upon the conditions annexed.

GEO. M. ROBESON,

Acting Secretary of War.

HENRY O. FLIPPER, Atlanta, Georgia.

Through HON. J. C. FREEMAN, M.C.

CIRCULAR.

I. Candidates *must* be actual *bona fide* residents of the Congressional district or Territory for which their appointments are made, and must be over *seventeen* and under *twenty-two* years of age at the time of entrance into the Military Academy ; but any person who has served honorably and faithfully not less than one year as an officer or enlisted man in the army of the United States, either as a Volunteer, or in the Regular service, during the war for the suppression of the rebellion, shall be eligible for appointment up to the age of twenty-four years. They must be at least five feet in height, and free from any infectious or immoral disorder, and, generally, from any deformity, disease, or infirmity which may render them unfit for arduous military service. They must be proficient in *Reading* and *Writing ;* in the elements of *English Grammar ;* in *Descriptive Geography,* particularly of our own country, and in the *History of the United States.*

In *Arithmetic,* the various operations in *addition, subtraction, multiplication,* and *division, reduction,* simple and compound *proportion,* and vulgar and decimal *fractions,* must be thoroughly understood and readily performed.

The following are the leading physical disqualifications :

1. Feeble constitution and muscular tenuity ; unsound health from whatever cause ; indications of former disease ; glandular swellings, or other symptoms of scrofula.

2. Chronic cutaneous affections, especially of the scalp.

3. Severe injuries of the bones of the head ; convulsions.

4. Impaired vision, from whatever cause ; inflammatory affections of the eyelids ; immobility or irregularity of the iris ; fistula, lachrymalis, etc., etc.

5. Deafness ; copious discharge from the ears.

6. Loss of many teeth, or the teeth generally unsound.

7. Impediment of speech.

8. Want of due capacity of the chest, and any other indication of a liability to a pulmonic disease.

9. Impaired or inadequate efficiency of one or both of the superior extremities on account of fractures, especially of the clavicle, contraction of a joint, extenuation, deformity, etc., etc.

10. An unusual excurvature or incurvature of the spine.

11. Hernia.

12. A varicose state of the veins of the scrotum or spermatic cord (when large), sarcocele, hydrocele, hemorrhoids, fistulas.

13. Impaired or inadequate efficiency of one or of both of the in-

ferior extremities on account of varicose veins, fractures, malformation (flat feet, etc.), lameness, contraction, unequal length, bunions, overlying or supernumerary toes, etc., etc.

14. Ulcers, or unsound cicatrices of ulcers likely to break out afresh.

Every person appointed, upon arrival at West Point, is submitted to a rigid medical examination, and if any causes of disqualification are found to exist in him to such a degree as may now or hereafter impair his efficiency, he is rejected.

No person who has served in any capacity in the military or naval service of the so-called Confederate States during the late rebellion can receive an appointment as cadet at the Military Academy.

II. The pay of a cadet is $500 per annum, with one ration per day, to commence with his admission into the Military Academy, and is sufficient, with proper economy, for his support.

III. Each cadet must keep himself supplied with the following mentioned articles, viz. :

One gray cloth coatee ; one gray cloth riding-jacket ; one regulation great-coat ; two pairs of gray cloth pantaloons, for winter ; six pairs of drilling pantaloons for summer ; one fatigue-jacket for the encampment ; one black dress cap ; one forage cap ; one black stock ; *two pairs of ankle-boots ; *six pairs of white gloves ; two sets of white belts ; *seven shirts and twelve collars ; *six pairs winter socks ; *six pairs summer socks ; *four pairs summer drawers ; *three pairs winter drawers ; *six pocket-handkerchiefs ; *six towels ; *one clothes-bag, made of ticking; *one clothes-brush ; *one hair-brush ; *one tooth-brush ; *one comb ; one mattress ; one pillow ; *two pillow-cases ; *two pairs sheets ; *one pair blankets ; *one quilted bed-cover ; one chair; one tumbler ; *one trunk ; one account-book ; and will unite with his room-mate in purchasing, for their common use, one looking-glass, one wash-stand, one wash-basin, one pail, and one broom, and shall he required to have one table, of the pattern that may be prescribed by the Superintendent.

The articles marked thus * candidates are required to bring with them ; the others are to be had at West Point at regulated prices, and it is better for a candidate to take with him as little clothing of any description as is possible (excepting what is marked), and no more money than will defray his travelling expenses ; but for the parent or guardian to send to " The Treasurer of the Military Academy" a sum sufficient for his necessary expenses until he is admitted, and for his clothes, etc., thereafter.

The expenses of the candidate for board, washing, lights, etc., prior to admission, will be about $5 per week, and immediately after being admitted to the Institution he must be provided with an outfit of uniform, etc., the cost of which will be $88.79. If, upon arrival, he has the necessary sum to his credit on the books of the Treasurer, he will start with many advantages, in a pecuniary point of view, over those whose means are more limited, and who must, if they arrive, as many do, totally unprovided in this way, go in debt on the credit of their pay—a burden from which it requires many months to free themselves ; while, if any accident compels them to leave the Academy, they must of necessity be in a destitute condition.

No cadet can receive money, or any other supplies, from his parents, or from any person whomsoever, without permission from the Superintendent.

IV. If the candidate be a minor, his acceptance must be accompanied by the written consent of his parent or guardian to his signing articles, binding himself to serve the United States eight years from the time of his admission into the Military Academy, unless sooner discharged.

V. During the months of July and August the cadets live in camp, engaged only in military duties and exercises and receiving practical military instruction.

The academic duties and exercises commence on the 1st of September, and continue till about the end of June.

The newly appointed cadets are examined at the Academy prior to admission, and those not properly qualified are rejected.

Examinations of the several classes are held in January and June, and at the former such of the new cadets as are found proficient in studies and have been correct in conduct are given the particular standing in their class to which their merits entitle them. After either examination cadets found deficient in conduct or studies are discharged from the Academy, unless, for special reasons in each case, the Academic Board should otherwise recommend.

These examinations are very thorough, and require from the cadet a close and persevering attention to study, without evasion or slighting of any part of the course, as no relaxations of any kind can be made by the examiners.

VI. A sound body and constitution, a fixed degree of preparation, good natural capacity, an aptitude for study, industrious habits, perseverance, an obedient and orderly disposition, and a correct moral deportment are such essential qualifications that candidates knowingly deficient in any of these respects should not, as many do, subject themselves and their friends to the chances of future mortification and disappointment, by accepting appointments to the Academy and entering upon a career which they can not successfully pursue.

Method of Examining Candidates for Admission into the Military Academy.

Candidates must be able to *read* with facility from any book, giving the proper intonation and pauses, and to *write* portions that are read aloud for that purpose, spelling the words and punctuating the sentences properly.

In ARITHMETIC they must be able to perform with facility examples under the four ground rules, and hence must be familiar with the tables of addition, subtraction, multiplication, and division, and be able to perform examples in reduction and in vulgar and decimal fractions, such as—

Add $\frac{2}{3}$ to $\frac{3}{4}$; subtract $\frac{2}{3}$ from $\frac{5}{8}$; multiply $\frac{3}{4}$ by $\frac{7}{8}$; divide $\frac{2}{3}$ by $\frac{3}{4}$.

Add together two hundred and thirty-four thousandths (.234), twenty-six thousandths (.026), and three thousandths (.003).

Subtract one hundred and sixty-one ten thousandths (.0161) from twenty-five hundredths (.25).

Multiply or divide twenty-six hundredths (.26) by sixteen thousandths (.016).

They must also be able to change vulgar fractions into decimal fractions, and decimals into vulgar fractions, with examples like the following:

Change $\frac{15}{8}$ into a decimal fraction of the same value.

Change one hundred and two thousandths (.102) into a vulgar fraction of the same value.

In simple and compound proportion, examples of various kinds will be given, and candidates will be expected to understand the principles of the rules which they follow.

In ENGLISH GRAMMAR candidates will be required to exhibit a familiarity with the nine parts of speech and the rules in relation thereto ; must be able to parse any ordinary sentence given to them, and, generally, must understand those portions of the subject usually taught in the higher academies and schools throughout the country, comprehended under the heads of Orthography, Etymology, Syntax, and Prosody.

In DESCRIPTIVE GEOGRAPHY they are to name, locate, and describe the natural grand and political divisions of the earth, and be able to delineate any one of the States or Territories of the American Union, with its principal cities, rivers, lakes, seaports, and mountains.

In HISTORY they must be able to name the periods of the discovery and settlement of the North American continent, of the rise and progress of the United States, and of the successive wars and political administrations through which the country has passed.

THE COURSE OF STUDY AND BOOKS USED AT THE MILITARY ACADEMY.

[Books marked thus * are for reference only.]

First Year—Fourth Class.

DEPARTMENT.	TEXT-BOOKS.
Mathematics....................	Davies' Bourdon's Algebra. Davies' Legendre's Geometry and Trigonometry. Church's Descriptive Geometry.
French Language..............	Bolmar's Levizac's Grammar and Verb Book. Agnel's Tabular System. Berard's Leçons Françaises. * Spier's and Surenne's Dictionary.
Tactics of Artillery and Infantry.	Practical Instruction in the Schools of the Soldier, Company, and Battalion. Practical Instruction in Artillery.
Use of Small Arms............	Instruction in Fencing and Bayonet Exercise.

Second Year—Third Class.

Mathematics....................	Church's Descriptive Geometry, with its application to Spherical Projections. Church's Shades, Shadows, and Perspective. Davies' Surveying. Church's Analytical Geometry. Church's Calculus.
French Language..............	Bolmar's Levizac's Grammar and Verb Book. Berard's Leçons Françaises. Chapsal's Leçons et Modéles de Littérature Française. Agnel's Tabular System. Rowan's Morceaux Choisis des Auteurs Modernes. * Spier's and Surenne's Dictionary.
Spanish......	Josse's Grammar. Morales' Progressive Reader. Ollendorff's Oral Method applied to the Spanish, by Velasquez and Simonné. * Seoane's Neuman and Baretti's Dictionary.
Drawing.....................	Topography, etc. Art of Penmanship.
Tactics of Infantry, Artillery, and Cavalry.	Practical Instruction in the Schools of the Soldier, Company, and Battalion. Practical Instruction in Artillery and Cavalry.

Third Year—Second Class.

Natural and Experimental Philosophy.	Bartlett's Mechanics. Bartlett's Acoustics and Optics. Bartlett's Astronomy.
Chemistry.....................	Fowne's Chemistry. Chemical Physics, from Miller.
Drawing..	Landscape. Pencil and Colors.
Tactics of Artillery, Cavalry, and Infantry.	United States Tactics for Garrison, Siege, and Field Artillery. United States Tactics for Infantry. Practical Instruction in the Schools of the Soldier, Company, and Battalion. Practical Instruction in Artillery and Cavalry.
Practical Military Engineering.	Myers' Manual of Signals. Practical and Theoretical Instruction in Military Signaling and Telegraphy.

Fourth Year—First Class.

Military and Civil Engineering, and Science of War.	Mahan's Field Fortification. Mahan's Outlines of Permanent Fortification. Mahan's Civil Engineering. Mahan's Fortification and Stereotomy. Mahan's Advanced Guard and Outpost, etc * Moseley's Mechanics of Engineering.
Mineralogy and Geology.......	Dana's Mineralogy. Hitchcock's Geology.
Ethics and Law...............	French's Practical Ethics. Halleck's International Law. Kent's Commentaries (portion on Constitutional Law). Law and Military Law, by Prof. French. Benét's Military Law and the Practice of Courts-Martial.
Tactics of Artillery, Cavalry, and Infantry.	United States Tactics for Cavalry. Practical Instruction in the Schools of the Soldier, Company, and Battalion. Practical Instruction in Artillery and Cavalry.
Ordnance and Gunnery........	Benton's Ordnance and Gunnery. Practical Pyrotechny.
Practical Military Engineering.	Practical Instruction in fabricating Fascines, Sap Faggots, Gabions, Hurdles, Sap-rollers, etc.; manner of laying out and constructing Gun and Mortar Batteries, Field Fortifications and Works of Siege; formation of Stockades, Abatis, and other military obstacles; and throwing and dismantling Pontoon Bridges. Myers' Manual of Signals. Practical Instruction in Military Signaling and Telegraphy.

The second paper was a printed blank, a letter of acceptance or non-acceptance, to be filled up, as the case may be, signed by myself, countersigned by my father, and returned to Washington, D. C.

The third, which follows, is simply a memorandum for use of the candidate.

MEMORANDUM.

It is suggested to all candidates for admission into the Military Academy that, before leaving their place of residence for West Point, they should cause themselves to be thoroughly examined by a competent physician, and by a teacher or instructor in good standing By such an examination any *serious* physical disqualification, or deficiency in mental preparation, would be revealed, and the candidate probably spared the expense and trouble of a useless journey and the mortification of rejection. The circular appended to the letter of appointment should be carefully studied by the candidate and the examiners.

It should be understood that the informal examination herein recommended is solely for the convenience and benefit of the candidate himself, and can in no manner affect the decision of the Academic and Medical Examining Boards at West Point.

NOTE.—There being no provision whatever for the payment of the travelling expenses of either accepted or rejected candidates for admission, no candidate should fail to provide himself in advance with the means of returning to his home, in case of his rejection before either of the Examining Boards, as he may otherwise be put to considerable trouble, inconvenience, and even suffering, on account of his destitute situation. If admitted, the money brought by him to meet such a contingency can be deposited with the Treasurer on account of his equipment as a cadet, or returned to his friends.

After I had secured the appointment the editor of one of our local papers, which was at the time publishing — weekly, I think—brief biographies of some of the leading men of the city, together with cuts of the persons themselves, desired to thus bring me into notoriety. I was duly consulted, and, objecting, the publication did not occur. My chief reason for objecting was merely this : I feared some evil might befall me while passing through Georgia *en route* for West Point, if too great a knowledge of me should precede me, such, for instance, as a publication of that kind would give.

At this interview several other persons—white, of course—were present, and one of them—after relating the trials of Cadet Smith and the circumstances of his dismissal, which, *apropos*, had not yet occurred, as he would have me believe—advised me to abandon altogether the idea of going to West Point, for, said he, " Them northern boys wont treat you right." I have a due proportion of stubbornness in me, I believe, as all of the negro race are said to have, and my Southern friend might as well have advised an angel to rebel as to have counselled me to resign and not go. He was convinced, too, before we separated, that no change in my determination

was at all likely to occur.   Next day, in a short
article, the fact of my appointment was mentioned,
and my age and degree of education.   Some days
after this, while in the post-office, a gentleman beck-
oned to me, and we withdrew from the crowd.   He
mentioned this article, and after relating—indeed, repeating, to my amusement, the many hardships to
which I should be subjected, and after telling me he
had a very promising son—candid, wasn't he ?—whom
he desired to have educated at West Point, offered
me for my appointment the rather large sum of five
thousand dollars.   This I refused instantly.   I had so
set my mind on West Point that, having the appointment, neither threats nor excessive bribes could in-
duce me to relinquish it, even if I had not possessed
sufficient strength of character to resist them otherwise.   However, as I was a minor, I referred him to
my father.   I have no information that he ever consulted him.   If he had, my reply to him would have
been sustained.   I afterward had reason to believe
the offer was made merely to test me, as I received
from strangers expressions of confidence in me and
in my doing faithfully all that might devolve upon
me from my appointment.

CHAPTER III.

MAY 20th, 1873 ! Auspicious day ! From the
deck of the little ferry-boat that steamed its way
across from Garrison's on that eventful afternoon
I viewed the hills about West Point, her stone struc-
tures perched thereon, thus rising still higher, as
if providing access to the very pinnacle of fame, and
shuddered. With my mind full of the horrors of
the treatment of all former cadets of color, and the
dread of inevitable ostracism, I approached trem-
blingly yet confidently.

The little vessel having been moored, I stepped
ashore and inquired of a soldier there where candidates should report. He very kindly gave me all
needed information, wished me much success, for
which I thanked him, and set out for the designated
place. I soon reached it, and walked directly into
the adjutant's office. He received me kindly, asked
for my certificate of appointment, and receiving that
—or assurance that I had it : I do not now remember
which—directed me to write in a book there for the
purpose the name and occupation of my father, the
State, Congressional district, county and city of his
residence, my own full name, age, State, county, and
place of my birth, and my occupation when at home.
This done I was sent in charge of an orderly to cadet

2

barracks, where my " plebe quarters" were assigned me.

The impression made upon me by what I saw while going from the adjutant's office to barracks was certainly not very encouraging. The rear windows were crowded with cadets watching my unpretending passage of the area of barracks with apparently as much astonishment and interest as they would, perhaps, have watched Hannibal crossing the Alps. Their words, jeers, etc., were most insulting.

Having reached another office, I was shown in by the orderly. I walked in, hat in hand—nay, rather started in—when three cadets, who were seated in the room, simultaneously sprang to their feet, and welcomed me somewhat after this fashion :

" Well, sir, what do you mean by coming into this office in that manner, sir ? Get out of here, sir."

I walked out, followed by one of them, who, in a similar strain, ordered me to button my coat, get my hands around—" fins" he said—heels together, and head up.

" Now, sir," said he, leaving me, " when you are ready to come in, knock at that door," emphasizing the word " knock."

The door was open. I knocked. He replied, " Come in." I went in. I took my position in front of and facing him, my heels together, head up, the palms of my hands to the front, and my little fingers on the seams of my pantaloons, in which position we habitually carried them. After correcting my position and making it sufficiently military to suit himself, one of them, in a much milder tone,

asked what I desired of them. I told him I had
been sent by the adjutant to report there. He arose,
and directing me to follow him, conducted me to the
bath-rooms. Having discharged the necessary duty
there, I returned and was again put in charge of the
orderly, who carried me to the hospital. There I
was subjected to a rigid physical examination, which
I "stood" with the greatest ease. I was given a
certificate of ability by the surgeon, and by him sent
again to the adjutant, who in turn sent me to the
treasurer. From him I returned alone to barracks.

The reception given to "plebes" upon reporting
is often very much more severe than that given me.
Even members of my own class can testify to this.
This reception has, however, I think, been best described in an anonymous work, where it is thus set
forth :

"How dare you come into the presence of your
superior officer in that grossly careless and unmili-
tary manner? I'll have you imprisoned. Stand,
attention, sir!" (Even louder than before.) "Heels-
together-and-on-the-same-line, toes-equally-turned-
out, little-fingers-on-the-seams-of-your-pantaloons,
button-your-coat, draw-in-your-chin, throw-out-
your-chest, cast-your-eyes-fifteen-paces-to-the-front,
don't-let-me-see-you-wearing-standing-collars-again.
Stand-steady, sir. You've evidently mistaken your
profession, sir. In any other service, or at the seat
of war, sir, you would have been shot, sir, without
trial, sir, for such conduct, sir."

The effect of such words can be easily imagined.
A "plebe" will at once recognize the necessity for
absolute obedience, even if he does know all this is

hazing, and that it is doubtless forbidden. Still "plebes" almost invariably tremble while it lasts, and when in their own quarters laugh over it, and even practise it upon each other for mutual amusement.

On the way to barracks I met the squad of "beasts" marching to dinner. I was ordered to fall in, did so, marched to the mess hall, and ate my first dinner at West Point. After dinner we were marched again to barracks and dismissed. I hastened to my quarters, and a short while after was turned out to take possession of my baggage. I lugged it to my room, was shown the directions on the back of the door for arrangement of articles, and ordered to obey them within half an hour. The parts of the regulations referred to are the following :

SPECIAL REGULATIONS FOR BARRACKS.

ORDERLIES OF ROOMS.

The particular attention of Orderlies is directed to those paragraphs of the Regulations for the U. S. Military Academy specifying their duties.

CADETS.

The hours of Recitation of each Cadet will be posted on the back of the door of his room. When a room is being washed out by the policeman, on reporting to the Officer of the Day, and stating to him the number of some room in his own Division he wishes to visit, a Cadet will be permitted to visit that particular room until his own can be occupied. The uniform coat will be worn from 8 till 10 A.M.; at Inspection before 10 A.M. the coat will be buttoned throughout ; at Sunday Morning Inspection gloves and side-arms will also be worn. After 10 A.M. any uniform garment or dressing-gown may be worn in their own rooms, but at no time will Cadets be in their shirt-sleeves unnecessarily. During the "Call to Quarters," between "Inspection Call" in the morning and "Tattoo," the following Arrangement of Furniture, etc., will be required :

ACCOUTREMENTS.

Dress Cap—On gun-rack shelf.
Cartridge Boxes, Waist Belts, Sabres, Forage Caps—Hung on pegs near gun-rack shelf.

Muskets—In gun-rack, Bayonets in the scabbards.
Spurs—Hung on peg with Sabres.

BEDSTEADS AND BEDDING.

Bedsteads—In alcove, against side wall of the room, the head against the back wall.

Bedding—Mattress to be folded once ; Blankets and Comforters, each one to be neatly and separately folded, so that the folds shall be of the width of an ordinary pillow, and piled at the head of the BEDSTEAD in the following order, viz.: MATTRESS, SHEETS, PILLOWS, BLANKETS, and COMFORTERS, the front edge of sheets, pillows, etc., to be vertical. On Sunday afternoons the BEDS may be made down and used.

CLOTHES-PRESS.

Books—On the top of the Press, against the wall, and with the backs to the front. BRUSHES (tooth and hair), COMBS, SHAVING IMPLEMENTS and MATERIALS, such small boxes as may be allowed, vials, etc., to be neatly arranged on the upper shelf. BELTS, COLLARS, GLOVES, HANDKERCHIEFS, SOCKS, etc., to be neatly arranged on the second shelf from the top. SHEETS, PILLOW-CASES, SHIRTS, DRAWERS, WHITE PANTS, etc., to be neatly arranged on the other shelves, the heaviest articles on the lower shelves.

Arrangement—All articles of the same kind are to be carefully and neatly placed in separate piles. The folded edges of these articles to be to the front, and even with the front edge of the shelf. Nothing will be allowed between these piles of clothing and the back of the press, unless the want of room on the front edge renders it necessary.

Dirty Clothes—To be kept in clothes-bag.

Shoes and Over-Shoes—To be kept clean, dusted, and arranged in a line where they can be seen by the Inspector, either at the foot of the bedstead or at the side near the foot.

Woollen Clothing, Dressing-Gown, and Clothes-Bag—To be hung on the pegs in alcove in the following general order, from the front of the alcove to the back : Over-Coat, Dressing-Gown, Uniform Coats, Jackets, Pants, Clothes-Bag.

FURNITURE.

Broom—To be kept behind the door. TIN BOX for CLEANING MATERIALS—To be kept clean and in the fire-place. SPITTOON—To be kept on one side of the hearth near mantel-piece. CHAIRS and TABLES—On no occasion to be in alcoves, the chairs, when not in use, to be against the owners' tables. LOOKING-GLASS—At the centre of the mantel-piece. WASH-STAND—To be kept clean, in front and against alcove partition. WASH-BASIN—To be kept clean, and inverted on the top of the wash-stand. WATER-BUCKET—To be kept on shelf of wash-stand. SLOP-BUCKET—To be kept near to and on side of wash-stand, opposite door. Baskets, Pictures, Clocks, Statues, Trunks, and large Boxes will NOT be allowed in quarters.

Curtains—WINDOW-CURTAINS—Only uniform allowed, and to be kept drawn back during the day. ALCOVE-CURTAINS—Only uniform allowed, and to be kept drawn, except between "Tattoo" and "Reveille" and when dressing. CURTAINS OF CLOTHES-PRESS— To be kept drawn, except when policing room.

FLOOR.
To be kept clean, and free from grease-spots and stains.

WALLS AND WOOD-WORK.
To be kept free from cobwebs, and not to be injured by nails or otherwise.

HEATING APPARATUS, SCREEN AND TOP.
To be kept clean, and not to be scratched or defaced.

These Regulations will be strictly obeyed and enforced.

By order of LIEUT.-COLONEL UPTON,

GEORGE L. TURNER,

Cadet Lieut. and Adjutant.

HEADQUARTERS, CORPS OF CADETS,

West Point, N. Y., Sept. 4, 1873.

At the end of the time specified every article was arranged and the cadet corporal returned to inspect. He walked deliberately to the clothes-press, and, informing me that every thing was arranged wrong, threw every article upon the floor, repeated his order, and withdrew. And thus three times in less than two hours did I arrange and he disarrange my effects. I was not troubled again by him till after supper, when he inspected again, merely opening the door, however, and looking in. He told me I could not go to sleep till "tattoo." Now tattoo, as he evidently used it, referred in some manner to time, and with such reference I had not the remotest idea of what it meant. I had no knowledge whatever of military terms or customs. However, as I was also told that I could do any thing—writing, etc. —I might wish to do, I found sufficient to keep me awake until he again returned and told me it was then tattoo, that I could retire then or at any time within half an hour, and that at the end of that time the light *must* be extinguished and I *must* be in bed. I instantly extinguished it and retired.

Thus passed my first half day at West Point, and thus began the military career of the fifth colored cadet. The other four were Smith of South Carolina, Napier of Tennessee, Howard of Mississippi, and Gibbs of Florida.

What I had seen and experienced during the few hours from my arrival till tattoo filled me with fear and apprehension. I expected every moment to be insulted or struck, and was not long in persuading myself that the various reports which I had heard concerning Smith were true—I had not seen him yet, or, if I had, had not recognized him—and that my life there was to be all torture and anguish. I was uneasy and miserable, ever thinking of the regulations, verbal or written, which had been given me. How they haunted me! I kept repeating them over and over, fearful lest I might forget and violate them, and be dismissed. If I wanted any thing or wished to go anywhere, I must get permission of the cadet officers on duty over us. To get such permission I must enter their office cleanly and neatly dressed, and, taking my place in the centre of the room, must salute, report my entrance, make known my wants, salute again, and report my departure.*

---

* Somewhat after this fashion :

"Candidate F—, United States Military Academy, reports his entrance into this office, sir."

"Well, sir, what do you want in this office ?"

"I desire permission, sir, to walk on public lands till retreat."

At the instant I heard the sound of a drum I must turn out at a run and take my place in the ranks.

At five o'clock the next morning two unusual sounds greeted my ears—the *reveille,* and a voice in the hall below calling out in a loud martial tone :

"Candidates, turn out promptly!" In an astonishingly short time I had dressed, "turned out," and was in ranks. We stood there as motionless as statues till the fifers and drummers had marched up to barracks, the rolls of the companies had been called, and they themselves dismissed. We were then dismissed, our roll having been also called. We withdrew at a run to our quarters and got them ready for inspection, which, we were informed, would take place at the expiration of half an hour. At the end of this time our quarters were inspected by a corporal. In my own room he upset my bedding, kicked my shoes into the middle of the room, and ordered me to arrange them again and in better order. This order was obeyed immediately. And this upsetting was done in every room, as I learned afterward from the occupants, who, strange to say, manifested no prejudice then. 'Twas not long ere they learned that they were prejudiced, and that they abhorred even the sight of a " *d—d nigger.*"

Just before, or perhaps just after breakfast, our quarters were again inspected. This time I was somewhat surprised to hear the corporal say, " Very well, Mr. Flipper, very well, sir."

And this, with other things, shows there was a

" No, sir, you can't walk on public lands till retreat. Get out of my sight."

" Candidate F—, United States Military Academy, reports his departure from this office, sir."

friendly feeling toward me from the first. After having thus expressed himself, he directed me to print my name on each of four pieces of paper, and to tack them up in certain places in the room, which he indicated to me. I did this several times before I could please him ; but at last succeeded. Another corporal visited me during the day and declared everything out of order, although I had not touched a single thing after once satisfying the first corporal. Of course I had to rearrange them to suit him, in which I also finally succeeded.

At eleven o'clock the mail came. I received a letter, and to my astonishment its postmark was " West Point, N. Y., May 21st." Of course I was at a loss to know who the writer was. I turned it over and over, looked at it, studied the postmark, finally opened it and read it.*

This was another surprise—a welcome surprise, however. I read it over several times. It showed me plainly that Smith had not been dismissed, as had been reported to me at home. I at once formed

---

* This letter by some means has been misplaced, and all efforts to find it, or to discover what its exact contents were, have failed. However, it was from James Webster Smith, the first and then only cadet of color at West Point. It reassured me very much, telling me not to fear either blows or insults, and advising me to avoid any forward conduct if I wished also to avoid certain consequences. " which," said the writer, " I have learned from sad experience," would be otherwise inevitable. It was a sad letter. I don't think any thing has so affected me or so influenced my conduct at West Point as its melancholy tone. That " sad experience" gave me a world of warning. I looked upon it as implying the confession of some great error made by him at some previous time, and of its sadder consequences.

a better opinion of West Point than I before had, and from that day my fears gradually wore away.

The candidates now reported rapidly, and we, who had reported the day previous, were comparatively undisturbed. At four o'clock I visited Smith at his quarters by permission. My visit was necessarily a short one, as he was then preparing for drill. It sufficed, however, for us to become acquainted, and for me to receive some valuable advice. An hour and place were designated for us to meet next day, and I took my leave of him. The "plebes" turned out *en masse*, walked around the grounds and witnessed the drilling of the battalion. We enjoyed it immensely. They were that day skirmishing and using blank cartridges. We thought the drill superb. I was asked by a fellow-"plebe," "Think you'll like that?"

"Oh yes," said I, "when I can do it as easily as they do."

We had quite a lengthy conversation about the fine appearance of the cadets, their forms, so straight and manly, evoking our greatest admiration. This, alas! was our only conversation on any subject. The gentleman discovered ere long that he too was prejudiced, and thus one by one they "cut" me, whether for prudential reasons or not I can not presume to say.

I went into the office one day, and standing uncovered at about the middle of the room, in the position of the soldier, saluted and thus addressed a cadet officer present:

"Candidate Flipper, United States Military Academy, reports his entrance into this office, sir."

" Well, what do you want ?" was the rather gruff reply.

" I desire permission to visit Smith, sir," answered I, thoughtlessly saying " Smith," instead of " Mr." or " Cadet Smith."

He instantly sprang from his seat into rather close proximity to my person and angrily yelled :

" Well, sir, I want to hear you say 'Mr. Smith.' I want you to understand, sir, he is a cadet and you're a ' plebe,' and I don't want to see such familiarity on your part again, sir," putting particular emphasis on " Mr."

Having thus delivered himself he resumed his seat, leaving me, I imagine, more scared than otherwise.

" What do you want ?" asked he again, after a pause of a moment or so.

" Permission to visit Mr. Smith."

Without condescending to notice for the time my request he gave the interview a rather ludicrous turn, I thought, by questioning me somewhat after this manner :

" Can you dance, Mr. Flipper ?"

Having answered this to his entire satisfaction, he further asked :

" Expect to attend the hops this summer ?"

" Oh no, sir," replied I, smiling, as he also was, for I had just discovered the drift of his questions. After mischievously studying my countenance for a moment, he returned to the original subject and queried, " Where do you want to go.?"

I told him.

" Well, get out of my sight."

I considered the permission granted, and hastily withdrew to take advantage of it.

Between breakfast and supper those of us who had been there at least a day had quite a pleasant time. We were not troubled with incessant inspections or otherwise. We either studied for examination or walked around the grounds. At or near seven o'clock, the time of retreat parade, we were formed near our barracks and inspected. Our ranks were opened and the cadet lieutenant inspected our clothing and appearance generally. A not infrequent occurrence on these occasions was :

" Well, mister, what did you shave with—a shoehorn ?"

At this we would smile, when the lieutenant, sergeant, or corporal would jump at us and yell :

" Wipe that smile off your face, sir ! What do you mean, sir, by laughing in ranks ?"

If any one attempted to reply he was instantly silenced with—

" Well, sir, don't reply to me in ranks."

The inspection would be continued. Some one, unable to restrain himself—the whole affair was so ridiculous — would laugh right out in ranks. He was a doomed man.

" What do you mean, sir, by laughing in ranks, sir ?"

Having been once directed not to reply in ranks, the poor " plebe" would stand mute.

" Well, sir, don't you intend to answer me ?"

" Yes, sir."

" Well, sir, step it out. What were you grinning at ?"

" Nothing, sir."

" Nothing ! Well, sir, you're a pretty thing to be grinning at nothing. Get in ranks."

The inspection would, after many such interruptions, be continued. Ranks would at length be closed and the command, " In place, rest !" given. The battalion would march in from parade at double time and form in the area to our rear. The delinquencies of the day previous would then be published by the cadet adjutant.

What most strikes a " plebe" is this same publication. He hasn't the remotest idea of what it is. Not a word uttered by the adjutant is understood by him. He stands and wonders what it is. A perfect jargon of words, unintelligible and meaningless to him ! I remember distinctly how I used to wonder, and how I was laughed at when I asked for information concerning it. We " plebes" used to speak of it often, and wonder if it was not French. When we were better acquainted with the rules and customs of the Academy we learned what it was. It was something of this nature, read from the " Delinquency Book :"

DELINQUENCIES, TUESDAY, OCT. 12.

ADAMS.—Late at reveille roll-call.

BEJAY.—Sentinel not coming to " Arms, Port," when addressed by the officer of the day.

SAME.—Not conversant with orders at same.

BARNES.—Same at same.

SAME.—Sentinel, neglect of duty, not requiring cadet leaving his post to report his departure and 'destination.

SAME.—Hanging head, 4 P.M.

BULOW.—Dust on mantel at inspection, 9.30 A.M.

SAME.—Executing manual of arms with pointer in section-room, 9 A.M.

SAME.—Using profane expression, 1 P.M.
CULLEN.—Out of bed at taps.
DOUNS.—Light in quarters, 11 P.M.
SAME.—Not prepared on 47 Velasquez.*

On the 26th of May, another colored candidate reported. It is said he made the best show at the preliminary examination. Unfortunately, however, he was " found " at the following semi-annual examination. He was brought up to my quarters by a corporal, and I was ordered to give him all instruction which had previously been given me. This I did, and his first days at West Point were much more pleasant than mine had been.

The candidates had now all reported, and Monday afternoon, May 28th, we were each given by the Adjutant in person a slip of paper upon which was written the number of each man's name in an alphabetically arranged roll. This we had special directions to preserve. The next day we were marched up to the Drawing Academy, and examined in grammar, history, and geography ; the following day in orthography and reading. On the same day, also, we were required to write out a list of all the text-books we had used in our previous school-days. The day following we were divided into sections and marched to the library, where the Academic Board

---

* For these delinquencies the cadets are allowed to write explanations. If the offence is absence from quarters or any duty without authority, or is one committed in the Academical Department, called an Academical Delinquency, such as not being prepared on some lesson, an explanation is required and must be written. For all other offences the cadet can write an explanation or not as he chooses. If the explanation is satisfactory, the offence is removed and he gets no demerits, otherwise he does. For form of explanation see Chapter X., latter part.

was in readiness to examine us in mathematics. It
took quite a while to examine our class of more
than one hundred members thus orally. I am not
positive about the dates of the examination. I
know it occurred in the immediate vicinity of those
named.

Not many days after this the result of the examination was made known to us. The familiar cry,
"Candidates, turn out promptly," made at about
noon, informed us that something unusual was about
to occur. It was a fearful moment, and yet I was
sure I had "passed." The only questions I failed
on were in geography. I stood motionless while the
order was being read until I heard my name among
the accepted ones. I felt as if a great burden had
been removed from my mind. It was a beginning,
and if not a good one, certainly not a bad one.
What has been the ending? Let the sequel show.

Now that the examination was over and the deficient ones gone, we were turned out for drill every
morning at half-past five o'clock and at four in the
afternoon. We were divided into squads of one
each, and drilled twice a day in the "settings up"
until about June 20th. After a few drills, however,
the squads were consolidated into others of four,
six, and eight each. The surplus drill-masters were
"turned in." Their hopes were withered, for it was
almost a certainty that those who were "turned in"
would not be "made." They expected to be
"made" on their proficiency in drilling, and when
it was shown by being "turned in" that others had
been thought better drill-masters, they were not a
little disappointed. How they "boned" tactics!

What proficiency they manifested ! How they yelled out their commands ! What eagerness they showed to correct errors, etc. And yet some could not overcome their propensity for hazing, and these were of course turned in. Not always thus, however. Those who were not " turned in" were not always " made" corporals. Often those who were so treated " got the chevrons" after all.

" Plebe drill," or, more familiarly, " squad drill," has always been a source of great amusement to citizens, but what a horror to plebes. Those torturous twistings and twirlings, stretching every nerve, straining every sinew, almost twisting the joints out of place and making life one long agonizing effort. Was there ever a " plebe," or recruit, who did not hate, did not shudder at the mere mention of squad drill ? I did. Others did. I remember distinctly my first experience of it. I formed an opinion, a morbid dislike of it then, and have not changed it. The benefit, however, of " squad drill" can not be overestimated. It makes the most crooked, distorted creature an erect, noble, and manly being, provided, of course, this distortion be a result of habit and not a natural deformity, the result of laziness in one's walking, such as hanging the head, dropping the shoulders, not straightening the legs, and crossing them when walking.

Squad drill is one of the painful necessities of military discipline, and no one regrets his experience of it, however displeasing it may have been at the time. It is squad drill and hazing that so successfully mould the coarser characters who come to West Point into officers and gentlemen. They teach him how to govern and be governed. They are more effectual in polishing his asperities of disposition and forming his character than any amount of regulations could be. They tame him, so to speak.

Squad drill was at once a punishment, a mode of hazing, and a drill. For the least show of grossness one was sure to be punished with " settings up, second time !" "settings up, fourth time !" " Continue the motion, settings up second (or fourth) time !" We would be kept at these motions until we could scarcely move. Of course all this was contrary to orders. The drill-master would be careful not to be " hived." If he saw an officer even looking at him, he would add the command " three," which caused a discontinuance of the motion. He would change, however, to one of the other exercises immediately, and thus keep the plebes continually in motion. When he thought the punishment sufficient he would discontinue it by the command " three," and give " place, rest." When the " place, rest" had been just about sufficient to allow the plebe to get cool and in a measure rested, the drill would be resumed by the command " 'tion, squad " (abbreviated from " attention" and pronounced " shun"). If the plebe was slow, " place, rest" was again given, and

" When I give the command ' 'tion, squad,' I want to see you spring up with life."

" 'Tion, squad !"

Plebe is slow again.

" Well, mister, wake up. This is no trifling matter. Understand ?"

" Yes, sir."

" Well, sir, don't reply to me in ranks."

And many times and terms even more severe than these.

Now that Williams and myself were admitted, the newspapers made their usual comments on such occurrences. I shall quote a single one from *The New National Era and Citizen,* published in Washington, D. C., and the political organ of the colored people. The article, however, as I present it, is taken from another paper, having been by it taken from the *Era and Citizen :*

"COLORED CADETS AT WEST POINT.

"The *New National Era and Citizen,* which is the national organ of the colored people, contains a sensible article this week on the status of colored cadets at West Point. After referring to the colored young men, 'Plebes' Flipper of Georgia, and Williams of Virginia, who have passed the examination requisite for entering the Academy, the *Era and Citizen* says : 'Now that they are in, the stiff and starched protégés of the Government make haste to tell the reporters that "none of the fellows would hurt them, but every fellow would let them alone." Our reporter seems to think that "to be let alone " a terrible doom. So it is, if one is sent to Coventry by gentlemen. So it is, if one is neglected by those who, in point of education, thrift, and morality are our equals or superiors. So it is not, if done by the low-minded, the ignorant, and the snobbish. If it be possible, among the four hundred young charity students of the Government, that Cadet Smith, for instance, finds no warm friends, and has won no respect after the gallant fight he has made for four years --a harder contest than he will ever have in the sterner field—then we despair of the material which West Point is turning out. If this be true, it is training selfish, snobbish martinets—not knightly soldiers, not Havelocks, Hardinges, and Kearneys—but the lowest type of disciplined and educated force and brutality—the Bluchers and Marlboroughs. We scarcely believe this, however, and we know that any young man, whether he be poor or black, or both, may enter any first-class college in America and find warm sympathetic friends, both among students and faculty, if he but prove himself to be possessed of some good qualities. . . . . If the Smiths, Flippers, and Williamses in their .honorable school-boy careers can not meet social as well as intellectual recognition while at West Point, let them study on and acquit themselves like men, for they will meet, out in the world, a worthy reception among men of worth, who have put by the prejudices of race and the shackles of ignorance. Emerson says somewhere that " Solitude, the nurse of Genius, is the foe of mediocrity." If our young men of ability have the stuff in them to make men out of, they need not fear " to be let alone" for a while ; they will ultimately come to the surface and attain worthy recognition.'

" That is plain, practical talk. We like it. It has the ring of the true metal. It shows that the writer has faith in the ultimate triumph of manhood. It is another form for expressing a firm belief that real worth will find a reward. Never has any bond people emerged from slavery into a condition full of such grand opportunities and splendid possibilities as those which are within the reach of the colored people of the United States ; but if those opportunities are to be made available, if those possibilities are to be realized, the colored people must move into the fore-front of action and study and work in their own behalf. The colored cadets at West Point, the colored students in the public schools, the colored men in the professions, the trades, and on the plantations, can not be idlers if they are to compete with the white race in the acquisition of knowledge and property. But they have examples of notable achievements in their own ranks which should convince them that they have not the slightest reason to despair of success. The doors stand wide open, from the plantation to the National Capitol, and every American citizen can, if he will, attain worthy recognition."

And thus, ere we had entered upon our new duties, were we forewarned of the kind of treatment we should expect. To be " sent to Coventry," " to be let severely alone," are indeed terrible dooms, but we cared naught for them. " To be let alone" was what we wished. To be left to our own re- sources for study and improvement, for enjoyment in whatever way we chose to seek it, was what we desired. We cared not for social recognition. We did not expect it, nor were we disappointed in not getting it. We would not seek it. We would not obtrude ourselves upon them. We would not accept recognition unless it was made willingly. We would be of them at least independent. We would mark out for ourselves a uniform course of conduct and follow it rigidly. These were our resolutions. So long as we were in the right we knew we should be recognized by those whose views were not limited or bound by such narrow confines as prejudice and caste, whether they were at West Point or elsewhere. Confident that right on our own part would secure us just treatment from others, that " if we but prove ourselves possessed of some good qualities" we could find friends among both faculty and students.

I came to West Point, notwithstanding I had heard so much about the Academy well fit to dishearten and keep one away. And then, too, at the time I had no object in seeking the appointment other than to gratify an ordinary ambition. Several friends were opposed to my accepting it, and even persuaded me, or rather attempted to persuade me, to give up the idea altogether. I was inexorable. I had set my mind upon West Point, and no amount of persuasion, and no number of harrowing narratives of bad treatment, could have induced me to relinquish the object I had in view. But I was right. The work I chose, and from which I could not flinch without dishonor, proved far more important than either my friends or myself at first thought it would be.

Let me not, however, anticipate. Of this importance more anon.

CHAPTER IV.

AS a narrative of this description is very apt to be dry and uninteresting, I have thought it possible to remove in a measure this objection by using as often as convenient the cant lingo of the corps. A vocabulary which shall contain it all, or nearly all, becomes necessary. I have taken great care to make it as full as possible, and at the same time as intelligible as possible.

There are a few cant words and expressions which are directly personal, and in many cases self-explanatory. They are for such reasons omitted.

" Animal," " animile," " beast," " reptile."— Synonymous terms applied to candidates for admission into the Academy.

" Plebe."—A candidate after admission, a new cadet. After the candidates are examined and the proficient ones admitted, these latter are known officially as " new cadets," but in the cant vernacular of the corps they are dubbed " plebes," and they retain this designation till the candidates of the next year report. They are then called " yearlings," a title applied usually to them in camp only. After the encampment they become " furloughmen" until they return from furlough in August of the following year. They then are " second-classmen," and are so officially and *à la cadet* throughout the year.

From this time till they graduate they are known as the " graduating class," so that, except the second class, each class has its own peculiar cant designation.

Candidates generally report in May—about the 20th—and during July and August are in camp. This is their " plebe camp." The next is their " yearling camp." During the next they are *en congé*, and the next and last is their " first-class camp." Of " plebe camp," " yearling camp," and " first-class camp," more anon.

" Rapid."— A " plebe" is said to be " rapid " when he shows a disposition to resist hazing, or to " bone familiarity" with older cadets—*i.e.*, upper classmen.

" Sep."—A cadet who reported for admission in September.

" Fins."—A term applied to the hands generally, of course to the hands of " plebes."

" Prelim."—A preliminary examination.

" Pred."—A predecessor.

" Pony."—A key, a *corrigé*.

" To bone."—To study, to endeavor to do well in any particular ; for instance, to " bone demerits" is to strive to get as few as possible.

" To bone popularity."—This alludes to a habit practised, especially by " yearlings" while in camp, and is equivalent to our every-day expression in civil life, viz., " to get in with."

" To bugle it."—To avoid a recitation. To avoid a recitation is an act seldom done by any cadet. It is in fact standing at the board during the whole time of recitation without turning around, and thus making known a readiness to recite. At the Academy a bugle takes the place of the bell in civil schools. When the bugle is blown those sections at recitation are dismissed, and others come in. Now, if one faces the board till the bugle blows, there is not then enough time for him to recite, and he is said to have "bugled it." Some instructors will call on any one who shows a disposition to do so, and will require him to tell what he knows about his subject.

"Busted," "broken."—These words apply only to cadet officers who are reduced to ranks.

"A cold case."—A sure thing, a foregone conclusion.

"To get chevrons."—To receive an appointment in the battalion organization. Each year, on the day the graduates receive their diplomas, and just after —possibly just before—they are relieved from further duty at the Academy, the order fixing the appointments for the next year is read, and those of the year previous revoked. It has been customary to appoint the officers, captains, and lieutenants from the first class, the sergeants from the second, and the corporals from the third. This custom has at times, and for reasons, been departed from, and the officers chosen as seemed best.

For any offence of a grave nature, any one who has chevrons is liable to lose them, or, in other words, to be reduced to ranks.

"A cit."—Any citizen.

"To crawl over."—To haze, generally in the severest manner possible.

"A chapel."—An attendance at church.

"To curse out."—To reprimand, to reprove, and

also simply to interview. This expression does not by any means imply the use of oaths.

" To cut," " To cut cold."—To avoid, to ostracize.

" Debauch." — Any ceremony or any thing unusual. It may be a pleasant chat, a drill, or any thing that is out of the usual routine.

" To drive a squad."—To march it.

" Dropped."—Not promoted.

" To eat up."—See " To crawl over."

" Exaggerations."—It is a habit of the cadets to exaggerate on certain occasions, and especially when policing. " A log of wood," " a saw-mill," " a forest," and kindred expressions, are applied to any fragment of wood of any description that may be lying about. A feather is " a pillow ;" a straw, " a broom factory ;" a pin, an " iron foundry ;" a cotton string, " a cotton factory ;" and I have known a " plebe" to be told to " get up that sugar refinery," which " refinery" was a cube of sugar crushed by some one treading upon it.

Any thing—whatever it may be—which must be policed, is usually known by some word or term suggested by its use or the method or the place of its manufacture.

" To find." — To declare deficient in studies or discipline.

An " extra" is an extra tour of guard duty given as punishment. Cadets on " extra" are equipped as for parade, and walk in the area of Cadet Barracks from two o'clock until retreat, or from two to five hours, on Saturday or other days of the week. An " extra" is sometimes called a " Saturday Punishment."

" A fem," " femme."—Any female person.

" A file."—Any male person.

" Fessed," " fessed cold," " fessed frigid," " fessed out," and " fessed through."—Made a bad recitation, failed.

" To get off."—To perpetrate.

" A gag," " Grin," " Grind."—Something witty, a repartee.

" To hive."—To detect, used in a good and bad sense. Also to take, to steal.

" To hoop up."—To hasten, to hurry.

" H. M. P."—Hop manager's privileges.

" A keen."—See " Gag," etc.

" To leap on."—See " To crawl over."

" Made."—Given an appointment, given chevrons as an officer in the battalion organization.

" A make."—Such an appointment.

" Maxed."—Made a thorough recitation.

" Ath."—The last one.

" To pile in."—To retire.

" To pink."—To report for any offence.

" To plant."—To bury with military honors.

" To police one's self."—To bathe.

" To pot."—" To pink," which see.

" Prof."—Professor.

" To put in."—To submit in writing.

" To put into the battalion."—To assign to a company, as in case of new cadets.

" Ragged," " ragged out."—Made a good recitation.

" Reveilles."—Old shoes, easy and comfortable, worn to reveille roll-call.

" Reckless, ricochet."—Careless, indifferent.

3

"To run it."—To do any thing forbidden.   To risk.

"To run it on."—To impose upon.

"Shout."—Excellent, *i.e.*, will create much comment and praise.

"Sketch-house."—The Drawing Academy.

"To skin."—See "To pink" (most common).

"To be spooney."—To be gallant.

"To spoon."—To be attentive to ladies.

"A spoon."—A sweetheart.

"Shungudgeon."—A stew.

"Supe."—Superintendent.

"To step out."—See "To hoop up."

"Topog."—A topographical drawing.

"To turn in."—To repair to one's quarters.

"To be sent in."—To order any thing sent in.

"To turn out."—To come out, or send out.

"To be white," "To treat white."—To be polite, courteous, and gentlemanly.

"To wheaten."—To be excused by surgeon.

"To yank."—To seize upon violently.

"O. G. P."—Old guard privileges.

"Chem."—Chemistry.

"Math."—Mathematics.

"Phil."—Philosophy.

"Rocks."—Mineralogy.

"Wigwag."—Signalling.

"To get out of."—To shun, to shirk.

"Thing."—A "plebe."

"To extinguish."—To distinguish.

"To go for."—To haze.

"House."—Room, quarters.

"To freeze to."—To hold firmly.

" To wipe out."—To destroy.

" Limbo."—Confinement.

" Solemncholy."—Sad, dejected.

" Plebeskin."—A rubber overcoat issued to new cadets.

" Turnbacks."—Cadets turned back to a lower class.

" Div," subdiv."—Division, subdivision.

" Devils."—Fellows familiarly.

" Tab."—Tabular system of French.

" To celebrate."—To do.

" A stayback."—A graduate detained at graduation to instruct the new cadets.*

" Scratch day."—A day when lessons are hard or numerous.

" Gum game."—A joke.

" To fudge."—To copy.

BENNY HAVENS O.

[A number of cadets sitting or lounging about the room. One at table pouring out the drinks. As soon as he is done he takes up his own glass, and says to the others, " Come, fellows," and then all together standing :]

—— Stand up in a row,
For sentimental drinking we're going for to go ;
In the army there's sobriety, promotion's very slow,
So we'll cheer our hearts with choruses of Benny Havens' O.
Of Benny Havens' O, of Benny Havens' O,
We'll cheer our hearts with choruses of Benny Havens' O.

* When the cadets are in barracks, the officer of the guard on Sundays either has or assumes authority to detain from church, for any emergency that might arise, one or two or more members of his guard, in addition to those on post on duty. Cadets so detained are called " staybacks."

When you and I and Benny, and General Jackson too,
Are brought before the final Board our course of life t' review,
May we never " fess" on any point, but then be told to go
To join the army of the blest at Benny Havens' O.
At Benny Havens' O, at Benny Havens' O,
To join the army of the blest at Benny Havens' O.

To the ladies of the army let our bumpers ever flow,
Companions of our exile, our shield 'gainst every woe,
May they see their husbands generals with double pay to show,
And indulge in reminiscences of Benny Havens' O.
Of Benny Havens O, of Benny Havens' O,
And indulge in reminiscences of Benny Havens' O.

'Tis said by commentators, in the land where we must go
We follow the same handicraft we followed here below ;
If this be true philosophy (the sexton, he says no),
What days of dance and song we'll have at Benny Havens' O.
At Benny Havens' O, at Benny Havens' O,
What days of dance and song we'll have at Benny Havens' O !

To the ladies of the Empire State, whose hearts and albums too
Bear sad remembrance of the wrongs we stripling soldiers do,
We bid you all a kind farewell, the best recompense we know—
Our loves and rhymings had their source at Benny Havens' O.
At Benny Havens' O, at Benny Havens' O,
Our loves and rhymings had their source at Benny Havens' O.

[Then, with due solemnity, every head uncovered and bowed
low, they sing :]

There comes a voice from Florida, from Tampa's lonely shore ;
It is the wail of gallant men, O'Brien is no more ;
In the land of sun and flowers his head lies pillowed low,
No more to sing *petite coquille* at Benny Havens' O.
At Benny Havens' O, at Benny Havens' O.
No more to sing *petite coquille* at Benny Havens' O, etc.

CHAPTER V.

PLEBE CAMP.

"PLEBE CAMP!" The very words are suggestive. Those who have been cadets know what "plebe camp" is. To a plebe just beginning his military career the first experience of camp is most trying. To him every thing is new. Every one seems determined to impose upon him, and each individual "plebe" fancies at times he's picked out from all the rest as an especially good subject for this abuse (?). It is not indeed a very pleasant prospect before him, nor should he expect it to be. But what must be his feelings when some old cadet paints for his pleasure camp scenes and experiences? Whatever he may have known of camp life before seems as naught to him now. It is a new sort of life he is to lead there, and he feels himself, although curious and anxious to test it, somewhat shy of entering such a place. There is no alternative. He accepts it resignedly and goes ahead. It is not always with smiling countenance that he marches out and surveys the site after reveille. Indeed, those who do have almost certainly received a highly colored sketch of camp life, and are hastening to sad disappointment, and not at all to the joys they've been led to expect. He marches into the company streets. He surveys them carefully and recognizes what is meant by "the plebes have to do all the

policing," servants being an unknown luxury.   He
also sees the sentry-boxes and the paths the sentinels tread, and shudders as he recollects the tales
of midnight adventure which some wily cadet has
narrated to him.   Imagination begins her cruel
work.   Already he sees himself lying at the bottom
of Fort Clinton Ditch tied in a blanket, or perhaps
fetterless and free, but helpless.   Or he may imagine
his hands are tied to one, and his feet to the other
tent-pole, and himself struggling for freedom as he
recognizes that the reveille gun has been fired and
those merciless fifers and drummers are rapidly
finishing the reveille.   And, horror of horrors!
mayhap his fancies picture him standing trembling-
ly on post at midnight's solemn hour, his gun just
balanced in his hands, while numbers of cadets in
hideous sheets and other ghostly garb approach or
are aleady standing around torturing him.   And
again, perchance, he challenges some approaching
person in one direction, and finds to his dismay the
officer of the day, the officer of the guard, and a corporal are crossing and recrossing his post, or having
already advanced without being challenged, are
demanding why it is, and why he has been so neg-
ligent.

Just after reveille on the morning of June 22d
the companies were marched to their company
streets, and the " plebes" assigned to each followed
in rear.   At the time only the tent floors and cord
stays were on the ground.   These former the
" plebes" were ordered to align.   This we did while
the old cadets looked on, occasionally correcting or
making some suggestion.   It required considerable

time to do this, as we were inexperienced and had to await some explanation of what we were to do.

When at last we were done, tents, or rather tent floors, were assigned to us. We thence returned to barracks and to breakfast. Our more bulky effects were carried into camp on wagons before breakfast, while the lighter articles were moved over by our own hands. By, or perhaps before, eleven o'clock every thing had been taken to camp. By twelve we were in ranks ready to march in. At the last stroke of the clock the column was put in march, and we marched in with all the "glory of war." We stacked arms in the company streets, broke ranks, and each repaired to the tent assigned him, which had by this time been brought over and placed folded on the tent floors. They were rapidly prepared for raising, and at a signal made on a drum the tents were raised simultaneously, 'mid rousing cheers, which told that another "camp" was begun.

After this we had dinner, and then we put our tents in order. At four o'clock the police-call was sounded, and all the "plebes" were turned out to police the company streets. This new phase of West Point life—and its phases rapidly developed themselves — was a hard one indeed. The duties are menial, and very few discharge them without some show of displeasure, and often of temper. None are exempt. It is not hard work, and yet every one objects to doing it. The third and fourth classes, by regulations, are required to do the policing. When I was a plebe, the plebes did it all. Many indeed tried to shirk it, but they were invariably "hived." Every plebe who attempted any such

thing was closely watched and made to work. The
old cadets generally chose such men for " special
dutymen," and required them to bring water, pile
bedding, sweep the floor, and do all sorts of menial
services. Of course all this last is prohibited, and
therefore risky. Somebody is " hived " and severely
punished almost every year for allowing plebes to
perform menial duties for him. But what of that ?
The more dangerous it becomes the more is it practised. Forbidden things always have an alluring
sweetness about them. More caution, however, is
observed. If, for instance, a cadet should want a
pail of water, he causes a plebe to empty his (the
plebe's) into his own (the cadet's). If it should be
empty, he sends him to the hydrant to fill it, and,
when he returns, gets possession of it as before. An
officer seeing a plebe with his own pail—recognizable
by his own name being on it in huge Roman characters—going for water would say nothing to him.
If the name, however, should be that of a cadet, the
plebe would be fortunate if he escaped an investigation or a reprimand on the spot, and the cadet, too,
if he were not put in arrest for allowing a new cadet
to perform menial services for him. If he wants a
dipper of iced-water, he calls out to the first plebe
he sees in some such manner as this : " Oh ! Mr.
——, don't you want to *borrow* my dipper for a
little while ?" The plebe of course understands
this. He may smile possibly, and if not serving
some punishment will go for the water.

Plebes are also required to clean the equipments
of the older cadets. They do it cheerfully, and,
strange to say, are as careful not to be "hived " as

the cadet whose accoutrements they are cleaning. I say " required." I do not mean that regulations or orders require this of the new cadets, but that the cadets by way of hazing do. From the heartrending tales of hazing at West Point, which citizens sometimes read of, one would think the plebes would offer some resistance or would complain to the authorities. These tales are for the most part untrue. In earlier days perhaps hazing was practised in a more inhuman manner than now. It may be impossible, and indeed is, for a plebe to cross a company street without having some one yell out to him : " Get your hands around, mister. Hold your head up ;" but all that is required by tactics. Perhaps the frequency and unnecessary repetition of these cautions give them the appearance of hazing. However that may be, there seems to be no way to impress upon a plebe the necessity of carrying his " palms to the front," or his " head up." To report him and give him demerits merely causes him to laugh and joke over the number of them that have been recorded against him.

I do not mean to defend hazing in any sense of the word ; but I do believe that it is indispensable as practised at the Academy. It would simply be impossible to mould and polish the social amalgamation at West Point without it. Some of the rough specimens annually admitted care nothing for regulations. It is fun to them to be punished. Nothing so effectually makes a plebe submissive as hazing. That contemptuous look and imperious bearing lowers a plebe, I sometimes think, in his own estimation. He is in a manner cowed and made to feel that he must obey, and not disobey ; to feel that he is a plebe, and must expect a plebe's portion. He is taught by it to stay in his place, and not to "bone popularity" with the older cadets.

It is frequently said that "plebe camp" and "plebe life" are the severest parts of life at West Point. To some they are, and to others they are not. With my own self I was almost entirely free from hazing, and while there were features in "plebe life" which I disliked, I did nevertheless have a far easier and better time than my own white classmates. Even white plebes often go through their camp pleasantly and profitably. Only those who shirk duty have to suffer any unusual punishment or hazing.

I have known plebes to be permitted to do any thing they chose while off duty. I have known others to have been kept working on their guns or other equipments whole days for several days at a time. It mattered not how clean they were, or how soon the work was done. I've known them to be many times interrupted for the mere sake of hazing, and perhaps to be sent somewhere or to do something which was unnecessary and would have been as well undone. Plebes who tent with first-classmen keep their own tents in order, and are never permitted by their tentmates to do any thing of the kind for others unless when wanted, are entirely unoccupied, and then usually their services are asked for. A classmate of mine, when a plebe, tented with a first-classman. He was doing something for himself one day in a free-and-easy manner, and had no thought of disturbing any one. A yearling corporal, who was passing, saw him, thought he was having too good and soft a time of it, and ordered him out to tighten cords, an act then highly uncalled for, save as a means of hazing. The first-classman happened to come up just as the plebe began to interfere with the cords, and asked him who told him to do that. He told him, and was at once directed to leave them and return to whatever he was doing before being interrupted. The yearling, confident in his red tape and his mightiness, ordered the plebe out again. His corporalship soon discovered his mistake, for the first-classman gave the plebe full information as to what could be required of him, and told him to disobey any improper order of the corporal's which was plainly given to haze him. The affair was made personal. A fight ensued. The corporal was worsted, to the delight, I imagine, of the plebes.

Again, I've known plebes to be stopped from work—if they were doing something for a cadet—to transfer it to some other one who was accustomed to shirk all the duty he could, or who did things slowly and slovenly. Indeed I may assert generally that plebes who are willing to work have little to do outside of their regular duty, and fare in plebe camp quite as well as yearlings ; while those who are stubborn and careless are required to do most all the work. Cadets purposely select them and make them work. They, too, are very frequently objects of hazing in its severest form. At best, though, plebe camp is rather hard, its numerous drills, together with guard and police duty, make it the severest and most undesirable portion of the four years a cadet spends at the Academy.

To get up at five o'clock and be present at reveille roll-call, to police for half an hour, to have squad drill during the next hour, to put one's tent in order after that, and then to prepare one's self for breakfast at seven, make up a rather trying round of duties To discharge them all—and that must certainly be done—keeps one busy ; but who would not prefer little extra work—and not hard work at that—in the cooler part of the day to an equal amount in the heated portion of it ? I am sure the plebes do. I know the corporals and other officers who drill them do, although they lose their after-reveille sleep.

After breakfast comes troop parade at eight o'clock, guard mounting immediately after, and the establishment of the "color line." Arms and accoutrements must be in perfect order. The plebes clean them during the afternoon, so that before parade it is seldom necessary to do more than wipe off dust, or adjust a belt, or something of the kind.

After establishing the "color line," which is done about 8.30 A.M., all cadets, save those on guard and those marching on, have time to do whatever they choose. The cadets generally repair to the guard tents to see lady friends and other acquaintances, while the plebes either interest themselves in the inspection of "color men," or make ready for artillery drill at nine. The latter drill, commencing at 9 A.M., continues for one hour. The yearlings and plebes receive instruction in the manual and nomenclature of the piece. The drill is not very trying unless the heavy guns are used—I mean unless they are drilled at the battery of twelve-pounders. Of late both classes have been drilled at batteries of three-inch rifles. These are light and easily manœuvred, and unless the heat be intense the drill is a very pleasant one.

The first class, during this same hour, are drilled at the siege or seacoast battery. The work here is sometimes hard and sometimes not. When firing, the drill is pleasant and interesting, but when we have mechanical manœuvres all this pleasantness vanishes. Then we have hard work. Dismounting and mounting is not a very pleasant recreation.

At eleven o'clock, every day for a week or ten days, the plebes have manual drill. This is entirely in the shade, and when "In place, rest," is frequently given, is not at all displeasing, except when some yearling corporal evinces a disposition to haze. At five o'clock this drill is repeated. Then comes parade, supper, tattoo, and best of all a long night's rest. The last two drills continue for a few days only, and sometimes do not take place at all.

The third class, or the yearlings, have dancing from eleven to twelve, and the plebes from then till one. In the afternoon the plebes have nothing to do in the way of duty till four o'clock. The camp is then policed, and when that is done there may or may not be any further duty to discharge till retreat parade. After the plebes are put in the battalion— that is, after they begin drilling, etc., with their companies—all cadets attend company drill at five o'clock. After attending a few of these drills the first class is excused from further attendance during the encampment. One officer and the requisite number of privates, however, are detailed from the class each day to act as officers at these drills.

I omitted to say that the first class received in the forenoon instruction in practical military engineering and ordnance.

What most tries plebes, and yearlings, too, is guard duty. If their classes are small, each member of them is put on guard every third or fourth day. To the plebes, being something entirely new, guard duty is very, very obnoxious.

During the day they fare well enough, but as soon as night comes "well enough" disappears. They are liable at any moment to be visited by cadets on a hazing tour from the body of the camp, or by the officers and non-commissioned officers of the guard. The latter generally leave the post of the guard in groups of three or four. After getting into camp they separate, and manage to come upon a sentinel simultaneously and from all points of the compass. If the sentinel isn't cool, he will challenge and advance one, and possibly let the others come upon him unchallenged and unseen even. Then woe be to him! He'll be "*crawled over*" for a certainty, and to make his crimes appear as bad as possible, will be reported for "neglect of duty while a sentinel, allowing the officers and non-commissioned officers of the guard to advance upon him, and to cross his post repeatedly without being challenged." He knows the report to be true, and if he submits an explanation for the offence his inexperience will be considered, and he will probably get no demerits for his neglect of duty.

But the best joke of all is in their manner of calling off the half-hours at night, and of challenging. Sometimes we hear No. 2 call off, " No. 2, ten o'clock, and all is well," in a most natural and unconcerned tone of voice, while No. 3 may sing out, " No. 3, ten o'clock and all is well-l-l," changing his tone only on the last word. Then No. 4, with another variation, may call off, " No. 4, ten o'clock, and all-l-l-l's well," changing his tone on " all-l-l-l's," and speaking the rest, especially the last word, in a low and natural manner of voice, and sometimes abruptly. And so on along the entire chain of sentinels, each one calls off in a manner different from that of the rest. Sometimes the calling off is scarcely to be heard, sometimes it is loud and full, and again it is distinct but squeakish. It is indeed most delightful to be in one's tent and here the plebes call off in the still quiet hours of the night. One can't well help laughing, and yet all plebes, more or less, call off in the same manner.

Plebe sentinels are very troublesome sometimes to the non-commissioned officers of the guard. They receive their orders time after time, and when inspected for them most frequently spit them out with ease and readiness ; but just as soon as night comes, and there is a chance to apply them, they " fess utterly cold," and in the simplest things at that. Nine plebes out of ten almost invariably challenge thus, " Who comes *here* ?" " Who stands *here* ?" " Who goes *here* ?" as the case may be, notwithstanding they have been repeatedly instructed orally,

and have seen the words, as they should be, in the
regulations. If a person is going, and is a hundred
yards or so off, it is still, "Who goes *here ?*"
Everything is "*here.*"

One night the officer of the day concealed himself
near a sentinel's post, and suddenly appeared on
it. The plebe threw his gun down to the proper
position and yelled out, "Who comes here ?" The
officer of the day stopped short, whereupon the
plebe jumped at him and shouted, "Who stands
here ?" Immediately the officer started off, saying as he did so, "I'm not standing; I'm going."
Then of course the challenge was again changed to,
"Who goes *here ?* "I'm not going; I'm coming,"
said the officer, facing about and approaching the
sentinel. This was kept up for a considerable time,
till the officer of the 'day got near a sentry-box and
suddenly disappeared. The plebe knew he was
there, and yelled in a louder tone than before, "Who
stands *here ?* "Sentry-box," was the solemn and
ghostly response.

It is hardly reasonable, I think, to say the plebe
was frightened; but he actually stood there motionless, repeating his challenge over and over again,
"Who stands *here ?*"

There was a light battery in park near by, and
through this, aided by the gloom, the officer of the
day managed to pass unobserved along, but not on
the sentinel's post. He then got upon it and advanced on him, making the while much noise with
his sword and his heavy tread. He walked directly
up to the sentinel unchallenged, and startled him by
asking, "What are you standing here yelling for ?"

The plebe told him that the officer of the day had been upon his post, and he had seen him go behind the sentry-box. And all this to the officer of the day, standing there before him, " Well, sir, whom do you take me to be ?"

The plebe looks, and for the first time brought to full consciousness, recognizes the officer of the day. Of course he is surprised, and the more so when the officer of the day inspects for his—the plebe's — satisfaction the sentry-box, and finds no one there. He " eats" that plebe up entirely, and then sends a corporal around to instruct him in his orders. When the corporal comes it may be just as difficult to advance him. He may, when challenged, advance without replying, or, if he replies, he may say, " Steamboat," " Captain Jack, Queen of the Modocs," as one did say to me, or something or somebody else not entitled to the countersign. Possibly the plebe remembers this, and he may command " Halt !" and call another corporal. This latter may come on a run at " charge bayonets," and may not stop till within a foot or so of the sentinel. He then gets another " cursing out." By this time the corporal who first came and was halted has advanced unchallenged and unnoticed since the arrival of the second. And then another cursing out. Thus it is that plebe camp is made so hard.

Surely the officers and non-commissioned officers are right in testing by all manner of ruses the ability of the sentinels. It is their duty to instruct them, to see that they know their orders, and are not afraid to apply them.

Sometimes plebes enjoy it, and like to be cursed out. Sometimes they purposely advance toward a party improperly, to see what will be said to them. It is fun to some, and to others most serious. At best it gives a plebe a poor opinion of West Point, and while he may bear it meekly he nevertheless sighs for the

"——touch of a vanished hand,"

the caressing hand of a loving mother or sister. I know I used to hate the very name of camp, and I had an easier time, too, than the other plebes.

Of course the plebes, being inexperienced for the most part, are "high privates in the rear rank." For another reason, also, this is the case. The first and second classes have the right established by immemorial custom of marching in the front rank, which right necessarily keeps the plebes in the rear rank, and the yearlings too, except so many as are required in the front rank for the proper formation of the company. Another reason, perhaps, may be given to the same end. We have what we call class rank, or, in other words, class standing. Every class has certain privileges and immunities, which the junior classes do not enjoy ; for example, first-classmen, and second-classmen too—by General Orders of September, 1876—are excused from guard duty in the capacity of privates, and are detailed—first-classmen for officers of the day and officers of the guard, and second-classmen for non-commissioned officers of the guard. All members of the third and fourth classes are privates, and from them the privates of the guard are detailed. All officers, commissioned and non-commissioned, are exempt from

"*Saturday punishment.*" I mean they do not walk extra tours of guard for punishment. The non-commissioned officers are sometimes required to serve such punishments by discharging the duties of corporal or sergeant in connection with the punishment squad. Third- and fourth-classmen enjoy no such immunities. Plebes, then, having no rank whatever, being in fact conditional cadets until they shall have received their warrants in the following January, must give way to those who have. One half or more of the privates of the company must be in the front rank. This half is made up of those who rank highest, first-classmen and second-classmen, and also, if necessary, a number of third classmen. Plebes must then, except in rare cases, march in the rear rank, and from the time they are put in the battalion till the close of the summer encampment, they are required to carry their hands with palms to the front as prescribed in the tactics.

All this is kept up till the close of camp, and makes, I think, plebe camp the most trying part of one's cadet life.

On the 28th of August the furloughmen return, and report to the commandant at two o'clock for duty.

In the afternoon the battalion is sized and quarters are assigned under the supervision of the assistant-instructors of tactics.

At parade the appointment of officers and non-commissioned officers for the ensuing year is published, and also orders for the discontinuance of the encampment.

In the evening the "twenty-eighth hop" takes

place, and is the last of the season. On the 29th—
and beginning at reveille—the cadets move their
effects into winter quarters in barracks. All heavy
articles are moved in on wagons, while all lighter
ones are carried over by cadets themselves. By
seven o'clock every thing is moved away from camp,
save each cadet's accoutrements.

Breakfast is served at 7 A.M., and immediately
afterward comes " troop" and guard-mounting, after
which the entire camp is thoroughly policed. This
requires an hour or more, and when all is done the
" general " is sounded. At this the companies are
formed under arms in their respective company
streets. The arms are then stacked and ranks broken.
At least two cadets repair to each tent, and at the first
tap of the drum remove and roll up all the cords
save the corner ones. At the second tap, while one
cadet steadies the tent the other removes and rolls
the corner cords nearest him. The tents in the body
of the encampment are moved back two feet, more
or less, from the color line, while the guard tents
and those of the company officers are moved in a
northerly direction. At the third tap the tents fall
simultaneously toward the color line and the south
cardinal point, amid rousing cheers. The tents
being neatly rolled up and placed on the floors, the
companies are reformed and on the centre. The
battalion then marches out to take up its winter
quarters in barracks.

When camp is over the plebes are no longer required to depress their toes or to carry their hands
with palms to the front. They are, in fact, " cadets
and gentlemen," and must take care of themselves.

CHAPTER VI.

STUDIES, ETC.

THE academic year begins July 1st, and continues till about June 20th the following year. As soon after this as practicable—depending upon what time the examination is finished—the corps moves into camp, with the exception of the second class, who go on furlough instead.

Between the 20th of August and the 1st of September, the "Seps," or those candidates who were unable to do so in the spring previous, report. Before the 1st they have been examined and the deficient ones dismissed. On the 1st, unless that be Sunday, academic duties begin. The classes are arranged into a number of sections, according to their class rank, as determined at the previous annual examination, or according to rank in some particular study—for instance, for instruction in engineering the first class is arranged according to merit in philosophy, and not according to general merit or class rank. The fourth, or "plebe" class, however, is arranged alphabetically since they as yet have no class rank.

The first class study, during the first term, engineering, law, and ordnance and gunnery. They recite on civil engineering from 8 to 11 A.M. daily, on ordnance and gunnery from 2 to 4 P.M., alternating with law.

The second class have natural and experimental philosophy from 8 to 11 A.M. daily, and chemistry, alternating with riding, from 11 A.M. to 1 P.M.; also drawing in pencil from 2 to 4 P.M. For instruction in this department the class is divided into two as nearly equal parts as practicable, which alternate in attendance at the Drawing Academy.

The third class have pure mathematics, analytical geometry, descriptive geometry, and the principles of shades, shadows, and perspective, from 8 to 11 A.M. daily. They also have French from 11 A.M., till 1 P.M., alternating with Spanish.

The entire class attend drawing daily till November 1st, when it is divided into two equal parts or platoons, which attend drawing and riding on alternate days. Riding! "Yearling riding!" I must advert to that before I go further. First let me describe it. A platoon of yearlings, twenty, thirty, forty perhaps; as many horses; a spacious riding-hall, with galleries that seat but too many mischievous young ladies, and whose interior is well supplied with tan bark, make up the principal objects in the play. Nay, I omit the most important characters, the Instructor and the necessary number of enlisted men.

ACT I.

Scene I.

Area of barracks. At guard-house door stands an orderly, with drum in hands. In the area a number of cadets, some in every-day attire, others dressed *à la cavalier*. These *à la cavalier* fellows are going to take their first lesson in riding. About four-fifths of them were never on a horse in their lives, and hence what dire expectations hover over their ordinarily placid heads! They have heard from the upper classmen what trials the novice experiences in his

first efforts, and they do not go to the riding-hall without some dread.
Four o'clock and ten minutes. The drum is beaten.

Officer of the Day.—Form your platoon ! Right,
face ! Call your roll !

Section Marcher.—Bejay ! Barnes ! Du Furing !
Swikeheimer ! Du Flicket, etc.

Platoon (answering to their names).—Here ! here-
re-re ! ho-o-o ! hi-i-i ! har-ar-ar ! heer-r !

Section Marcher (facing about salutes).—All are
present, sir !

Officer of the Day (returning salute).—March off
your platoon, sir !

Section Marcher (facing about).—Left, face ! forward. March ! (Curtain falls.)

ACT II.

SCENE I.

The riding-hall, a large, spacious, rectangular structure, door on
each side and at each end, floor well covered with tan bark, spacious
gallery over each side door, staircases outside leading to them. Galleries are occupied, one by ladies, and, perhaps a number of gentlemen, and the other by enlisted men usually. In the centre of the
hall are a number of horses, each equipped with a surcingle, blanket,
and watering bridle. A soldier stands at the head of each one of
them. As curtain rises enter platoon by side door, and marches
around the left flank of the line of horses and as far forward as necessary.

Section Marcher. — Platoon, halt ! left, face !
(Saluting Instructor) All are present, sir !

Instructor (saluting).—The Section Marcher will
take his place on the left.

He then gives all necessary instruction.

" To mount the trooper the Instructor first causes
him to stand to horse by the command ' *Stand to*

horse!' At this command—" Well, see "Cavalry Tactics."

We've got the trooper mounted now. After some further explanation the Instructor forms them into a column of files by the commands :

"By file, by the right (or left) flank. March!"

They are now going around the hall at a walk, a slow, snail-like pace, but what figures some of them present! Still all goes on quite well. The Instructor is speaking :

"To trot," says he, "raise the hands" ("yearlings" use both hands) "slightly. This is to apprise the horse that you want his attention. Then lower the hands slightly, and at the same time gently press the horse with the legs until he takes the gait desired. As soon as he does, relax the pressure." A long pause. The occupants of the galleries are looking anxiously on. They know what is coming next. They have seen these drills over and over again. And so each trooper awaits anxiously the next command. Alas! it comes! "Trot!"

What peals of laughter from that cruel gallery! But why? Ah! See there that trooper struggling in the tan bark while a soldier pursues his steed. He is not hurt. He gets up, brushes away the tan bark, remounts and starts off again. But there, he's off again! He's continually falling off or jumping off purposely (?). What confusion! There comes one at a full gallop, sticking on as best he can ; but there, the poor fellow is off. The horses are running away. The troopers are dropping off everywhere in the hall. No one is hurt. Alas! they pressed too hard to keep on, and instead of relaxing the pressure at the desired gait, the trot, they kept on pressing, the horse taking the trot, the gallop, the run, and the trooper, alas ! the dust. Again they had the reins too long, and instead of holding on by the flat of the thighs with their feet parallel to the horse, we see them making all sorts of angles. But that gallery ! that gallery ! how I used to wish it wasn't there ! The very sight of a lady under such circumstances is most embarrassing.

Fair ones, why will you thus torture the " yearlings" by your at other times so desirable presence ?

The fourth class have pure mathematics, and algebra, daily from 8 to 11 A. M., and French also, daily, from 2 to 4 P. M. Beginning on October 15th, or as near that time as practicable, they have fencing, and the use of the bayonet and small-sword.

During the month of September cadets of all classes, or the battalion, are instructed in the infantry tactics in the " School of the Battalion." Near the end of the month it is customary to excuse the officers of the first class from these drills, and to detail privates to perform their duties for one drill only at a time. The other classes are in ranks, or the line of file-closers, according as they are sergeants, guides, or privates.

During October the several classes receive practical instruction as follows : The first class in military engineering, the manner of making and recording the details of a military reconnoissance, and field sketching ; the second class in siege and sea-coast artillery, and military signalling and telegraphy. The class is divided into two parts, composed of the odd and even numbers, which attend drills on alter-

4

nate days—that is, artillery one day and signalling
the next ; the third class in light or field artillery,
and the theory and principles of "target practice."
Sometimes this latter is given during camp, as is
most convenient. Sometimes, also, they receive instruction in ordnance. This, however, is generally
deferred till they become first-classmen.

For further instruction of the first class the following part of the *personnel* of a light battery is detailed from that class, viz. : three chiefs of platoon,
one chief of caissons, one guidon, and six chiefs of
section. Each member of the class is detailed for
each of these offices in his proper order.

The fourth class receives instruction in field artillery at the "foot batteries." This instruction is limited to the nomenclature and manual of the piece. Here,
also, to assist the instructor, a chief of piece for each
piece is detailed. They are required to correct all
errors made by the plebes, and sometimes even to
drill them. Hence a knowledge of tactics is indispensable, and the means of fixing such knowledge in
the mind is afforded.

Sometimes also two first-classmen are required
to assist at the siege or sea-coast batteries.

Every day throughout the year a guard is
mounted. It consists of two officers of the guard—
sometimes only one—one sergeant, three corporals—
or more—and twenty-four privates—sometimes, also,
eighteen or twenty-one in camp, and twenty-seven in
barracks. Every day, also, there is one officer of
the day detailed from the first class.

The weather permitting, we have "dress parade"
daily. When unfavorable, on account of snow, rain,

or severe cold, we have "undress parade"—that is, parade without arms and in undress or fatigue uniform, the object being to get us all together to publish the orders, etc., for the morrow. After November 1st we usually have "undress parade," and then "supper mess parade." Between these two ceremonies the cadets amuse themselves at the gymnasium, dancing or skating, or "spooneying," or at the library; generally, I think—the upper classmen at any rate—at the library. After supper we have recreation and then study. And thus we "live and do" till January.

The semi-annual examination begins January 1st, or as soon thereafter as practicable. The plebes are examined first, and started in their new studies as soon as possible. After the plebes the other classes are examined in the order of their rank—that is, first class, second class, and third class—and of the importance of their studies, engineering being first, then philosophy, and mathematics, etc.

The examination being over, the deficient ones, after receiving orders from the Secretary of War, are dismissed. Studies are then resumed as follows:

For the first class military engineering, ordnance, and gunnery, constitutional law, military law, rules of evidence, practice of courts-martial, mineralogy, and geology, strategy, and grand tactics, and the throwing and dismantling of pontoon bridges. For the second class, acoustics and optics, astronomy, analytical mechanics in review; infantry, artillery, and cavalry tactics; drawing, riding, and signalling. For the third class, calculus, surveying, geometry, and riding. Immediately after the examination the entire third class receive instruction in mechanical drawing before they begin their other mathematical studies. For the fourth class the studies are plane geometry, trigonometry, descriptive geometry, and fencing, including the use of the small-sword, broad-sword, and bayonet.

Parades, guard duty, etc., remain as previously described until about the middle of March usually. At that time the ordinary routine of drills, dress parades, etc., is resumed ; but drills in this order, viz., from March 15th to April 1st instruction in the school of the company ; in artillery tactics, as before described during April ; and in infantry tactics, in the " School of the Battalion," during May. The annual examination takes place in June. The following diary, made for the purpose of insertion here, will best explain what generally occurs during the month :

MEMORANDA.

Thursday, June 1, 1876.—Resumed white pants at 5.10 P.M. Received Board of Visitors by a review at 5.10 P.M. Examination begun at 9 A.M. First class, engineering. Salute of fifteen guns at meridian to Board of Visitors.

Friday, June 2.—First class, engineering finished. Second class, philosophy commenced. Siege battery drill at 5.10 P.M.

Saturday, June 3. — Second class, philosophy continued.

Monday, June 5. — Light battery at 5.10 P.M. A yearling lost his " white continuations." Plebes went to parade.

Tuesday, June 6.—Fourth class, entire in French. Examination written. Second class, philosophy finished. First class, mineralogy and geology begun. Third class, mathematics begun. Battalion drill at 5.10 P.M.

Wednesday, June 7.—Second class turned out, marched to sea-coast battery at 11 A.M. Three detachments selected. Rest marched back and dismissed. Cavalry drill at 5.10 P.M. Six secondclassmen turned out. Plebes put in battalion.

Thursday, June 8.—Plebes put on guard. Pontoon bridging, 5.10 P.M.

Friday, June 9.—Battalion skirmish drill 5.10 P.M. Deployed to front at double time. Second, fourth, and seventh companies reserve. Almost all manœuvres at double time. Deployed by numbers and charged. Marched in in line, band on right. Broke into column of companies to the left, changed direction to the right, obliqued to the left, moved forward and formed " front into line, faced to the rear." Arms inspected, ammunition returned. Dismissed.

Saturday, June 10.—Third class, mathematics finished. Miss Philips sang to cadets in mess hall after supper. First class, ordnance begun.

Sunday, June 11.—Graduating sermon by Hon. ——, of Princeton, N. J., closing "hime," "When shall we meet again ?" Graduating dinner at 2 P.M.

Monday, June 12.—Detail from first class to ride in hall. Use of sabre and pistol on horseback. First class, ordnance finished. Law begun.

Tuesday, June 13.—First class finished. Board divided into committees. Second class, chemistry begun. Graduating parade. Corps cheered by graduates after parade. Hop in evening; also German; whole continuing till 3 A.M. Rumor has it two first-classmen, Slocum and Guilfoyle, are "found" in ordnance and engineering.

Wednesday, June 14.—Fourth class, mathematics begun. Salute seventeen guns at 10 A.M. in honor of arrival at post of General Sherman and Colonel Poe of his staff. Graduating exercises from 11 A.M. till near 1 P.M. Addresses to graduates. Mortar practice and fireworks at night.

This ended the "gala" days at West Point in '76.

Thursday, June 15.—Usual routine of duties resumed. Company drills in the afternoon from 5.10 to 6.10 P.M. Rather unusual, but we're going to the Centennial. Rumor has it we encamp Saturday the 17th for ten days.

Friday, June 16.—Dom Pedro, emperador de la Brasil estaba recibiado para un "review" a las cuatro horas y quarenta y cinco minutos. El em-

barcó por la ciudad de Nueva York inmediatemente
Second class, chemistry finished. Third class, French
begun.

Saturday, June 17.—Third class, French finished.
Third class, Spanish begun. " Camp rumor" not
true.

Monday, June 19.—Moved into camp, aligned
tent floors at 5 A.M. in the rain. Required by order
to move in effects at 9 A.M., and to march in and
pitch tents at 12 M. Rained in torrents. Marched
in, etc., at 9 A.M. Effects moved in afterwards.
Rain ceased by 12 M. Marched in. Second class,
tactics finished. Third class, Spanish finished.

Ordinarily as soon as the examination is over the
third class take advantage of the two months' furlough allowed them, while other classes go into
camp. This encampment begins June 17th, or a day
or two earlier or later, according to circumstances.
This brings me to the end of the first year. I have
described camp life, and also, I observe, each of the
remaining years of cadet life. On July 1st the
plebes become the fourth class ; the original fourth
the third ; the third, now on furlough, the second ;
and the second the first. I have given in an earlier
part of my narrative the studies, etc., of these several classes.

The plebe, or fourth class of the previous year,
are now become yearlings, and are therefore in their
" yearling camp." At the end of every month an

extract from the class and conduct report of each cadet is sent to his parents or guardian for their information.   I insert a copy of one of these monthly reports.

United States Military Academy,

West Point, N. Y., March 26, 1875.

EXTRACT from the Class and Conduct Reports of the MILITARY
ACADEMY for the month of February, 1875, furnished for
the information of Parents and Guardians,

THIRD CLASS—Composed of 83 Members.

Cadet Henry O. Flipper

Was, in Mathematics.................No. 48
"   French.....................No. 48
"   Spanish,....................No. 37
"   Drawing....................No. 40

His demerit for the month is 2, and since the commencement of the
academic half year, 23.

Robt. N. Hall,

Captain 10th Infantry,
Adjutant Military Academy.

REGULATIONS FOR THE MILITARY ACADEMY.

Par. 71.—When any Cadet shall have a total of numbers [*of demerit*] thus
recorded, exceeding one hundred in six months, he shall be declared deficient in
discipline.

Par. 153.—No Cadet shall apply for, or receive money, or any other supplies
from his parents, or from any person whomsoever, without permission of the Superintendent.

Note.—The attention of Parents and Guardians is invited to the foregoing Regulations. The permission referred to in paragraph 153 must be obtained before the
shipment to the Cadet of the supplies desired.

STEREOTOMY AND CIVIL ENGINEERING.

September, 1876.

Day	Date	Section	No. in do.	Lesson To Art.	Lesson Page	Subject of Recitation.	Pp.
S.	30	:	:	182	109	Differential equation of curve of mean fibre.	101
F.	29	:	:	173	99	No recitation (*i.e.*, *a*).	... .
T.	28	:	:	162	86	Classification of strains.	73–6
W.	27	:	:	147	72	*a.*	. ...
T.	26	:	:	93	44	Limes, limestones, and tests.	42–3
M.	25	:	:	+43	23	*a.*	....
S.	23	:	:	265	198	*a.*	....
F.	22	:	:	250	191	Strains on an inclined beam.	183–6
T.	21	:	:	252	181	Questions.	....
W.	20	:	:	237	168	Fish and scarf joints combined.	167–8
T.	19	:	:	223	152	*a.*	....
M.	18	*6	:	210	138	Strength of beams, influence of form of cross-section on.	137–8
S.	16	:	:	195	125	Bending moment, shearing strain and equation of mean fibre of beam, general case	114–6
F.	15	:	:	184	113	Do. of beam uniformly loaded.	104–6
T.	14	:	:	178	107	Questions.	....
W.	13	:	:	174	100	Force of compression and shearing strain.	89–92
T.	12	:	:	168	92	*a.*	....
M.	11	:	:	161	85	Questions.	....
S.	9	:	:	147	72	Sand and manipulation of mortar.	61–3
F.	8	:	:	119	57	*a.*	....
T.	7	:	:	93	44	Steel.	36–8
W.	6	:	:	63	33	Brick.	23–5
T.	5	:	:	43	23	*a.*	....
M.	4	:	:	26	13	Durability and decay of timber under certain conditions.	8–11
S.	2	:	:	25	9	To find where a given line pierces a given plane.	8
F.	1	5	12	19	7	*a.*	....

Maximum.....		6							15		12				12			12
Mark per recitation....	2·6	2·3	2·6	2·4	2·5	2·5	2·3	2·3	2·0	2·4	2·6	2·9	2·9	2·8	2·6	2·5	2·6	2·6
Do. per week...	10·3	5·2			9·8				11·5					11·2				
Average per w'k...	2·5	2·6			2·4				2·3					2·8				
Do. per month....	2·5																	
Rank in section....	8	3			5				12					2				
Do. per month....	5																	
Do. class.....	60																	
Demerit.....	3																	

REMARK.—Omit Arts. 160, 169, 223, 224, 225, 296, and 227, also pp. 119, 120, 125, 126, 127.

All figures in text-book were required to be drawn in blank-books for the purpose.

The lesson each day included that of the preceding day. The first lessons were in one plane descriptive geometry. There were two of them in this month.

* Transferred to 6th section, September 16th.

+ Review, omitting Arts. as above.

The maximum is equal the greatest number of times any one has recited multiplied by three (3), and such an one's weekly mark is the sum of his daily marks.

For any other we have : As the number of days he recited is to the greatest number, so is the sum of his daily marks to his total marks.

Text-books used : Wheeler's "Civil Engineering" and Mahan's "Fortification and Stone-cutting."

For a thorough recitation the mark is 3.

CIVIL ENGINEERING.

October, 1876.

Day	Date	Section	No. in do	Lesson To Art.	Lesson Page	Subject of Recitation.	Pp.
T.	31	:	:	467	350	Strains on "Warren girder" due to weight at middle point.	334–5
M.	30	:	:	453	335	Questions.	....
S.	28	:	:	434	318	Cofferdams.	297–302
F.	27	:	:	413	297	Foundations under water, water excluded.	290–292
T.	26	:	:	377	277	a.	....
W.	25	:	:	330	243	Rubble, ashlar, and cutstone masonry.	237–243
T.	24	:	:	†299	222	a.§	....
M.	23	:	:	12	57	Construction of geometrical stairway.	55–6
S.	21	:	:	9	47	Dimensions of voussoirs of groined arch, construction of.	43–4
F.	20	:	:	8	43	a.	....
T.	19	:	:	*5	31	Right section, plan, and elevation of a given wall.	23–4
W.	18	:	:	434	318	a.	....
T.	17	:	:	421	302	Questions.	....
M.	16	:	:	402	290	Grillage and platform.	288–9
S.	14	:	:	377	277	Masonry, its preservation, etc.	274–6
F.	13	:	:	358	263	Ovals of three centres.	259–60
T.	12	:	:	337	251	a.	....
W.	11	:	:	317	236	Retaining walls, face and back parallel.	220
T.	10	:	:	302	224	Reservoir walls and dams.	222–3
M.	9	:	:	289	211	a.	....
S.	7	:	:	265	198	Strains on given inclined beam.	183–6
F.	6	:	:	253	183	a.	....
T.	5	·	:	230	163	Strains on curved beam, approximate.	160–1
W.	4	:	:	219	147	a.	. . ..
T.	3	:	:	205	134	Questions.	....
M.	2	6	12	187	117	Beam, one end fixed, other resting on support, bending m't, shearing strain, etc., of.	113–4

Maximum......		12			12			12			6				12		
Mark per recitation	2·8	2·8	2·0	2·5	2·8	2·8	2·5	2·6	2·8	2·6	2·7	2·7	5·4	2·7	2·7	2·6	
Do. per week...		11·3				10·1				10·7							
Average per w'k		2·8				2·5				2·6		2·7					
Do. per month...																	
Rank in section.		1				2				2		1					
Do. per month.																	
Do. class......																2	
Demerit.........																53	1

REMARK.—Omit Art. 538.

* Transferred back from 6th to 5th section, November 11th.

† Review.

‡ From this date till December 7th the class was instructed in mechanical drawing. The drawings made were one king-post and one queen-post roof truss, the dimensions, etc., being given; and also one railroad bridge, Howe truss pattern, dimensions, etc., being calculated.

CIVIL ENGINEERING.

November, 1876.

Day	Date	Section	No. in do	Lesson — To Art.	Lesson — Page	Subject of Recitation	Pp.
W.	1	6	12	485	365	a.	....
T.	2			505	381	Britannia bridge.	365–6
F.	3			535	395	Suspension bridges.	372–9
S.	4			545	410	a.	....
M.	6			578	425	Strains graphically.	407–8
T.	7			600	439	Sidewalks and tramroads.	437–9
W.	8			631	453	a.	....
T.	9			End	472	Canal locks.	457–61
F.	10			†468	347	Questions.	....
S.	11			505	381	a.	....
M.	13	*5		545	410	a.	....
T.	14			600	439	Surveys for roa	425–30
W.	15			End	472	Canal locks.	457–61
T.	16			++	:		....
F.	17			:	:		....
S.	18			:	:		....
M.	20			:	:		....
T.	21			:	:		....
W.	22			:	:		....
T.	23			:	:		....
F.	24			:	:		....
S.	25			:	:		....
M.	27			:	:		....
T.	28			:	:		....
W.	29			:	:		....
T.	30			:	:		....

Maximum				12				12				12				12				12			
Mark per recitation	2·0	2·5	2·7	2·9	2·3	†	2·9	2·7	2·9	2·0	3·0	3·0	2·5	2·7	2·7	2·5	2·7	3·0
Do. per week	10·1	10·5	10·9	10·4
Average per w'k	2·5	2·6	2·7	2·6	2·6
Do. per month	
Rank in section	4	2	1	4	1
Do. per month	
Do. class	65
Demerit	2

REMARK.—Omit Arts. 188, 195, 196, 197; Figs. 80, 81, 83, 114, 115, 116, 130, 131, 188, 149, 150, 153, 154 in note-books; Arts. 293, 308, 309, 315, 356, Case II., p. 26, Stereotomy, and also pp. 35, 36, 37, 38, and Fig. of Prob. 11.

* These Nos. 5, 8, 9, and 12 are numbers of problems in stone-cutting, and not articles.
† Review.
‡ "Bugled it,"

December, 1876.

CIVIL ENGINEERING.

Day	Date	Section	No. in do.	To Art. Lesson	Page	Subject of Recitation.	Pp.
S.	30	:	:	End	:	Kinds of canals.	453–4
F.	29	:	:	600	439	Roads generally.	410–14
T.	28	:	:	545	410	Strains on roof-truss rafters trisected by struts.	403–5
W.	27	:	:	495	372	Burr and New York canal trusses.	359–60
T.	26	:	:	463	347	α	....
M.	25	:	:	8	:	α	....
S.	23	:	:	434	318	Questions.	....
F.	22	:	:	387	282	Foundations in compressible soils and firm ones, but affected by water.	280–2
T.	21	:	:	346	255	Stability of arches against rotation and sliding.	224–7
W.	20	:	:	301	224	Open-built beam, triangular bracing, uniform load, strains.	193
T.	19	:	:	263	194	Inclined beam.	183–6
M.	18	:	:	230	163	Solid of equal resistance.	140–1–3
S.	16	:	:	210	139	Questions.	....
F.	15	:	:	187	117	*M.S. and Y. of horizontal beam, uniformly loaded, one end fixed, other not.	113
T.	14	:	:	176	103	α	....
W.	13	:	:	164	88	Bar of uniform strength to resist elongation.	86–7
T.	12	:	:	147	72	Perpetual kilns, products of calcination, pozzuolana. "Bugled it."	46–51
M.	11	:	:	†56	32	Concrete and patent stones.	28–31
S.	9	:	:	End	:	α	....
F.	8	:	:	:	:	Groined arch.	434
T.	7	:	:	†1	35	Questions.	....
W.	6	:	:	:	:		....
T.	5	:	:	:	:		....
M.	4	:	:	.	:		...
S.	2	:	:	:	:		...
F.	1	5	12	*	:		....

Maximum......	6					9					12					12					9
Mark per recitation......	2·7		2·8	2·5	2·7	2·5		2·5		2·6	2·6		2·5		2·6	2·7 2·04				2·0 2·08	2·4
Do. per week...	5·4					8·0					10·2					10·2					7·2
Average per w'k...	2·7					2·6					2·5					2·5					2·4
Do. per month..																					2·5
Rank in section.	1					3					3					4					6
Do. per month..																					5
Do. class........																					58
Demerit........																					2

REMARK.—Omissions same as on advance.

* Mechanical drawing.

+ General review, beginning with stone-cutting.

++ In civil engineering.

§ Absent in New York City from 1 P.M. Saturday, December 23d, till 7 P.M. Tuesday, December 26th, on Christmas leave.

LAW

September, 1876.

Day	Date	Section	No. in do	To Sec.	Page	Subject of Recitation	Pp.
M.	4		7	9	36	Questions.	....
W.	6				53	States surrendering rights in part or whole, how.	51
F.	8				63	Protection to individual aliens.	96–8
T.	12				73	α	....
T.	14				86	Laws governing marriage and guardianship.	121–2
M.	18				Page 164	Right of sending ambassadors.	145–6
W.	20				108	Questions.	....
F.	22				122	Interpretation of treaties.	185–6
T.	26				136	No recitation.	....
T.	28				147	Complete title to prizes, how given.	239–40

Metric						
Maximum	6	9	6	6	9	9
Mark per recitation	2·3	2·9	2·8	2·7	2·7	2·9	2·5
Do. per week		8·0		5·4		8·3	5·0
Average per w'k		2·6		2·7		2·7	2·5
Do. per month							2·6
Rank in section		5		1		4	2
Do. per month							3
Do. class							61

REMARKS.—Text-book used, Woolsey's "International Law." Omissions: Sections 1, 2, 4, 6, 9, 10, 11, 12, 13, 14, 15, 16, 31, 34, 35, and their foot-notes, 44, 46 to Congress of Verona; 55 from middle page 83, and foot-notes on pp. 90 and 95, 63, "rules, etc." pp. 105, 106, foot-notes on pp. 180, 136; sec. 86, 89 de 3d line to 9th, p. 143, de 3d line p. 158 to sec. 93, and 93 de 23d line to sec. 94, foot-notes pp. 145, 146, 148, 150, 151, 152, 155, 156; sec. 95 de mid. p. 166; sec. 100 de mid. p. 175; 105 de 4th line, p. 180 to 7th line p. 181, and from top p. 162 to sec. 106, foot-notes pp. 165, 183; sec. 114 de top p. 194, except last sentence; 115 de 11th line p. 196 to 4th p. 198 of 118, first 27 lines p. 203. De 25th line p. 208 to 6th p. 209, de 18th p. 209 to 15th p. 210; sec. 222, first three lines sec. 223, de 6th to 21st line p. 221; last ten lines p. 215; first eleven p. 216, 10 p. 218, 15 p. 219, p. 235; sec. 139, first eleven lines p. 236, foot-notes 202, 204, 209, 210, 211, 212, 215, 225, 234, 244, 245,

LAW.

REMARKS.—Of section 161 omit all save first three and last three lines; omit secs. 172, 173, and of 174 to "First Armed Neutrality," p. 289, and foot-notes pp. 284, 285, 286; sec. 176 from 5th line from bottom p. 294; of 179 from 5th line p. 301; 181 from 5th line from bottom p. 303 to 9th p. 305, and from 7th to 27th line p. 310.

* Lesson extends from sec. 200 to Appendix p. 357, including "c," p. 434, Appendix II., first two thirds of page; notes 12, 13, 17, 20, and 21 Appendix III., omitting secs. 197, 198, 199, 206, 209.

† Review. Omissions same as on advance.

‡ Was absent from recitation, being officer of the day.

October, 1876.

Day	Date	Section	No. in do	Lesson To Sec.	Lesson Page	Maximum	Mark per recitation	Do. per week	Average per w'k	Do. per month	Rank in section	Do. per month	Do. class	Subject of Recitation	?p.
M.	30	:	:	164	272	3·0	2·7	:	:	:	:	3	61	Effects of temporary conquests.	247–8
T.	26	:	:	137	232	2·9	2·9	5·8	2·9	:	1	:	:	Questions.	....
T.	24	:	:	110	187	:	:	:	:	:	:	:	:	α‡	....
F.	20	:	:	91	144	:	:	8·5	2·8	:	1	:	:	α	....
W.	18	:	:	67	107	2·9	:	:	:	:	:	:	:	Protection to aliens.	96–8
M.	16	:	:	†48	71	2·8	:	:	:	:	:	:	:	Balance of power.	53–9
T.	12	:	:	*a	357	2·6	:	5·3	2·6	:	5	:	:	Questions.	....
T.	10	:	:	197	331	2·7	:	:	:	:	:	:	:	The right of search.	323–45
F.	6	:	:	185	313	2·9	8·1	2·7	:	2	:	:	:	Questions.	....
W.	4	:	:	175	291	2·5	:	:	:	:	:	:	:	Nationality of vessels and goods liable to capture and convoy of hostile goods.	280–2
M.	2	7	9	161	269	2·7	:	:	:	:	:	:	:	Obligations of neutrals.	233–6

LAW.

November, 1876.

Day	Date	Section	No. in do	To Sec.	Page	Subject of recitation	Pp
W.	29			92	63	Questions.	....
M.	27			57	40	Questions.	....
T.	23			All		Powers of the President.	....
T.	21			All‡		Questions.	....
F.	17			Adts		Questions.	...
W.	15			IV.		α	....
M.	13			‡ II.	555	Powers of Congress.	551–2
T.	9			End		Deserters, prisoners of war, hostages, and booty on battle-field.	15–21
T.	7			V.	23	α	....
F.	3			a*	357	Is there a right of convoy ?	325–8
W.	1	6	9	187	317	Liability of vessels to capture.	277–80

Statistic										
Maximum......	:	:	6	:	9	:	6	:	9	:
Mark per reci-tation......	2·7	2·6	2·9	3·0	2·9	3·0	2·5	2·9	2·9	2·6
Do. per week...	:	:	8·6	:	8·8	:	5·0	:	5·9	:
Average per w'k	:	:	2·8	:	2·9	:	2·5	:	2·9	:
Do. per month..	:	:	:	:	1	:	8	:	:	2·7
Rank in section.	:	11	:	:	:	:	:	:	2	:
Do. per month..	:	:	:	:	:	:	:	:	:	1
Do. class......	:	:	:	:	:	:	:	:	:	50

REMARKS.—* This lesson begins at section 187, and includes notes, etc., as given in lesson for October 12th, *q. v.*

† That is, to sec. 2, art. II. of the U. S. Constitution. The two lessons before this one were in "Instructions for the government of armies," being general order 100 from A. G. O., April 24th, 1863.

‡ Of Constitution, omit par. 3, sec. 1, art. II. Omit sec. 35 of text, and from sec. 151 to sec. 106 inclusive, and sec. 250. Text book used, Pomeroy's "Constitutional Law."

LAW.

December, 1876.

	Dec. 29 (F.)	Dec. 27 (W.)	Dec. 25 (M.)	Dec. 21 (T.)	Dec. 19 (T.)	Dec. 15 (F.)	Dec. 13 (W.)	Dec. 11 (M.)	Dec. 7 (T.)	Dec. 5 (T.)	Dec. 1 (F.)
Maximum	6	:	:	6	:	9	:	:	6	:	9
Mark per recitation	2·5	2·7	·	2·9	2·7	2·9	2·6	2·8	2·8	2·9	2·8
Do. per week	5·2	:	:	5·6	:	8·3	:	:	5·7	:	8·3
Average per w'k	2·6	:	:	2·8	:	2·7	:	:	2·8	:	2·7
Do. per month	2·7	:	:	:	:	:	:	:	:	:	:
Rank in section	4	:	:	1	:	1	:	:	1	:	2
Do. per month	:	:	:	:	:	:	:	:	:	:	:
Do. class	:	:	:	:	:	:	:	:	:	:	:

Day	Date	Section	No. in do.	Lesson To Sec.	Lesson Page	Subject of recitation	Pp.
F.	29			U. S. Con.		Questions.	....
W.	27			269	171	Questions.	....
M.	25					(Christmas.)	....
T.	21			231	145	Bill of rights.	143–5
T.	19			177	113	Questions.	....
F.	15			92	†63	Adoption of U. S. Constitution.	53–7
W.	13			243–269	171	Questions.	....
M.	11			184–226	142	Choosing President and Vice-President.	126–9
T.	7			243	*155	Questions.	....
T.	5			177	113	Questions.	....
F.	1	6	9	129	84	Questions.	....

REMARKS.—For omissions, see "Remarks" for November.
* The sections from 188 to 226 inclusive were omitted in this lesson, but were the lesson of the following day.
† Review.

ORDNANCE AND GUNNERY.

September, 1876.

Day	Date	Section	No. in do.	Lesson To Art.	Lesson Page	Subject of Recitation	Pp.	Maximum	Mark per recitation	Do. per week	Average per w'k	Do. per month	Rank in section	Do. per month	Do. class
F.	29			144	190	α	....	9		7·2	2·4	2·4	4	8	66
W.	27			113-125	165	Exterior form of cannon, and pressure of gas theoretically and experimentally.	151-3		3·0						
M.	25			36	62	Questions.	....		1·8						
T.	21			26-30	52	α	....	6		5·6	2·8		2		
T.	19			†	9	Sulphur.	2		2·8						
F.	15			*113	151	α	....	6		5·0	2·5		5		
W.	13			96-111	145	Strength of cannon metal.	132-4		2·9						
M.	11			103	137	Windage.	124-6		2·1						
T.	7			86	120	"System, materiel, and personnel of artillery."	108-12	6	2·6	3·1	1·5		6		
T.	5			52-60	100	Hale rocket.	98-9		0·5						
F.	1	7	9	50	84	Questions.	....	3	2·9	2·9	2·9		2		

REMARKS.—* This lesson includes section 1, 6, 7, 8, 9, and 10.

† This lesson is taken from a printed pamphlet furnished by the Ordnance Department, U. S. M. A. Omit chapter 1, part I., except articles above given, and "Oblong Bullet," p. 77; arts. 50, 51, 54, 55; 64, 65, 66, 6*, 08, 69; pp. 122, 123, 124, to "Windage." Also latter half of p. 125 and first half p. 126; arts. 139, 140.

Text book used, "Benton's Ordnance and Gunnery."

ORDNANCE AND GUNNERY.

October, 1876.

Day	Date	Section	No. in do.	Max.	Mark per recitation	Do. per week	Average per w'k	Do. per month	Rank in section	Do. per month	Do. class	Lesson — To Art.	Lesson — Page	Subject of Recitation	Pp.
T.	31				2·1			2·7		6	64	190	230	Questions.	....
F.	27			9		8·3	2·7		5			179	217	α	....
W.	25				2·6							166	204	Star gauge, trunnion rule, and trunnion square.	200–3
M.	23				2·9							152	189	Three-inch rifle-gun.	181
T.	19			6		5·2	2·6		6			136	174	Trunnions, preponderance, rimbases, cascabel, and handles on guns.	160–3
T.	17				2·6							117	154	Wrought iron.	143–4
F.	13			9		8·9	2·9		1			106	138	α	....
W.	11				2·9							83	116	Inspection of projectiles.	90–2
M.	9				3·0							53	90	Questions.	....
T.	5			6	2·8	5·4	2·7		3			26–4	58	General formula for quantity of powder consumed in a given time.	46–7
T.	3	7	9		2·6							*11	20	Inspection of powder and densimeter.	6–7

REMARKS.—* Review. This lesson includes pamphlet. Omissions same as on advance, and arts. 155, 156, to "In 1860," p. 192, art. 189, "Lance," pp. 279, 280, arts. 239–52, inclusive, and 259.

ORDNANCE AND GUNNERY.

November, 1876.

Day	Date	Section	No. in do.	Lesson To Art.	Lesson Page	Maximum	Mark per recitation	Do. per week	Average per w'k	Do. per month	Rank in section	Do. per month	Do. class	Subject of Recitation.	Pp.
T.	30	:	:	:	:	3	:	:	:	:	:	:	:	(Thanksgiving.)	....
T.	28	:	:	264 / 340–6	†290 / 346	:	:	:	:	:	:	:	:	Manufacture of sword blades.	287–90
F.	24	:	:	260	287	:	:	:	:	:	:	:	:	α	....
W.	22	:	:	225	259	9	2.9	:	:	:	:	:	:	Gins and iron sling cart.	248–50
M.	20	:	:	205	239	:	2.5	:	:	:	:	:	:	Field gun carriage.	225–7
T.	16	:	:	181	220	6	2.9	5·8	2·9	:	3	:	:	α	....
T.	14	:	:	*144 / 164	200	6	2.7	5·6	2·8	:	3	:	:	Siege mortars and Coehorn mortars.	187–8
F.	10	.	:	264	290	:	:	8.1	2.7	:	4	:	:	Thrusting swords.	277–8
W.	8	:	:	239	270	:	2.5	:	:	:	:	:	:	α	....
M.	6	:	:	224	256	6	2·9	5·0	2·5	:	5	:	:	Sea-coast gun carriage.	243–5
T.	2	7	9	211	243	3	:	2.5	2.5	2.8	4	6	64	Field caisson and mountain carriage.	235–8

REMARKS.—* This lesson extends from art. 144, p. 180, to art. 164, p. 200.
† This one from 264, p. 290, and from 340, p. 342, to 346, p. 346, and pamphlet on metallic cartridges.

ORDNANCE AND GUNNERY.

December, 1876.

Day	Date	Section	No. in do.	Lesson To Art.	Lesson Page	Subject of Recitation.	Pp.
T.	28			‡403	381	Combustion of gunpowder.	39–44
T.	26			376	366	*On leave of absence to New York.*	....
F.	22			360	353	Construction of case and anvil of the metallic case cartridge.	*
W.	20			229	261	Seacoast carriage.	243–4–5
M.	18			187	225	α	....
T.	14			152	189	Strains due to action of powder.	154–5–6
T.	12			113	151	Questions.	....
F.	8			183	116	Shrapel shell.	82–3
W.	6			403	381	Concussion and percussion fuses.	364–5
M.	4	7	9	371	390	Military fireworks.	356–8

Summary columns:

	Maximum	Mark per recitation	Do. per week	Average per w'k	Do. per month	Rank in section	Do. per month	Do. class
	6	2·0	4·0	2·0	1·98	9	13	71
	9	2·9	8·4	2·8		3		
		2·7						
	6	2·3	4·5	2·2		5		
	9	3·0	7·4	2·4		6		
		2·9						
		1·5						

REMARKS.—Omit arts. 349, 350, 351, 352, 353, 354, 355, 377, 378, last half of 382, 383, 384, 335, 386, 387, 389, 393, 394, 395, 396.

† General review. This lesson commences at art. 39, p. 71; omits arts. 75 to 79, inclusive.

‡ In addition this lesson includes from beginning of text to art. 39, p. 71.

* This lesson included a pamphlet furnished by the Ordnance Department.

5

CHAPTER VII.

YEARLING CAMP.

IN this chapter I shall describe only those phases of cadet life which are experienced by "yearlings" in their "yearling camp."

Beginning July 5th, or as soon after as practicable, the third class receive practical instruction in the nomenclature and manual of the field-piece. This drill continues till August 1st, when they begin the "School of the Battery."

The class attend dancing daily. Attendance at dancing is optional with that part of the third class called "yearlings," and compulsory for the "Seps," who of course do not become yearlings till the following September. The third class also receive instruction in the duties of a military laboratory, and "target practice." These instructions are not always given during camp. They may be given in the autumn or spring.

Another delight of the yearling is to "bone colors." Immediately in front of camp proper is a narrow path extending entirely across the ground, and known as the "color line." On the 1st of August — sometimes before — the "color line" is established, this name being applied also to the purpose of the color line. This ceremony consists in stacking arms just in rear of the color line, and placing the colors on the two stacks nearest the centre of the line.

From the privates of the guard three are chosen to guard the stacks and to require every one who crosses the color line or passes within fifteen paces of the colors to salute them. These three sentinels are known as "the colors," or "color men," and are numbered "first," "second," and "third."

Those are chosen who are neatest and most soldier-like in their appearance. Cadets prepare themselves specially for this, and they toss up their guns to the adjutant at guard-mounting. This signifies that they intend competing for "colors." The adjutant falls them out after the guard has marched to its post, and inspects them. Absolute cleanliness is necessary. Any spot of dirt, dust, or any thing unclean will often defeat one. Yearlings "bone" their guns and accoutrements for "colors," and sometimes get them every time they toss up.

A "color man" must use only those equipments issued to him. He cannot borrow those of a man who has "boned them up" and expect to get colors. Sometimes—but rarely—plebes compete and win.

The inducement for this extra labor is simply this : Instead of being on duty twenty-four hours, color men are relieved from 4 P.M. till 8 A.M. the next day, when they march off. They of course enjoy all other privileges given the "Old Guard."

"*Sentinels for the Color Line.*—The sentinels for the color line will be permitted to go to their tents from the time the stacks are broken till 8 A.M. the following morning, when they will rejoin the guard. They will be excused from

marching to meals, but will report to the officer
of the guard at the roll-call for each meal, and also
at tattoo and reveille."—(From Résumé of Existing
Orders, U. S. C. C.)

It is the yearling who does most of the hazing.
Just emerged from his chrysalis state, having the
year before received similar treatment at the hands of
other yearlings, he retaliates, so to speak, upon the
now plebe, and finds in such retaliation his share of
enjoyment.

The practice, however, is losing ground. The
cadets are more generous, and, with few exceptions,
never interfere with a plebe. This is certainly an
advance in the right direction ; for although hazing
does comprise some good, it is, notwithstanding, a
low practice, one which manliness alone should condemn. None need information and assistance more
than plebes, and it is unkind to refuse it ; nay, it is
even not humane to refuse it and also to haze the
asker. Such conduct, more than any thing else, dis-
courages and disheartens him. It takes from him
all desire to do and earn, to study or strive for success. At best it can be defended only as being
effective where regulations are not, viz., in the cases
of rough specimens who now not infrequently manage to win their appointments.

Formerly in yearling camp the corporals were
all " acting sergeants." They were so acting in the
absence of the *de facto* sergeants. These corporals
got the idea into their heads that to retain their appointments they had to do a certain amount of
" skinning," and often " skins" were more fancied
than real. This was a rather sad condition of affairs.

Plebes would find their demerits accumulating and become disheartened. It was all due to this unnecessary rigor, and "being military," which some of the yearling corporals affected. No one bears, or rather did bear, such a reputation as the yearling corporal. As such he was disliked by everybody, and plebes have frequently fought them for their unmanly treatment. This, however, was. It is no more. We have no yearling corporals, and plebes fare better generally than ever before. Not because all yearling corporals thus subserved their ambition by reporting men for little things that might as well have been overlooked, did they get this bad reputation, but rather because with it they coupled the severest hazing, and sometimes even insults. That was unmanly as well as mean. Hazing could be endured, but not always insults.

Whether for this reason or not I cannot say, the authorities now appoint the corporals from the second class, men who are more dignified and courteous in their conduct toward all, and especially toward plebes. The advantages of this system are evident.

One scarcely appreciates cadet life—if such appreciation is possible—till he becomes a yearling. It is not till in yearling camp that a cadet begins to "spoon." Not till then is he permitted to attend the hops, and of course he has but little opportunity to cultivate female society, nor is he expected to do so till then, for to assume any familiarity with the upper classes would be considered rather in advance of his "plebeship's" rights. How then can he—he is little more than a stranger—become acquainted with the fair ones who either dwell at or are visiting

West Point. Indeed, knowing " femmes" are quite as prone to haze as the cadets, and most unmercifully cut the unfortunate plebe. Some are also so very haughty : they will admit only first-classmen to their acquaintance and favor.

But Mr. Plebe, having become a yearling finds that the " Mr." is dropped, and that he is allowed all necessary familiarity. He then begins to enjoy his cadetship, a position which for pleasure and happiness has untold advantages, for what woman can resist those glorious buttons ? A yearling has another advantage. The furlough class is absent, and the plebes—well, they are " plebes." Sufficient, isn't it ? The spooneying must all be done, then, by the first and third classes. Often a great number of the first class are bachelors, or not inclined to be spooney ; and that duty then of course devolves on the more gallant part of that class and the yearlings.

The hop managers of the third class have been mentioned elsewhere. They enjoy peculiar facilities for pleasure, and, where a good selection has been made, do much to dispel the monotony of academic military life. Indeed, they do very much toward inducing others to cultivate a high sense of gallantry and respect for women. The refining influence of female society has greater play, and its good results are inevitable.

But what a wretched existence was mine when all this was denied me ! One would be unwilling to believe I had not, from October, 1875, till May, 1876, spoken to a female of any age, and yet it was so. There was no society for me to enjoy—no friends, male or female, for me to visit, or with whom I could have any social intercourse, so absolute was my isolation.* Indeed, I had friends who often visited me, but they did so only when the weather was favorable. In the winter season, when nature, usually so attractive, presented nothing to amuse or dispel one's gloom, and when, therefore, something or some one suited for that purpose was so desirable, no one of course visited me. But I will not murmur. I suppose this was but another constituent of that mechanical mixture of ills and anxieties and suspense that characterized my cadet life. At any rate I can console myself in my victory over prejudice, whether that victory be admitted or not. I know I have so lived that they could find in me no fault different from those at least common to themselves, and have thus forced upon their consciences a just and merited recognition whether or not they are disposed to follow conscience and openly accept my claim to their brotherly love.

---

* I could and did have a pleasant chat every day, more or less, with "Bentz the bugler," the tailor, barber, commissary clerk, the policeman who scrubbed out my room and brought around the mail, the treasurer's clerk, cadets occasionally, and others. The statement made in some of the newspapers, that from one year's end to another I never heard the sound of my own voice, except in the recitation room, is thus seen to be untrue.

CHAPTER VIII.

FIRST-CLASS CAMP.

IT is a common saying among cadets that "first-class camp is just like furlough." I rather think the assertion is an inheritance from former days and the cadets of those days, for the similarity at present between first-class camp and furlough is beyond our conception. There is none, or if any it is chimerical, depending entirely on circumstances. In the case of a small class it would be greater than in that of a large one. For instance, in "train drill" a certain number of men are required. No more are necessary. It would be inexpedient to employ a whole class when the class had more men in it than were required for the drill. In such cases the supernumeraries are instructed in something else, and alternate with those who attend train drill. In the case of a small class all attend the same drill daily, and that other duty or drill is reserved for autumn. Thus there is less drill in camp, and it becomes more like furlough when there is none at all.

Again, first-classmen enjoy more privileges than others, and for this reason their camp is more like furlough. If, however, there are numerous drills, the analogy will fail ; for how can duty, drills, etc., coexist with privileges such as first-class privileges ?

Time which otherwise would be devoted to enjoyment of privileges is now consumed in drills. Still
there is much in it which makes first-class. camp the
most delightful part of a cadet's life. There are
more privileges, the duties are lighter and more
attractive, and make it withal more enjoyable.
First, members of the class attend drill both as
assistants and as students. They are detailed as
chiefs of platoon, chiefs of section, chiefs of caissons,
and as guidons at the light battery ; as chiefs of
pieces at the several foot batteries ; attend themselves
at the siege or sea-coast batteries, train drill, pontoon
drill, engineering, ordnance, and astronomy, and
they are also detailed as officers of the guard. These
duties are generally not very difficult nor unpleasant
to discharge. Second, from the nature of the privileges allowed first-classmen, they have more opportunity for pleasure than other cadets, and therefore
avoid the rather serious consequences of their
monotonous academic military life. A solitary
monotonous life is rather apt to engender a dislike
for mankind, and no high sense of honor or respect
for women. I deem these privileges of especial importance, as they enable one to avoid that danger
and to cultivate the highest possible regard for
women, and those virtues and other Christian attributes of which they are the better exponents. A
soldier is particularly liable to fall into this *sans-
souci* way of looking at life, and those to whom its
pleasures, as well as its ills, are largely due. We
are indebted to our fellows for every thing which
affects our life as regards its happiness or unhappi-

ness, and this latter misfortune will rarely be ours if we properly appreciate our friends and those who can and will make life less wretched. To shut one's self up in one's self is merely to trust, or rather to set up, one's own judgment as superior to the world's. That cannot be, nor can there be happiness in such false views of our organization as being of and for each other.

At this point of the course many of the first-class have attained their majority. They are men, and in one year more will be officers of the army. It becomes them, therefore, to lay aside the ordinary student's *rôle*, and assume a more dignified one, one more in conformity with their age and position. They leave all cadet *rôles*, etc., to the younger classes, and put on the proper dignity of men.

There are for them more privileges. They are more independent — more like men ; and consequently they find another kind of enjoyment in camp than that of the cadet. It is a general, a proper, a rational sort of pleasure such as one would enjoy at home among relatives or friends, and hence the similarity between first-class camp and furlough.

But it is not thus with all first-classmen. Many, indeed the majority, are cadets till they graduate. They see every thing as a cadet, enjoy every thing as a cadet, and find the duties, etc., of first-class camp as irksome as those of plebe or yearling camp. Of course such men see no similarity between first-class camp and furlough. It is their misfortune. We should enjoy as many things as we can, and not sorrow over them. We should not make our life one of sorrow when it could as well be one of comfort and pleasure. I don't mean comfort and pleasure in an epicurean sense, but in a moral one. Still first-classmen do have many duties to perform, but there is withal one consolation at least, there are no upper classmen to keep the plebe or yearling in his place. There is no feeling of humbleness because of junior rank, for the first class is the first in rank, and therefore need humble itself to none other than the proper authorities.

Again, their honor, as " cadets and gentlemen," is relied upon as surety for obedience and regard for regulations. They are not subject to constant watching as plebes are. The rigor of discipline is not so severe upon them as upon others. It was expended upon them during their earlier years at the Academy, and, as a natural consequence, any violation of regulations, etc., by a first-classman, merits and receives a severer punishment than would be visited upon a junior classman for a like infringement on his part.

The duties of first-classmen in first-class camp are as follows : The officer of the day and two officers of the guard are detailed each day from the class. Their duties are precisely those of similar officers in the regular army. The junior officer of the guard daily reports to the observatory to find the error of the tower clock. Also each day are detailed the necessary assistants for the several light batteries, who are on foot or mounted, as the case may require. The remainder of the class receive instructions in the service of the siege and sea-coast artillery. These drills come in the early forenoon. After them come ordnance and engineering.

The entire class is divided as equally as may be into two parts, which alternate in attendance at ordnance and engineering.

In ordnance the instructions are on the preparation of military fireworks, fixing of ammunition and packing it, the battery wagon and forge. This instruction is thoroughly practical. The cadets make the cases for rockets, paper shells, etc., and fill them, leaving them ready for immediate use. The stands of fixed ammunition prepared are the grape and canister, and shell and shot, with their sabots.

The battery wagon and forge are packed as prescribed in the "Ordnance Manual."

The instructions in engineering are also practical and military. They are in the modes of throwing and dismantling pontoon bridges, construction of fascines, gabions, hurdles, etc., and revetting batteries with them. Sometimes also during camp, more often after, foot reconnoissances are made. A morning and night detail is made daily from the class to receive practical instruction in astronomy in the field observatory.

Night signalling with torches, and telegraphy by day, form other sources of instruction for the first class.

Telegraphy, or train drill, as the drill is called, consists in erecting the telegraph line and opening communication between two stations, and when this is done, in communicating so as to acquire a practical knowledge of the instruments and their use.

These various drills—all of them occurring daily, Sunday of course excepted, and for part of them Saturday also—complete the course of instruction given the first class only during their first - class camp. It will be observed that they all of them are of a military nature and of the greatest importance. The instruction is thorough accordingly.

I have sufficiently described, I think, a cadet's first-class camp. I shall, therefore, close the chapter here.

CHAPTER IX.

OUR FUTURE HEROES.

THE WEST POINT CADETS' VACATION.

Ten Days of Centennial Sport for Prospective Warriors—The Miseries of three hundred Young Gentlemen who are limited to Ten Pairs of White Trousers each.

" ALMOST at the foot of George's Hill, and not far to the westward of Machinery Hall, is the camp of the West Point cadets. From morning till night the domestic economy of the three hundred young gentlemen who compose the corps is closely watched, and their guard mountings and dress parades attract throngs of spectators. It would be hard to find anywhere a body of young men so manly in appearance, so perfect in discipline, and so soldier-like and intelligent. The system of competitive examination for admission, so largely adopted within the past few years in many of our large cities, has resulted in recruiting the corps with lads of bright intellect and more than ordinary attainments, while the strict physical examination has rigorously excluded all but those of good form and perfect health. The competitive system has also given to the Academy students who want to learn, instead of lads who are content to scramble through the prescribed course as best they can, escaping the disgrace of being " found" (a cadet term equivalent to the old college word " plucked") by nearly a hair's-breadth.

" *The camp.*—The camp is laid out in regulation style, and has four company streets. Near the western limit of the Centennial grounds are the tents of the commandant and the cadet captains and lieutenants. Below, on a gentle incline, are the wall tents, occupied by the cadets. Each of these has a board floor, and it is so arranged that when desired it may be thrown open on all sides. From two to four narrow iron cots, a bucket for water, an occasional chair, and now and then a mirror, comprise the furniture. But scanty as it is, every article of this little outfit has a place, and must be kept in it, or woe to the unlucky wight upon whom the duty of housekeeping devolves for the day. The bucket must stand on the left-hand side of the

tent, in front ; the beds must be made at a certain hour and in a certain style—for the coming heroes of America have to be their own
chambermaids ; while valises and other baggage must be stowed
away in as orderly a way as possible. Every morning the tents are
inspected, and any lack of neatness or order insures for the chamber-
maid of the day a misconduct mark. It may be easily conceived that
under a regime so strict as this the cadets are particularly careful as
to their quarters, inasmuch as one hundred of these marks mean dismissal from the Academy.

"At daybreak the reveille sounds, and the cadets turn out for roll-
call. Then come breakfast, guard mounting, and camp and general
police duty, which consume the time until 8.30 A.M., from which
hour those who are not on guard have the freedom of the Centennial
grounds. At 5 P.M. they must fall in for dress parade ; at 9 they
answer to 'tattoo' roll-call, and a few minutes later 'taps' or
'lights out' consigns them to darkness and quiet.

"*West Point Aristocracy.*—Small as is this corps, it is still patent
that the distinction of caste is very strong. A first-classman—cadet
officers are selected from this class—looks down upon lower grade
men, while second-class cadets view their juniors with something
nearly allied to contempt, and third-class men are amusingly patron-
izing in their treatment of 'plebes' or new-comers. For the first
year of their Academy life the 'plebes' have rather a hard time of it ;
but no sooner do they emerge from their chrysalis state than they
are as hard upon their unfortunate successors as the third-class men
of the year before were upon them.

"The cadets are delighted with their reception and kind treatment
in Philadelphia, and look upon their ten days' visit to the Centennial
as a most pleasant break in the monotony of Academy life. That
they maintain the reputation of the Academy for gallantry and devotion to the fair sex is evidenced by the presence of numbers of beautiful young ladies in their camp after dress parade every evening.
Given, a pretty girl, the twilight of a summer evening, and a youth
in uniform, and the result is easily guessed.

"The Cadet Corps is to return to West Point to-morrow morning.
There the cadets are to go into camp until September. General
Sherman at one time purposed to have them march from this city to
the Academy, but it was finally decided that the march would consume time which might be more profitably devoted to drill.

"One of the complaints of the cadets is that in the arrangements
for their visit, the Quartermaster's Department was stricken with a

spasm of economy as regarded transportation, and each of the future heroes was limited to the miserably insufficient allowance of ten pairs of white trousers.

"The cadets speak in warmly eulogistic terms of the Seventh New York, to whose kindly attentions, they say, much of their pleasure is due."

Of this article, which was taken from the Philadelphia *Times*, I need only say, those "two or four narrow iron cots" and that "occasional chair" existed solely in the imagination of the reporter, as they were nowhere visible within the limits of our encampment.

CHAPTER X.

"A brave and honorable and courteous man
Will not insult me ; and none other can."—COWPER.

"HOW do they treat you?" "How do you get along?" and multitudes of analogous questions have been asked me over and over again. Many have asked them for mere curiosity's sake, and to all such my answers have been as short and abrupt as was consistent with common politeness. I have observed that it is this class of people who start rumors, sometimes harmless, but more often the cause of needless trouble and ill-feeling. I have considered such a class dangerous, and have therefore avoided them as much as it was possible. I will mention a single instance where such danger has been made manifest.

A Democratic newspaper, published I know not where, in summing up the faults of the Republican party, took occasion to advert to West Point. It asserted in bold characters that I had stolen a number of articles from two cadets, had by them been detected in the very act, had been seen by several other cadets who had been summoned for the purpose that they might testify against me, had been

reported to the proper authorities, the affair had
been thoroughly investigated by them, my guilt
established beyond the possibility of doubt, and yet
my accusers had actually been dismissed while I
was retained.* This is cited as an example of Republican rule ;· and the writer had the effrontery to
ask, " How long shall such things be ?" I did not
reply to it then, nor do I intend to do so now.   Such
assertions from such sources need no replies.   I
merely mention the incident to show how wholly
given to party prejudices some men can be.   They
seem to have no thought of right and justice, but
favor whatever promotes the aims and interests of
their own party, a party not Democratic but hellish.
How different is the following article from the Philadelphia *North American*, of July 7th, 1876 :

" It is very little to the credit of the West Point cadets, a body of
young men in whose superior discipline and thoroughly excellent
deportment we feel in common with nearly all others a gratified
pride, that they should be so ungenerous and unjust as they confess
themselves to be in their treatment of the colored boy, who, like themselves, has been made a ward of the nation.   We know nothing of
this young man's personal character or habits, but we have seen no
unkind criticism of them.   For that reason we condemn as beneath
contempt the spirit which drives him to an isolation, in bearing
which the black shows himself the superior of the white.   We do
not ask nor do we care to encourage any thing more than decent
courtesy.   But the young gentlemen who boast of holding only official intercourse with their comrade should remember that no one of
them stands before the country in any different light from him.
West Point is an academy for the training of young men, presumably
representative of the people, for a career sufficiently honorable to

---

* This article was cut from a newspaper, and, together with the
name of the paper, was posted in a conspicuous place, where other
cadets, as well as myself, saw and read it.

gratify any ambition. The cadets come from all parts of the country, from all ranks of the social scale. Amalgamated by the uniform course of studies and the similarity of discipline, the separating fragments at the end of the student life carry similar qualities into the life before them, and step with almost remarkable social equality into the world where they must find their level. It would be expecting too much to hope that the companionship which surmounts or breaks down all the barriers of caste, should tread with equal heel the prejudices of color. But it would be more manly in these boys, if they would remember how easy ordinary courtesy would be to them, how much it would lighten the life of a young man whose rights are equal to their own. It is useless to ignore the inevitable. This colored boy has his place ; he should have fair encouragement to hold it. Heaping neglect upon him does not overcome the principle involved in his appointment, and while we by no means approve of such appointments we do believe in common justice.''

On the other hand, many have desired this information for a practical use, and that, too, whether they were prejudiced or not. That is, if friends, they were anxious to know how I fared, whether or not I was to be a success, and if a success to use that fact in the interest of the people ; and if enemies, they wanted naturally to know the same things in order to use the knowledge to the injury of the people if I proved a failure.

I have not always been able to distinguish one class from the other, and have therefore been quite reticent about my life and treatment at West Point. I have, too, avoided the newspapers as much as possible. I succeeded in this so well that it was scarcely known that I was at the Academy. Much surprise was manifested when I appeared in Philadelphia at the Centennial. One gentleman said to me in the Government building : '' You are quite an exhibition yourself. No one was expecting to see a colored cadet.''

But I wander from my theme. It is a remarkable fact that the new cadets, in only a very few instances, show any unwillingness to speak or fraternize. It is not till they come in contact with the rougher elements of the corps that they manifest any disposition to avoid one. It was so in my own class, and has been so in all succeeding classes.

When I was a plebe those of us who lived on the same floor of barracks visited each other, borrowed books, heard each other recite when preparing for examination, and were really on most intimate terms. But alas! in less than a month they learned to call me "nigger," and ceased altogether to visit me. We did the Point together, shared with each other whatever we purchased at the sutler's, and knew not what prejudice was. Alas! we were soon to be informed! In camp, brought into close contact with the old cadets, these once friends discovered that they were prejudiced, and learned to abhor even the presence or sight of a "d—d nigger."

Just two years after my entrance into the Academy, I met in New York a young man who was a plebe at the time I was, and who then associated with me. He recognized me, hurried to me from across the street, shook my hand heartily, and expressed great delight at seeing me. He showed me the photograph of a classmate, told me where I could find him, evidently ignorant of my ostracism, and, wishing me all sorts of success, took his leave. After he left me I involuntarily asked myself, "Would it have been thus if he had not been 'found on his prelim?'" Possibly not, but it is very, very doubtful.

There are some, indeed the majority of the corps
are such, who treat me on all occasions with proper
politeness. They are gentlemen themselves, and
treat others as it becomes gentlemen to do. They
do not associate, nor do they speak other than officially, except in a few cases. They are perhaps
as much prejudiced as the others, but prejudice does
not prevent all from being gentlemen. On the other
hand, there are some from the very lowest classes
of our population. They are uncouth and rough in
appearance, have only a rudimentary education,
have little or no idea of courtesy, use the very worst
language, and in most cases are much inferior to the
average negro. What can be expected of such
people ? They are low, and their conduct must be
in keeping with their breeding. I am not at all surprised to find it so. Indeed, in ordinary civil life I
should consider such people beneath me in the social
scale, should even reckon some of them as roughs,
and consequently give them a wide berth.

What surprises me most is the control this class
seems to have over the other. It is in this class I
have observed most prejudice, and from it, or rather
by it, the other becomes tainted. It seems to rule
the corps by fear. Indeed, I know there are many
who would associate, who would treat me as a
brother cadet, were they not held in constant dread
of this class. The bullies, the fighting men of the
corps are in it. It rules by fear, and whoever dis-
obeys its beck is " cut." The rest of the corps follows like so many menials subject to command. In
short, there is a fearful lack of backbone. There is,

it seems at first sight, more prejudice at West Point
than elsewhere. It is not really so I think.

The officers of the institution have never, so far
as I can say, shown any prejudice at all. They have
treated me with uniform courtesy and impartiality.
The cadets, at least some of them, away from West
Point, have also treated me with such gentlemanly
propriety. The want of backbone predominates to
such an alarming extent at West Point they are
afraid to do so there. I will mention a few cases under this subject of treatment.

During my first-class camp I was rather surprised
on one occasion to have a plebe—we had been to the
Centennial Exhibition and returned, and of course
my status must have been known to him—come to
my tent to borrow ink of me. I readily complied
with his request, feeling proud of what I thought
was the beginning of a new era in my cadet life. I
felt he would surely prove himself manly enough,
after thus recognizing me, to keep it up, and thus
bring others under his influence to the same cause.
And I was still further assured in this when I observed he made his visits frequent and open. At
length, sure of my willingness to oblige him, he
came to me, and, after expressing a desire to "bone
up" a part of the fourth-class course, and the need
he felt for such "boning," begged me to lend him
my algebra. I of course readily consented, gave
him my key, and sent him to my trunk in the trunk
rooms to get it. He went. He got it, and returned
the key. He went into ecstasies, and made no end
of thanks to me for my kindness, etc. All this naturally confirmed my opinion and hope of better

recognition ultimately. Indeed, I was glad of an opportunity to prove that I was not unkind or ungenerous. I supposed he would keep the book till about September, at which time he would get one of his own, as every cadet at that time was required to procure a full course of text - books, these being necessary for reference, etc., in future life. And so he did. Some time after borrowing the book, he came to me and asked for India ink. I handed him a stick, or rather part of one, and received as usual his many thanks. Several days after this, and at night, during my absence—I was, if I remember aright, at Fort Clinton making a series of observations with a zenith telescope in the observatory there —he came to the rear of my tent, raised the wall near one corner, and placed the ink on the floor, just inside the wall, which he left down as he found it.

I found the ink there when I returned. I was utterly disgusted with the man. The low, unmanly way in which he acted was wholly without my approval. If he was disposed to be friendly, why be cowardly about it ? If he must recognize me secretly, why, I would rather not have such recognition. Acting a lie to his fellow-cadets by appearing to be inimical to me and my interests, while he pretended the reverse to me, proved him to have a baseness of character with which I didn't care to identify myself.

September came at last, and my algebra was returned. The book was the one I had used my first year at the Academy. I had preserved it, as I have all of my books, for future use and as a sort of souvenir of my cadet life. It was for that sole reason of great value to me. I enjoined upon him to take care of the book, and in nowise to injure it. My name was on the back, on the cover, and my initial, "F," in two other places on the cover. When the book was returned he had cut the calfskin from the cover, so as to remove my name. The result was a horrible disfiguration of the book, and a serious impairment of its durability. The mere sight of the book angered me, and I found it difficult to refrain from manifesting as much. He undoubtedly did it to conceal the fact that the book was borrowed from me. Such unmanliness, such cowardice, such baseness even, was most disgusting ; and I felt very much as if I would like to—well, I don't know that I would. There was no reason at all for mutilating the book. If he was not man enough to use it with my name on it, why did he borrow it and agree not to injure it ? On that sole condition I lent it. Why did he not borrow some one else's and return mine ?

I have been asked, "What is the general feeling of the corps towards you ? Is it a kindly one, or is it an unfriendly one. Do they purposely ill-treat you or do they avoid you merely ?" I have found it rather difficult to answer unqualifiedly such questions ; and yet I believe, and have always believed, that the general feeling of the corps towards me was a kindly one. This has been manifested in multitudes of ways, on innumerably occasions, and under the most various circumstances. And while there are some who treat me at times in an unbecoming manner, the majority of the corps have ever treated me as I would desire to be treated. I mean, of course, by this assertion that they have treated me as I expected and really desired them to treat me, so long as they were prejudiced. They have held certain opinions more or less prejudicial to me and my interests, but so long as they have not exercised their theories to my displeasure or discomfort, or so long as they have "let me severely alone," I had no just reason for complaint. Again, others, who have no theory of their own, and almost no manliness, have been accustomed "to pick quarrels," or to endeavor to do so, to satisfy I don't know what; and while they have had no real opinions of their own, they have not respected those of others. Their feeling toward me has been any thing but one of justice, and yet at times even they have shown a remarkable tendency to recognize me as having certain rights entitled to their respect, if not their appreciation.

As I have been practically isolated from the cadets, I have had little or no intercourse with them. I have therefore had but little chance to know what was really the feeling of the corps as a unit toward myself. Judging, however, from such evidences as I have, I am forced to conclude that it is as given above, viz., a feeling of kindness, restrained kindness if you please.

Here are some of the evidences which have come under my notice.

I once heard a cadet make the following unchristian remark about myself when a classmate had been accidentally hurt at light-battery drill: "I wish it had been the nigger, and it had killed him." I couldn't help looking at him, and I did; but that, and nothing more. Some time after this, at cavalry drill, we were side by side, and I had a rather vicious horse,

6

one in fact which I could not manage. He gave a sudden jump unexpectedly to me. I almost lost my seat in the saddle. This cadet seized me by the arm, and in a tone of voice that was evidently kind and generous, said to me, "For heaven's sake be careful. You'll be thrown and get hurt if you don't." How different from that other wish given above!

Another evidence, and an important one, may be given in these words. It is customary for the senior, or, as we say, the first class, to choose, each member, a horse, and ride him exclusively during the term. The choice is usually made by lot, and each man chooses according to the number he draws. By remarkable good fortune I drew No. 1, and had therefore the first choice of all the horses in the stables.

As soon as the numbers drawn were published, several classmates hastened to me for the purpose of effecting an exchange of choice. It will at once be seen that any such change would in no manner benefit me, for if I lost the first choice I might also lose the chance of selecting a good horse. With the avowed intention of proving that I had at least a generous disposition, and also that I was not disposed to consider, in my reciprocal relations with the cadets, how I had been, and was even then treated by them, I consented to exchange my first choice for the fourteenth.

This agreement was made with the first that asked for an exchange. Several others came, and, when informed of the previous agreement, of course went their way. A day or two after this a number of cadets were discussing the choice of horses, etc., and reverted to the exchange which I had made. One of them suggested that if an exchange of a choice higher than fourteen were suggested to me, I might accept it.

What an idea he must have had of my character to suppose me base enough to disregard an agreement I had already made !

However, all in the crowd were not as base as he was, and one of them was man enough to say :

" Oh no ! that would be imposing upon Mr. Flipper's good nature." He went on to show how ungentlemanly and unbecoming in a " cadet and gentleman" such an act would be. The idea was abandoned, or at least was never broached to me, and if it had been I would never have entertained it. Such an act on the part of the cadet could have arisen only from a high sense of manly honor or from a feeling of kindness.

There are multitudes of little acts of kindness similar to these, and even different ones. I need not—indeed as I do not remember them all I cannot—mention them all. They all show, however, that the cadets are not avowedly inclined to ill-treat me, but rather to assist me to make my life under the circumstances as pleasant as can be. And there may be outside influences, such as relatives or friends, which bias their own better judgments and keep them from fully and openly recognizing me. For however hard either way may be, it is far easier to do as friends wish than as conscience may dictate, when conscience and friends differ. Under such conditions it would manifestly be unjust for me to expect recognition of them, even though they themselves were disposed to make it. I am sure this is at least a Christian view of the case, and with such view I have ever kept aloof from the cadets. I have not obtruded myself upon them, nor in any way attempted to force recognition from them. This has proved itself to be by far the better way, and I don't think it could well be otherwise.

The one principle which has controlled my conduct while a cadet, and which is apparent throughout my narrative, is briefly this : to find, if possible, for every insult or other offence a reason or motive which is consistent with the character of a gentleman. Whenever I have been insulted, or any thing has been done or said to me which might have that construction, I have endeavored to find some excuse, some reason for it, which was not founded on prejudice or on baseness of character or any other ungentlemanly attribute ; or, in other words, I wanted to prove that it was not done because of my color. If I could find such a reason —and I have found them—I have been disposed not only to overlook the offence, but to forgive and forget it. Thus there are many cadets who would associate, etc., were they not restrained by the force of opinion of relatives and friends. This cringing dependence, this vassalage, this mesmerism we may call it, we all know exists. Why, many a cadet has openly confessed to me that he did not recognize us because he was afraid of being " cut."

Again, I find some too high-toned, too punctilious, to recognize me. I attribute this not to the loftiness of their highnesses nor to prejudice, but to the depth of their ignorance, and of course I forgive and forget. Others again are so " reckless," so

"don't care" disposed, that they treat me as fancy
dictates, now friendly, now vacillating, and now inimical. With these I simply do as the Romans do.
If they are friendly, so am I ; if they scorn me I do
not obtrude myself upon them ; if they are indifferent, I am indifferent too.

There is a rather remarkable case under this subject which has caused me no little surprise and disappointment. I refer to those cadets appointed by
colored members of Congress.

It was quite natural to expect of them better
treatment than of others, and yet if in any thing at
all they differed from the former, they were the more
reserved and discourteous. They most "severely
let me alone." They never associated, nor did they
speak, except officially, and then they always spoke
in a haughty and insolent manner that was to me
most exasperating. And in one case in particular
was this so. One of those so appointed was the son
of the colored Congressman who sent him there, and
from him at least good treatment was reasonably expected. There have been only two such appointments to my knowledge, and it is a singular fact that
they were both overbearing, conceited, and by no
means popular with their comrades. The status of
one was but little better than my own, and only in
that his comrades would speak and associate. He
was not "cut," but avoided as much as possible
without making the offence too patent.

There was a cadet in the corps with myself who
invariably dropped his head whenever our eyes met.
His complexion was any thing but white, his features
were rough and homely, and his person almost en-

tirely without symmetry or beauty. From this singular circumstance and his physique, I draw the conclusion that he was more African than Anglo-Saxon. Indeed, I once heard as much insinuated by a fellow-cadet, to whom his reply was : " It's an honor to be black."

Near the close of this chapter I have occason to speak of fear. There I mean by fear a sort of shrinking demeanor or disposition to accept insults and other petty persecutions as just dues, or to leave them unpunished from actual cowardice, to which fear some have been pleased to attribute my generally good treatment. This latter fact has been by many, to my personal knowledge, attributed to fear in another quarter, viz., in the cadets themselves. It has many times been said to me by persons at West Point and elsewhere : " I don't suppose many of those fellows would care to encounter you ?"

This idea was doubtless founded upon my physical proportions — I am six feet one and three-quarter inches high, and weigh one hundred and seventy-five pounds. In behalf of the corps of cadets I would disclaim any such notions of fear,

First. Because the conception of the idea is not logical. I was not the tallest, nor yet the largest man in the corps, nor even did I give any evidence of a disposition to fight or bully others.

Second. Because I did not come to West Point purposely to " go through on my muscle." I am not a fighting character, as the cadets—those who know me—can well testify.

Third. Because it is ungenerous to attribute

what can result from man's better nature only to such base causes as fear or cowardice. This seems to be about the only way in which many have endeavored to explain the difference between my life at West Point and that of other colored cadets. They seem to think that my physique inspired a sort of fear in the cadets, and forced them at least to let me alone, while the former ones, smaller in size, did therefore create no such fear until by persistent retaliation it was shown they were able to defend themselves.

Now this, I think, is the most shallow of all reasoning and entirely unworthy our further notice.

Fourth. I should be grieved to suppose any one feared me. It is not my desire to go through life feared by any one. I can derive no pleasure from any thing which is accorded me through motives of fear. The grant must be spontaneous and voluntary to give me the most pleasure. I want nothing, not even recognition, unless it be freely given, hence have I not forced myself upon my comrades.

" But the sensible Flipper accepted the situation, and proudly refused to intrude himself on the white boys."—*Atlanta (Ga.) Herald.*

Fifth. Because it is incompatible with the dignity of a " cadet and a gentleman" for one to fear another.

Sixth. Because it is positively absurd to suppose that one man of three hundred more or less would be feared by the rest individually and collectively, and no rational being would for an instant entertain any such idea. There is, however, a single case which may imply fear on the part of the

cadet most concerned. A number of plebes, among
them a colored one, were standing on the stoop of
barracks. There were also several cadets standing
in the doorway, and a sentinel was posted in the
hall. This latter individual went up to one of the
cadets and said to him, " Make that nigger out there
get his hands around," referring to this plebe mentioned above.

I happened to come down stairs just at that time,
and as soon as he uttered those words he turned and
saw me. He hung his head, and in a cowardly manner sneaked off, while the cadets in the door also dis-
persed with lowered heads. Was it fear ? Verily I
know not. Possibly it was shame.

Again I recall a rather peculiar circumstance
which will perhaps sustain this notion of fear on the
part of the cadets. I have on every occasion when I
had command over my fellow-cadets in any degree,
noticed that they were generally more orderly and
more obedient than when this authority was exercised by another.

Thus whenever I commanded the guard there
were very few reports for offences committed by
members of the guard. They have ever been obedient and military. In camp, when I was first in command of the guard, I had a most orderly guard and
a very pleasant tour, and that too, observe, while some
of the members of it were plebes and on for the first
time. On all such occasions it is an immemorial
custom for the yearlings to interfere with and haze
the plebe sentinels. Not a sentinel was disturbed,
not a thing went amiss, and why ? Manifestly because it was thought—and rightly too—that I would

not connive at such interference, and because they feared to attempt it lest they be watched and reported. Later, however, even this semblance of fear disappeared, and they acted under me precisely as they do under others, because they are convinced that I will not stoop to spy or retaliate.

"The boys were rather afraid that when he should come to hold the position as officer of the guard that he would swagger over them ; but he showed good sense and taste, merely assuming the rank formally and leaving his junior to carry out the duty."—*New York Herald.*

And just here it is worthy of notice that the press, in commenting upon my chances of graduating, has never, so far as I know, entertained any doubts of my ability to do so. It has, on the contrary, expressed the belief that the probability of my graduating depended upon the officers of the Academy, and upon any others who, by influence or otherwise, were connected with the Academy. Some have even hinted at politics as a possible ground upon which they might drop me.

All such opinions have been created and nurtured by the hostile portion of the press, and, I regret to say, by that part also which ought to have been more friendly, if not more discreet. No branch of the government is freer from the influences and whims of politicians than the National Military Academy. Scarcely any paper has considered how the chances of any cadet depended upon himself alone. The authorities of the Academy are, or have been, officers of the army. They are, with one or two exceptions, graduates, and therefore, presumably, "officers and gentlemen." To transform young men into a like ilk as themselves is their duty. The country intrusts them with this great responsibility. To prove faithless to such a charge would be to risk position, and even those dearer attributes of the soldier, honor and reputation. They would not dare ill-treat a colored cadet or a white one. Of course the prejudice of race is not yet overcome entirely, and possibly they may be led into some indiscretion on account of it ; but I do not think it would be different at any other college in the country. It is natural.

There are prejudices of caste as well as prejudices of race, and I am most unwilling to believe it possible that any officer would treat with injustice a colored cadet who in true gentlemanly qualities, intelligence, and assiduousness equals or excels certain white ones who are treated with perfect equanimity. With me it has not been so. I have been treated as I would wish to be in the majority of cases. There have been of course occasions where I've fancied wrong had been done me. I expected to be ill-treated. I went to West Point fully convinced that I'd have "a rough time of it." Who that has read the many newspaper versions of the treatment of colored cadets, and of Smith in particular, would not have been so convinced ? When, therefore, any affront or any thing seemingly of that nature was offered me, I have been disposed, naturally I think, to unduly magnify it, because I expected it. This was hasty and unjust, and so I admit, now that I am better informed. What was apparently done to incommode or discourage me has been shown to have been done either for my own benefit or for some other purpose, not to my harm. In every single instance I have, after knowing better the reason for such acts, felt obliged to acknowledge the injustice of my fears. At other times I have been agreeably surprised at the kindnesses shown me both by officers and cadets, and have found myself at great loss to reconcile them with acts I had already adjudged as malicious wrongs.

I have, too, been particularly careful not to fall into an error, which, I think, has been the cause of misfortune to at least one of the cadets of color. If a cadet affront another, if a white cadet insult a colored one for instance, the latter can complain to the proper authorities, and, if there be good reason for it, can always get proper redress. This undoubtedly gives the consolation of knowing that the offence will not be repeated, but beyond that I think it a great mistake to have so sought it. A person who constantly complains, even with some show of reason, loses more or less the respect of the authorities. And the offenders, while they refrain from open acts, do nevertheless conduct their petty persecutions in such a manner that one can shape no charge against them, and consequently finds himself helpless. One must endure these little tortures—the sneer, the shrug of the shoulder, the epithet, the effort to avoid, to disdain, to ignore—and thus suffer ; for any of them are—to me at least—far more hard to bear than a blow. A blow I may resist or ignore. In either case I soon forget it. But a sneer, a shrug of the shoulder, mean more. Either is a blow at my sensitiveness, my inner feelings, and which through no ordinary effort of mind can be altogether forgotten. It is a sting that burns long and fiercely. How much better to have ignored the greater offences which could be reached, and to have thus avoided the lesser ones, which nothing can destroy ! How much wiser to stand like a vast front of fortification, on some rocky moral height absolutely unassailable, passively resisting alike the attack by open assault and the surer one by regular approaches ! The assault can be repulsed, but who can, who has ever successfully stopped the mines and the galleries through which an entrance is at length forced into the interior ?

" We cannot expect the sons to forget the lessons of the sires ; but we have a right to demand from the general government the rooting out of all snobbery at West Point, whether it is of that kind which sends poor white boys to Coventry, because they haven't a family name or wealth, or whether it be that smallest, meanest, and shallowest of all aristocracies—the one founded upon color.

" If the government is not able to root out these unrepublican seeds in these hotbeds of disloyalty and snobbery, let Congress shut up the useless and expensive appendages and educate its officers at the colleges of the country, where they may learn lessons in true Republican equality and nationality. The remedy lies with Congress. A remonstrance, at least, should be heard from the colored members of Congress, who are insulted whenever a colored boy is ill-treated by the students or the officers of these institutions. So far from being discouraged by defeats, the unjust treatment meted out to the young men should redouble the efforts of others of their class to conquer this new Bastile by storm. It should lead every colored Congressman to make sure that he either sends a colored applicant or a white one who has not the seeds of snobbery or caste in his soul."

I shall consider this last clause at the end of this chapter, where I shall quote at length the article from which this passage is taken.

If I may be pardoned an opinion on this article, I do not think the true remedy lies with Congress at all. I do not question the right to demand of Congress any thing, but I do doubt the propriety or need of such a proceeding, of course, in the case under consideration. As to "that kind which sends poor white boys to Coventry," because of their poverty, etc., I can say with absolute truthfulness it no longer exists. When it did exist the power to discontinue it did not lie with Congress. Congress has no control over personal whims or prejudices. But I make a slight mistake. There was a time when influence, wealth, or position was able to secure a cadetship. At that time poor boys very rarely succeeded in getting an appointment, and when they did they were most unmercifully "cut" by the snobs of aristocracy who were at the Academy. Then the remedy did lie with Congress. The appointments could have been so made as to exclude those snobs whose only recommendation was their position in society, and so also as to admit boys who were deserving, although they were perhaps poor. This remedy has been made, and all classes (white), whether poor or rich, influential or not, are on terms of absolute equality.

But for that other kind, "the one founded upon color," Congress has no remedy, no more than for fanaticism or something of that kind.

This article also tells us that "the government has been remiss in not throwing around them the protection of its authority." I disdainfully scout the idea of such protection. If my manhood cannot stand without a governmental prop, then let it fall.

If I am to stand on any other ground than the one white cadets stand upon, then I don't want the cadetship. If I cannot endure prejudice and persecutions, even if they are offered, then I don't deserve the cadetship, and much less the commission of an army officer. But there is a remedy, a way to root out snobbery and prejudice which but needs adoption to have the desired effect. Of course its adoption by a single person, myself for instance, will not be sufficient to break away all the barriers which prejudice has brought into existence. I am quite confident, however, if adopted by all colored cadets, it will eventually work out the difficult though by no means insoluble problem, and give us further cause for joy and congratulations.

The remedy lies solely in our case with us. We can make our life at West Point what we will. We shall be treated by the cadets as we treat them. Of course some of the cadets are low—they belong to the younger classes—and good treatment cannot be expected of them at West Point nor away from there. The others, presumably gentlemen, will treat everybody else as becomes gentlemen, or at any rate as they themselves are treated. For, as Josh Billings quaintly tells us, "a gentleman kant hide hiz true karakter enny more than a loafer kan."

Prejudice does not necessarily prevent a man's being courteous and gentlemanly in his relations with others. If, then, they be prejudiced and treat one with ordinary civility, or even if they let one "severely alone," is there any harm done? Is such a course of conduct to be denounced? Religiously,

yes ; but in the manner of every-day life and its con-
ventionalities, I say not by any means.   I have the
right—no one will deny it—of choosing or rejecting
as companions whomsoever I will.   If my choice be
based upon color, am I more wrong in adopting it
than I should be in adopting any other reason ?   It
may be an unchristian opinion or fancy that causes
me to do it, but such opinion or fancy is my own,
and I have a right to it.   No one objects to prejudice
as such, but to the treatment it is supposed to cause.
If one is disposed to ill-treat another, he'll do it,
prejudiced or not prejudiced.   Only low persons are
so disposed, and happily so for West Point, and indeed for the whole country.

"The system of competitive examination for admission, so largely adopted within the past few years
in many of our large cities, has resulted in recruiting
the corps with lads of bright intellect and more than
ordinary attainments, while the strict physical examination has rigorously excluded all but those of
good form and perfect health.   The competitive system has also given to the Academy students who
want to learn, instead of lads who are content to
scramble through the prescribed course as best they
can, escaping being 'found' (a cadet term equivalent to the old college word 'plucked') by merely
a hair's-breadth."

The old way of getting rid of the rough, uncouth
characters was to "find" them.   Few, very few of
them, ever got into the army.   Now they are excluded by the system of competitive examination
even from entering the Military Academy, and if

they should succeed in getting to West Point, they eventually fail, since men with no fixed purpose cannot graduate at West Point.

Now if the " colored cadets" be not of this class also, then their life at West Point will not be much harder than that of the others. The cadets may not associate, but what of that? Am I to blame a man who prefers not to associate with me? If that be the only charge against him, then my verdict is for acquittal. Though his conduct arises from, to us, false premises, it is to his sincere convictions right, and we would not in the slightest degree be justified in forcing him into our way of looking at it. In other words, the remedy does not lie with Congress.

The kind of treatment we are to receive at the hands of others depends entirely upon ourselves. I think my life at West Point sufficiently proves the truth of this assertion. I entered the Academy at a time when, as one paper had it, West Point was a " hotbed of disloyalty and snobbery, a useless and expensive appendage." I expected all sorts of ill-treatment, and yet from the day I entered till the day I graduated I had not cause to utter so much as an angry word. I refused to obtrude myself upon the white cadets, and treated them all with uniform courtesy. I have been treated likewise. It simply depended on me what sort of treatment I should receive. I was careful to give no cause for bad treatment, and it was never put upon me. In making this assertion I purposely disregard the instances of malice, etc., mentioned elsewhere, for the reason that I do not believe they were due to any deep personal convictions of my inferiority or personal desire to impose upon me, but rather were due to the fear of being " cut" if they had acted otherwise.

Our relations have been such, as any one will readily observe, that even officially they would have been obliged to recognize me to a greater or less extent, or at the expense of their consciences ignore me. They have done both, as circumstances and not inclination have led them to do.

A rather unexpected incident occurred in the summer of '73, which will show perhaps how intense is that gravitating force—if I may so term it—which so completely changes the feelings of the plebes, and even cadets, who, when they reported, were not at all prejudiced on account of color.

It was rather late at night and extremely dark. I was on guard and on post at the time. Approaching the lower end of my post, No. 5, I heard my name called in a low tone by some one whom I did not recognize. I stopped and listened. The calling was repeated, and I drew near the place whence it came. It proved to be a cadet, a classmate of mine, and then a sentinel on the adjacent post, No. 4. We stood and talked quite awhile, as there was no danger either of being seen by other cadets—an event which those who in any manner have recognized me have strenuously avoided—or "hived standing on post." It was too dark. He expressed great regret at my treatment, hoped it would be bettered, assured me that he would ever be a friend and treat me as a gentleman should.

Another classmate told me, at another time, in effect the same thing. I very naturally expected a fulfilment of these promises, but alas! for such hopes! They not only never fulfilled them, but treated me even as badly as all the others. One of them was assigned a seat next to me at table. He would eat scarcely anything, and when done with that he would draw his chair away and pretend to be imposed upon in the most degrading manner possible. The other practised similar manœuvres whenever we fell in at any formation of company or section. They both called me " nigger," or " d—d nigger," as suited their inclination. Yet this ought, I verily believe, to be attributed not to them, but to the circumstances that led them to adopt such a course.

On one occasion, however, one of them brought to my room the integration of some differential equation in mechanics which had been sent me by our instructor. He was very friendly then, apparently. He told me upon leaving, if I desired any further information to come to his " *house*," and he would give it. I observed that he called me " *Mr.* Flipper."

One winter's night, while on guard in barracks during supper, a cadet of the next class above my own stopped on my post and conversed with me as long as it was safe to do so. He expressed—as all have who have spoken to me—great regret that I should be so isolated, asked how I got along in my studies, and many other like questions. He spoke at great length of my general treatment. He assured me that he was wholly unprejudiced, and would ever be a friend. He even went far enough to say, to my great astonishment, that he cursed me and my race among the cadets to keep up appearances with them, and that I must think none the less well of him for so doing. It was a sort of necessity, he said, for he would not only be " cut," but would be treated a great deal worse than I was if he should fraternize with me. Upon leaving me he said, " I'm d—d sorry to see you come here to be treated so, but I am glad to see you stay."

Unfortunately the gentleman failed at the examination, then not far distant, and of course did not have much opportunity to give proof of his friendship. And thus,

> " The walk, the words, the gesture could supply,
> The habit mimic and the mien belie."

When the plebes reported in '76, and were given seats in the chapel, three of them were placed in the pew with myself. We took seats in the following order, viz., first the commandant of the pew, a sergeant and a classmate of mine, then a third-classman, myself, and the plebes. Now this arrangement was wholly unsatisfactory to the third-classman, who turned to the sergeant and asked of him to place a plebe between him and myself. The sergeant turned toward me, and with an angry gesture ordered me to " Get over there." I refused, on the ground that the seat I occupied had been assigned me, and I therefore had no authority to change it. Near the end of the service the third-classman asked the sergeant to tell me to sit at the further end of the seat. He did so. I refused on the same ground as before. He replied, " Well, it don't make any difference. I'll see that your seat is changed." I feared he would go to the cadet quartermaster, who had charge of the arrangement of seats, and have my seat changed without authority. I reported to the officer in charge of the new cadets, and explained the whole affair to him.

" You take the seat," said he, " assigned you in the guard-house" — the plan of the church, with names written on the pews, was kept here, so that cadets could consult it and know where their seats were—" and if anybody wants you to change it tell them I ordered you to keep it."

The next Sabbath I took it. I was ordered to change it. I refused on the authority just given above. The sergeant then went to the commandant of cadets, who by some means got the impression that I desired to change my seat. He sent for me and emphatically ordered me to keep the seat which had by his order been assigned me. Thus the effort to change my seat, made by the third-classman through the sergeant, but claimed to have been made by me, failed. It was out of the question for it to be otherwise. If the sergeant had wanted the seat himself he would in all probability have got it, because he was my senior in class and lineal rank. But the third-classman was my junior in both, and therefore could not, by any military regulation, get possession of what I was entitled to by my superior rank. And the effort to do so must be regarded a marvellous display of stupidity, or a belief on the part of the cadet that I could be imposed upon with impunity, simply because I was alone and had shown no disposition to quarrel or demand either real or imaginary rights.

While in New York during my furlough—summer of '75—I was introduced to one of her wealthy bankers. We conversed quite a while on various topics, and finally resumed the subject on which we began, viz., West Point. He named a cadet, whom I shall call for convenience John, and asked if I knew him. I replied in the affirmative. After asking various other questions of him, his welfare, etc., he volunteered the following bit of information :

" Oh ! yes," said he, " I've known John for several years. He used to peddle newspapers around the bank here. I was agreeably surprised when I heard he had been appointed to a cadetship at West Point. The boys who come in almost every morning with their papers told me John was to sell me no more papers. His mother has scrubbed out the office here, and cleaned up daily for a number of years. John's a good fellow though, and I'm glad to know of his success."

This information was to me most startling. There certainly was nothing dishonorable in that sort of labor—nay, even there was much in it that deserved our highest praise. It was honest, humble work. But who would imagine from the pompous bearing assumed by the gentleman that he ever peddled newspapers, or that his mother earned her daily bread by scrubbing on her knees office floors ? And how does this compare with the average negro ?

It is not to me very pleasant to thus have another's private history revealed, but when it is done I can't help feeling myself better in one sense at least than my self-styled superiors. I certainly am not really one thing and apparently another. The distant haughtiness assumed by some of them,

and the constant endeavor to avoid me, as if I were
"a stick or a stone, the veriest poke of creation,"
had no other effect than to make me feel as if I were
really so, and to discourage and dishearten me.   I
hardly know how I endured it all so long.   If I
were asked to go over it all again, even with the experience I now have, I fear I should fail.   I mean of
course the strain on my mind and sensitiveness
would be so great I'd be unable to endure it.

There is that in every man, it has been said,
either good or bad, which will manifest itself in his
speech or acts.   Keeping this in mind while I constantly study those around me, I find myself at
times driven to most extraordinary conclusions.   If
some are as good as their speech, then, if I may be
permitted to judge, they have most devoutly observed that blessed commandment, "Honor thy
father and thy mother, that thy days may be long
upon the land which the Lord thy God giveth thee,"
in that they have profited by their teaching both
mentally and morally.

On the other hand, we hear from many the very
worst possible language.   Some make pardonable
errors, while others make blunders for which there
can be no excuse save ignorance.   Judging their
character by their speech, what a sad condition must
be theirs ; and more, what a need for missionary
work !

This state of affairs gives way in the second, and
often in the first year, to instruction and discipline.
West Point's greatest glory arises from her unparal-
leled success in polishing these rough specimens and

sending them forth " officers and gentlemen." No college in the country has such a " heterogeneous conglomeration"—to quote Dr. Johnson—of classes. The highest and lowest are represented. The glory of free America, her recognition of equality of all men, is not so apparent anywhere else as at West Point. And were prejudice entirely obliterated, then would America in truth be that Utopia of which so many have but dreamed. It is rapidly giving way to better reason, and the day is not far distant when West Point will stand forth as the proud exponent of absolute social equality. Prejudice weakens, and ere long will fail completely. The advent of general education sounds its death knell. And may the day be not afar off when America shall proclaim her emancipation from the basest of all servitudes, the subservience to prejudice !

After feeling reasonably sure of success, I have often thought that my good treatment was due in a measure to a sort of apprehension on the part of the cadets that, when I should come to exercise command over them, I would use my authority to retaliate for any ill-treatment I had suffered. I have thought this the case with those especially who have been reared in the principles of prejudice, and often in none other, for " prejudices, it is well known, are the most difficult to eradicate from the heart whose soil has never been loosened or fertilized by education. They grow there as firm as weeds among rocks."

When the time did come, and I proved by purely gentlemanly conduct that it was no harder, no more dishonorable, to be under me than under others, this reserve vanished to a very great extent. I might mention instances in which this is evident.

At practical engineering, one day, three of us were making a gabion. One was putting in the watling, another keeping it firmly down, while I was preparing it. I had had some instruction on a previous day as to how it should be made, but the two others had not. When they had put in the watling to within the proper distance of the top they began trimming off the twigs and butt ends of the withes. I happened to turn toward the gabion and observed what they were doing. In a tone of voice, and with a familiarity that surprised my own self, I exclaimed, "Oh, don't do that. Don't you see if you cut those off before sewing, the whole thing will come to pieces? Secure the ends first and then cut off the twigs."

They stopped working, listened attentively, and one of them replied, "Yes, that would be the most sensible way." I proceeded to show them how to sew the watling and to secure the ends. They were classmates. They listened to my voluntary instruction, and followed it without a thought of who gave it, or any feeling of prejudice.

At foot battery drill one day I was chief of piece. After a time the instructor rested the battery. The cannoneers at my piece, instead of going off and sitting down, gathered around me and asked questions about the nomenclature of the piece and its carriage. "What is this?" "What is it for?" and many others. They were third-classmen. Certainly there was no prejudice in this. Certainly, too, it could only be due to good conduct on my part. And here is another.

Just after taps on the night of July 12th, 1876, while lying in my tent studying the stars, I happened to overhear a rather angry conversation concerning my unfortunate self.

It seems the cadet speaking had learned beforehand that he and myself would be on duty a few days hence, myself as senior and he as junior officer of the guard. His chums were teasing him on his misfortune of being under me as junior, which act caused him to enter into a violent panegyric upon me. He began by criticising my military aptitude and the manner in which I was treated by the authorities, that is, by the cadet officers, as is apparent from what follows :

" That nigger," said he, " don't keep dressed. Sometimes he's 'way head of the line. He swings his arms, and does other things not half as well as other ' devils,' and yet he's not ' skinned ' for it."

What a severe comment upon the way in which the file-closers discharge their duties ! Severe, indeed, it would be were it true. It is hardly reasonable, I think, to suppose the file-closers, in the face of prejudice and the probability of being " cut," would permit me to do the things mentioned with impunity, while they reported even their own classmates for them.

And here again we see the fox and sour grapes. The gentleman who so honored me with his criticism was junior to me in every branch of study we had taken up to that time except in French. I was his senior in tactics by—well, to give the number of files

7

would be to specify him too closely and make my narrative too personal.   Suffice it to say I ranked him, and I rather fancy, as I did not gain that position by favoritism, but by study and proficiency, he should not venture to criticise.   But so it is all through life, at West Point as well as elsewhere. Malcontents are ever finding faults in others which they never think of discovering in themselves.

When the time came the detail was published at parade, and next day we duly marched on guard. When I appeared on the general parade in full dress, I noticed mischievous smiles on more than one face, for the majority of the corps had turned out to see me.   I walked along, proudly unconscious of their presence.

Although I went through the ceremony of guard mounting without a single blunder, I was not at all at ease.   I inspected the front rank, while my junior inspected the rear.   I was sorely displeased to observe some of the cadets change color as they tossed up their pieces for my inspection, and that they watched me as I went through that operation. Some of them were from the South, and educated to consider themselves far superior to those of whom they once claimed the right of possession.   I know it was to them most galling, and although I fully felt the responsibility and honor of commanding the guard, I frankly and candidly confess that I found no pleasure in their apparent humiliation.

I am as a matter of course opposed to prejudice, but I nevertheless hold that those who are not have just as much right to their opinions on the matter as they would have to any one of the various religious creeds. We in free America at least would not be justified in forcing them to renounce their views or beliefs on race and color any more than those on religion.

We can sometimes, by so living that those who differ from us in opinion respecting any thing can find no fault with us or our creed, influence them to a just consideration of our views, and perhaps persuade them unconsciously to adopt our way of thinking. And just so it is, I think, with prejudice. There is a certain dignity in enduring it which always evokes praise from those who indulge it, and also often discovers to them their error and its injustice.

Knowing that it would be unpleasant to my junior to have to ask my permission to do this or that, and not wishing to subject him to more mortification than was possible, I gave him all the latitude I could, telling him to use his own discretion, and that he need not ask my permission for any thing unless he chose.

This simple act, forgotten almost as soon as done, was in an exceedingly short time known to every cadet throughout the camp, and I had the indescribable pleasure, some days after, of knowing that by it I had been raised many degrees in the estimation of the corps. Nor did this knowledge remain in camp. It was spread all over the Point. The act was talked of and praised by the cadets wherever they went, and their conversations were repeated to me many times by different persons.

When on guard again I was the junior, and of course subject to the orders of the senior. He came to me voluntarily, and in almost my own words gave me exactly the same privileges I had given my junior, who was a chum of my present senior. In view of the ostracism and isolation to which I had been subjected, it was expected that I would be severe, and use my authority to retaliate. When, however, I did a more Christian act, did to others as I would have them do to me, and not as they had sometimes done, I gave cause for a similar act of good-will, which was in a degree beyond all expectation accorded me.

Indeed, while we are all prone to err, we are also very apt to do to others as they really do to us. If they treat us well, we treat them well; if badly, we treat them so also. I believe such to be in accordance with our nature, and if we do not always do so our failure is due to some influence apart from our better reason, if we do not treat them well, or our first impulse if we do. If now, on the contrary, I had been severe and unnecessarily imperious because of my power, I should in all probability have been treated likewise, and would have fallen and not have risen in the estimation of the cadets.

It has often occurred to me that the terms " prejudice of race, of color," etc., were misnomers, and for this reason. As soon as I show that I have some good qualities, do some act of kindness in spite of insult, my color is forgotten and I am well treated. Again, I have observed that colored men of character and intellectual ability have been treated as men should be by all, whether friends or enemies; that is to say, no prejudice of color or race has ever been manifested.

I have been so treated by men I knew to be—to

use a political term—" vile democrats." Unfortunately a bad temper, precipitation, stubbornness, and like qualities, all due to non-education, are too often attributes of colored men and women. These characteristics lower the race in the estimation of the whites, and produce, I think, what we call prejudice. In fact I believe prejudice is due solely to non-education and its effects in one or perhaps both races.

Prejudice of—well, any word that will express these several characteristics would be better, as it would be nearer the truth.

There is, of course, a very large class of ignorant and partially cultured whites whose conceptions can find no other reason for prejudice than that of color. I doubt very much whether they are prejudiced on that account as it is. I rather think they are so because they know others are for some reason, and so cringing are they in their weakness that they follow like so many trained curs. This is the class we in the South are accustomed to call the " poor white trash," and speaking of them generally I can neglect them in this discussion of my treatment, and without material error.

In camp at night the duties of the officers of the guard are discharged part of the night by the senior and the other part by the junior officer. As soon as it was night—to revert to the subject of this article— my junior came to me and asked how I wished to divide the night tour.

" Just suit yourself. If you have any reason for wanting a particular part of the night, I shall be pleased to have you take it."

He chose the latter half of the night, and asked

me to wake him at a specified time. After this he discovered a reason for taking the first half, and coming to me said :

"If it makes no difference to you I will take the first half of the night."

"As you like," was my reply.

"You 'pile in' then, and I'll wake you in time," was his reply.

Observe the familiarity in this rejoinder.

The guard was turned out and inspected by the officer of the day at about 12.20 P.M. After the inspection I retired, and was awakened between 1 and 2 P.M. by my junior, who then retired for the night.

The officer in charge turned out and inspected the guard between 2 and 3 P.M.

Several of the cadets were reported to me by the corporals for violating regulations. The reports were duly recorded in the guard report for the day. I myself reported but one cadet, and his offence was "Absence from tattoo roll-call of guard."

These reports were put in under my signature, though not at all made by me, as also was another of a very grave nature.

It seems—for I didn't know the initial circumstances of the case—that a citizen visiting at West Point asked a cadet if he could see a friend of his who was a member of the corps. The cadet at once sought out the corporal then on duty, and asked him to go to camp and turn out this friend. The corporal did not go. The cadet who requested him to do so reported the fact to the officer of the day. The latter came at once to me and directed me, as officer of the guard, to order him to go and turn out the cadet, and to see that he did it. I did as ordered. The corporal replied, " I have turned him out." As the cadet did not make his appearance the officer of the day himself went into camp, brought him out to his citizen friend, and then ordered me in positive terms to report the corporal for gross disobedience of orders. I communicated to him the corporal's reply, and received a repetition of his order. I obeyed it, entering on my guard report the following :

" ——, disobedience of orders, not turning out a cadet for citizen when ordered to do so by the officer of the guard."

The commandant sent for me, and learned from me all the circumstances of the case as far as I knew them. He made similar requirements of the corporal himself.

Connected with this case is another, which, I think, should be recorded, to show how some have been disposed to act and think concerning myself. At the dinner table, and on the very day this affair above mentioned occurred, a cadet asked another if he had heard about ——, mentioning the name of the cadet corporal.

" No, I haven't," he replied ; " what's the matter with him ?"

" Why, the officer of the day ordered him reported for disobedience of orders, and served him right too."

" What was it ? Whose orders did he disobey ?"

" Some cit wanted to see a cadet and asked C—— if he could do so. C—— asked ——, who was then on duty, to go to camp and turn him out. He

didn't do it, but went off and began talking with
some ladies. The officer of the day directed the
senior officer of the guard to order him to go. He
did order him to go and —— replied, " I have turned
him out," and didn't go. The officer of the day
then turned him out, and ordered him to be reported
for disobedience of orders, and I say served him
right."

" I don't see it," was the reply.

" Don't see it ? Why ——'s relief was on post,
and it was his duty to attend to all such calls during
his tour ; and besides, I think ordinary politeness
would have been sufficient to make him go."

" Well, I can sympathize with him anyhow."

" Sympathize with him ! How so ?"

" *Because he's on guard to-day.*" What an excellent reason ! " Because he's on guard to-day,"
or, in other words, because *I* was in command of the
guard.

He then went on to speak of the injustice of the
report, the malice and spirit of retaliation shown in
giving it, and hoped that the report would not be
the cause of any punishment. And all this because
the report was under my signature.

When the corporal replied to me that he had
turned out the cadet, I considered it a satisfactory
answer, supposing the cadet's non-appearance was
due to delay in arranging his toilet. I had no intention of reporting him, and did so only in obedience to positive orders. There surely was nothing
malicious or retaliatory in that ; and to condemn me
for discharging the first of all military duties—viz.,
obedience of orders—is but to prove the narrowness

of the intellect and the baseness of the character which are vaunted as so far superior to those of the "negro cadet," and which condemn him and his actions for no other reason than that they are his. How could it be otherwise than that he be isolated and persecuted when such minds are concerned?

In his written explanation to the commandant the corporal admitted the charge of disobedience of orders on his part, but excused himself by saying he had delegated another cadet to discharge the duty for him. This was contrary to regulations, and still further aggravated his offence.

For an incident connected with this tour of guard duty, see chapter on "Incidents, Humor," etc.

The only case of downright malice that has come to my knowledge—and I'm sure the only one that ever occurred—is the following:

It is a custom, as old as the institution I dare say, for cadets of the first and second classes to march in the front rank, while all others take their places in the rear rank, with the exception that third-classmen may be in the front rank whenever it is necessary for the proper formation of the company to put them there. The need of such a custom is apparent. Fourth-classmen, or plebes not accustomed to marching and keeping dressed, are therefore unfit to be put in the front rank. Third-classmen have to give way to the upper classmen on account of their superior rank, and are able to march in the front rank only when put there or allowed to remain there by the file-closers. When I was a plebe, and also during my third-class year, I marched habitually in the rear rank, as stated with reason elsewhere. But when I became a second-classman, and had by class rank a right to the front rank, I took my place there.

Just about this time I distinctly heard the cadet captain of my company say to the first sergeant, or rather ask him why he did not put me in the rear rank. The first sergeant replied curtly, " Because he's a second-classman now, and I have no right to do it." This settled the question for the time, indeed for quite a while, till the incident above referred to occurred.

At a formation of the company for retreat parade in the early spring of '76, it was necessary to transfer some one from the front to the rear rank. Now instead of transferring a third-classman, the sergeant on the left of the company ordered me, a second-classman, into the rear rank. I readily obeyed, because I felt sure I'd be put back after the company was formed and inspected, as had been done by him several times before. But this was not done. I turned to the sergeant and reminded him that he had not put me back where I belonged. He at once did so without apparent hesitation or unwillingness. He, however, reported me for speaking to him about the discharge of his duties. For this offence, I submitted the following explanation :

WEST POINT, N. Y., April 11, 1876.

Offense : Speaking to sergeant about formation of company at parade.

Explanation : I would respectfully state that the above report is a mistake. I said nothing whatever about the formation of the company. I was put in the rear rank, and, contrary to custom, left there. As soon as the command " In place, rest," was given, I turned to the nearest sergeant and said, " Mr. ——, can I take my place in the front rank ?" He leaned to the front and looked along the line. I then said, "There are men in the front rank who are junior to me." I added, a moment after, "There is one just up there," motioning with my head the direction meant. He made the change.

Respectfully submitted,

HENRY O. FLIPPER,

Cadet Priv., Comp. " D," First Class.

To Lieut. Colonel ——,

Commanding Corps of Cadets.

This explanation was sent by the commandant to the reporting sergeant. He indorsed it in about the following words :

Respectfully returned with the following statement :

It was necessary in forming the company to put Cadet Flipper in the rear rank, and as I saw no third-classman in the front rank, I left him there as stated. I reported him because I did not think he had any right to speak to me about the discharge of my duty.

"—— —— ——,

Cadet Sergeant Company "D."

A polite question a reflection on the manner of discharging one's duty ! A queer construction indeed ! Observe, he says, he saw no third-classman in the front rank. It was his duty to be sure about it, and if there was one there to transfer him to the rear, and myself to the front rank. In not doing so he neglected his duty and imposed upon me and the dignity of my class. I was therefore entirely justified in calling his attention to his neglect.

This is a little thing, but it should be borne in mind that it is nevertheless of the greatest importance. We know what effect comity or international politeness has on the relations or intercourse between nations. The most trifling acts, such as congratulations on a birth or marriage in the reigning family, are wonderfully efficacious in keeping up that feeling of amity which is so necessary to peace and continued friendship between states. To disregard these little things is considered unfriendly, and may be the cause of serious consequences.

There is a like necessity, I think, in our own case. Any affront to me which is also an affront to my class and its dignity deserves punishment or satisfaction. To demand it, then, gives my class a better opinion of me, and serves to keep that opinion in as good condition as possible.

I knew well that there were men in the corps who would readily seize any possible opportunity to report me, and I feared at the time that I might be reported for speaking to the sergeant. I was especially careful to guard against anger or roughness in my speech, and to put my demand in the politest form possible. The offence was removed. I received no demerits, and the sergeant had the pleasure or displeasure of grieving at the failure of his report.

I am sorry to know that I have been charged, by some not so well acquainted with West Point and life there as they should be to criticise, with manifesting a lack of dignity in that I allowed myself to be insulted, imposed upon, and otherwise ill-treated. There appears to them too great a difference between the treatment of former colored cadets and that of myself, and the only way they are pleased to account for this difference is to say that my good treatment was due to want of " spunk," and even to fear, as some have said. It evidently never occurred to them that my own conduct determined more than all things else the kind of treatment I would receive.

Every one not stubbornly prejudiced against West Point, and therefore not disposed to censure or criticise every thing said or done there, knows how false the charge is. And those who make it scarcely deserve my notice. I would say to them, however, that true dignity, *selon nous*, consists in being above the rabble and their insults, and particularly in remaining there. To stoop to retaliation is not compatible with true dignity, nor is vindictiveness manly. Again, the experiment suggested by my accusers has been abundantly tried, and proved a most ridiculous failure, while my own led to a glorious success.

I do not mean to boast or do any thing of the kind, but I would suggest to all future colored cadets to base their conduct on the "$\dot{\alpha}\rho\iota\sigma\tau o\nu\mu\acute{\epsilon}\tau\rho o\nu$," the golden mean. It is by far the safer, and surely the most Christian course.

Before closing this chapter I would add with just pride that I have ever been treated by all other persons connected with the Academy not officially, as becomes one gentleman to treat another. I refer to servants, soldiers, other enlisted men, and employés. They have done for me whatever I wished, whenever I wished, and as I wished, and always kindly and willingly. They have even done things for me to the exclusion of others. This is important when it is remembered that the employés, with one exception, are white.

"NATIONAL SCHOOLS AND SNOBOCRACY.

" ' Cadet Smith has arrived in Columbia. He did not " pass." ' "
—*Phœnix.*

" ' Alexander Bouchet, a young man of color, graduates from Yale College, holding the fifth place in the largest class graduated from that ancient institution.'—*Exchange.*

" These simple announcements from different papers tersely sum up the distinction between the military and civil education of this country. One is exclusive, snobbish, and narrow, the other is liberal and democratic.

" No one who has watched the course of Cadet Smith and the un-democratic, selfish, and snobbish treatment he has experienced from the martinets of West Point, men educated at the expense of the government, supported by negro taxes, as well as white, who attempt to dictate who shall receive the benefits of an education in our national charity schools—no one who has read of his court-martialings, the degradations and the petty insults inflicted upon him can help feeling that he returns home to-day, in spite of the *Phœnix's* sneers, a young hero who has ' passed ' in grit, pluck, perseverance, and all the better qualities which go to make up true manhood, and only has been ' found ' because rebel sympathizers at West Point, the fledg-lings of caste, and the Secretary of War, do not intend to allow, if they can prevent it, a negro to graduate at West Point or Annapolis, *if he is known to be a negro.*

" Any one conversant with educational matters who has examined the examinations for entrance, or the curriculum of the naval and military academies, will not for a moment believe that their require-ments, not as high as those demanded for an ordinary New England high school, and by no means equal in thoroughness, quantity, or quality to that demanded for entrance at Yale, Amherst, Dartmouth, or Brown, are too high or abstruse to be compassed by negroes, some of whom have successfully stood all these, and are now pursuing their studies in the best institutions of the North.

" No fair-minded man believes that Smith, Napier and Williams, Conyers and McClellan, have had impartial treatment. The govern-ment itself has been remiss in not throwing about them the protec-tion of its authority. Had these colored boys been students at St. Cyr, in Paris, or Woolwich, in England, under despotic France and aristocratic England, they would have been treated with that cour-tesy and justice of which the average white American has no idea. The South once ruled West Point, much to its detriment in loyalty, however much, by reason of sending boys more than prepared. It dominated in scholarship. It seeks to recover the lost ground, and rightly fears to meet on terms of equality in the camp the sons of fathers to whom it refused quarter in the war and butchered in cold blood at Fort Pillow. We cannot expect the sons to forget the lessons of the sires ; but we have a right to demand from the general government the rooting out of all snobbery at West Point, whether it is of that kind which sends poor white boys to Coventry, because they haven't a family name or wealth, or whether it be that smallest, meanest, and shallowest of all aristocracies—the one founded upon color.

" If the government is not able to root out these unrepublican seeds in these hot-beds of disloyalty and snobbery, then let Congress shut up the useless and expensive appendages and educate its officers at the colleges of the country, where they may learn lessons in true republican equality and nationality. The remedy lies with Congress. A remonstrance at least should be heard from the colored members of Congress, who are insulted whenever a colored boy is ill-treated by the students or the officers of these institutions. So far from being discouraged by defeats, the unjust treatment meted out to these young men should redouble the efforts of others of their class to carry this new Bastile by storm. It should lead every colored Congressman to make sure that he either sends a colored applicant or a white one who has not the seeds of snobbery and caste in his soul. Smith, after four years of torture, comes home, is driven home, because, forsooth, he might attend the ball next year ! He is hounded out of the Academy because he would have to be assigned to a white regiment ! There are some negroes who feel that their rights in the land of their birth are superior to the prejudices of the enemies of the Union, and who dare to speak and write in behalf of these rights, as their fathers dared to fight for them a very few years ago.

" Bouchet, under civil rule, enters Yale College the best prepared student of one hundred and thirty freshmen, and all through his course is treated like a gentleman, both by the faculty and the students, men who know what justice means, and have some adequate idea of the true theory of education and gentlemanly conduct. Two freed boys, from North Carolina and South Carolina, slaves during the war, prepare at the best Northern academies, and enter, without remonstrance, Amherst and Dartmouth. What divinity, then, hedges West Point and Annapolis ? What but the old rebel spirit, which seeks again to control them for use in future rebellions as it did in the past. The war developed some unwelcome truths with regard to this snobbish and disloyal spirit of our national institutions, and the exploits of some volunteer officers showed that all manhood,

bravery, skill, and energy were not contained in West Point or Annapolis, or, if there, did not pertain solely to the petty cliques that
aim to give tone to those academies.   It is not for any officer, the
creature of the government—it is not for any student, the willing
ward of that government—to say who shall enter the national schools
and be the recipients of my bounty.   It is the duty of every member of Congress to see that the government sanctions no such spirit ;
and it becomes every loyal citizen who wishes to avoid the mistakes
of the former war to see to it that no class be excluded, and that every
boy, once admitted, shall have the strictest justice dealt out to him,
a thing which, thus far, has not been done in the case of the colored
cadets.

    " The true remedy lies in the feelings and sympathies of the officers
of these academies, in the ability and fair investigations of the board
of examiners ; not from such gentlemen as at present seem to rule
these institutions.

" NIGER NIGRORUM."

  This article was taken from some South Carolina
paper during the summer of '74.   Its tone is in accordance with the multitude of articles upon the
same subject which occurred about the same time,
and, like them all, or most of them, is rather far-
fetched.   It is too broad.   Its denunciations cover
too much ground.   They verge upon untruth.

  As to Conyers and McClellan at the Naval Academy I know nothing.   Of Napier I know nothing.
Of Smith I prefer to say nothing.   Of Williams I do
express the belief that his treatment was impartial
and just.   He was regularly and rightly found deficient and duly dismissed.   The article seems to
imply that he should not have been " found " and
dismissed simply because he was a negro.   A very
shallow reason indeed, and one " no fair - minded
man" will for an instant entertain.

  Of four years' life at the Academy, I spent the
first with Smith, rooming with him.   During the

first half year Williams was also in the corps with us. The two following years I was alone. The next and last year of my course I spent with Whittaker, of South Carolina.. I have thus had an opportunity to become acquainted with Smith's conduct and that of the cadets toward him. Smith had trouble under my own eyes on more than one occasion, and Whittaker[*] has already received blows in the face, but I have not had so much as an angry word to utter. There is a reason for all this, and had " Niger Nigrorum" been better acquainted with it he had never made the blunder he has.

I cannot venture more on the treatment of colored cadets generally without disregarding the fact that this is purely a narrative of my own treatment and life at West Point. To go further into that subject would involve much difference of opinion, hard feelings in certain quarters, and would cause a painful and needless controversy.

---

[*] Johnson Chestnut Whittaker, of Camden, South Carolina, appointed to fill vacancy created by Smith's dismissal, after several white candidates so appointed had failed, entered the Academy in September, 1876. Shortly after entering he was struck in the face by a young man from Alabama for sneering at him, as he said, while passing by him. Whittaker immediately reported the affair to the cadet officer of the day, by whose efforts this belligerent Alabama gentleman was brought before a court-martial, tried, found guilty, and suspended for something over six months, thus being compelled to join the next class that entered the Academy.

CHAPTER XI.

JULY 1, 1876 ! Only one year more ; and yet how wearily the days come and go ! How anxiously we watch them, how eagerly we count them, as they glimmer in the distance, and forget them as they fade ! What joyous anticipation, what confident expectation, what hope animates each soul, each heart, each being of us ! What encouragement to study this longing, this impatience gives us, as if it hastened the coming finale ! And who felt it more than I ? Who could feel it more than I ? To me it was to be not only an end of study, of discipline, of obedience to the regulations of the Academy, but even an end to isolation, to tacit persecution, to melancholy, to suspense. It was to be the grand realization of my hopes, the utter, the inevitable defeat of the minions of pride, prejudice, caste. Nor would such consummation of hopes affect me only, or those around me. Nay, even I was but the point of "primitive disturbance," whence emanates as if from a focus, from a new origin, prayer, friendly and inimical, to be focused again into realization on one side and discomfiture on the other. My friends, my enemies, centre their hopes on me. I treat them, one with earnest endeavor for realization, the other with supremest indifference. They are deviated with varying anxiety on either side, and hence my joy, my gratitude, when I find, July 1, 1876, that I am a first-classman.

A first-classman ! The beginning of realization, for had I not distanced all the colored cadets before me ? Indeed I had, and that with the greater prospect of ultimate success gave me double cause for rejoicing.

A first-classman ! " There's something prophetic in it," for behold

" The country begins to be agitated by the approaching graduation of young Flipper, the colored West Point cadet from Atlanta. If he succeeds in getting into the aristocratic circles of the official army there will be a commotion for a certainty. *Flipper is destined to be famous.*"

Such was the nature of the many editorials which appeared about this time, summer of '76. The circumstance was unusual, unexpected, for it had been predicted that only slaughter awaited me at that very stage, because Smith had failed just there, just where I had not.

" Henry Flipper, of Atlanta, enjoys the distinction of being the only negro cadet that the government is cramming with food and knowledge at West Point. He stands forty-sixth in the third class, which includes eighty-five cadets. A correspondent of the New York *Times* says that, while all concede Flipper's progress, yet it is not believed that he will be allowed to graduate. No negro has passed out of the institution a graduate, and it is believed that Flipper will be eventually slaughtered in one way or another. The rule among the regulars is : No darkeys need apply."

Or this :

" Smith's dismissal leaves Henry Flipper the sole cadet of color at West Point. Flipper's pathway will not be strewn with roses, and we shall be surprised if the Radicals do not compel him, within a year, to seek refuge from a sea of troubles in his father's quiet shoe shop on Decatur Street."

Isn't it strange how some people strive to drag every thing into politics! A political reason is assigned to every thing, and "every thing is politics."

The many editors who have written on the subject of the colored cadets have, with few exceptions, followed the more prejudiced and narrow-minded critics who have attributed every thing, ill-treatment, etc., to a natural aversion for the negro, and to political reasons. They seem to think it impossible for one to discharge a duty or to act with justice in any thing where a negro is concerned. Now this is unchristian as well as hasty and undeserved. As I have said elsewhere in my narrative, aside from the authorities being *de facto* "officers and gentlemen," and therefore morally bound to discharge faithfully every duty, they are under too great a responsibility to permit them to act as some have asserted for them, to compel me "to seek refuge from a sea of troubles," or to cause me to "be eventually slaughtered in one way or another." Who judges thus is not disposed to judge fairly, but rather as suits some pet idea of his own, to keep up prejudice and all its curses.

It would be more Christian, and therefore more just, I apprehend, to consider both sides of the question, the authorities and those under them. Other and better reasons would be found for some things which have occurred, and reasons which would not be based on falsehood, and which would not tend to perpetuate the conflict of right and prejudice. My own success will prove, I hope, not only that I had sufficient ability to graduate—which by the way none have questioned—but also that the authorities were not as some have depicted them. This latter proof is important, first, because it will remove that fear which has deterred many from seeking, and even from accepting appointments when offered, to which determent my isolation is largely due ; and second, because it will add another to the already long list of evidences of the integrity of our national army.

To return to the last quotation. Immediately after the dismissal of Smith, indeed upon the very day of that event, it was rumored that I intended to resign. I learned of the rumor from various sources, only one of which I need mention.

I was on guard that day, and while off duty an officer high in rank came to me and invited me to visit him at his quarters next day. I did so, of course. His first words, after greeting, etc., were to question the truth of the rumor, and before hearing my reply, to beg me to relinquish any such intention. He was kind enough to give me much excellent advice, which I have followed most religiously. He assured me that prejudice, if it did exist among my instructors, would not prevent them from treating me justly and impartially. I am proud to testify now to the truth of his assurance. He further assured me that the officers of the Academy and of the army, and especially the older ones, desired to have me graduate, and that they would do all within the legitimate exercise of their authority to promote that end. This assurance has been made me by officers of nearly every grade in the army, from the general down, and has ever been carried out by them whenever a fit occasion presented itself.

Surely this is not discouraging. Surely, too, it

is not causing me "to seek refuge from a sea of troubles." We need only go back to the article quoted from the *Era*, and given in Chapter III., to find an explanation for this conduct.

"We know that any young man, whether he be poor or black, or both, may enter any first-class college in America and find warm sympathetic friends, both among students and faculty, *if he but prove himself to be possessed of some good qualities.*"

This is the keynote to the whole thing. One must not expect to do as one pleases, whether that be right or wrong, or right according to some fanatical theory, and notwithstanding to be dealt with in a manner warranted only by the strictest notion of right. We must force others to treat us as we wish, by giving them such an example of meekness and of good conduct as will at least shame them into a like treatment of us. This is the safer and surer method of revenge.

"Therefore if thine enemy hunger, feed him ; if he thirst, give him drink ; for in so doing thou shalt heap coals of fire on his head."

To proceed : I am undoubtedly a first-classman. None other has enjoyed that eminence. There are many honors and responsibilities incident to that position or rank. First-classmen have authority at times over their fellow-cadets. How will it be when I come to have that authority ? Will that same coldness and distance be manifested as hitherto ? These are important questions. I shall be brought necessarily into closer relations with the cadets than before. How will they accept such relationship ? The greatest proof of their personal convictions will be

manifested in their conduct here.   If they evade my
authority, or are stubborn or disobedient, then are
their convictions unfriendly indeed.   But if kind,
generous, willing to assist, to advise, to obey, to respect myself as well as my office, then are they, as I
ever believed them to be, gentlemen in all that recognizes no prejudice, no caste, nothing inconsistent
with manhood.

There are certain privileges accorded to first-classmen which the other classes do not enjoy.   The privates of the first class do duty as officers of the
guard, as company officers at company and battalion
drills, at light battery drills, and at other drills and
ceremonies.   In all these cases they have command
of other cadets.   These cadets are subject to their
orders and are liable to be reported—indeed such is
required—for disobedience, stubbornness, or for any
thing prejudicial to good order and good discipline.

In this fact is a reason—the only one, I think,
which will in any manner account for the unpardon-
able reserve of many of the cadets.   To be subject to
me, to my orders, was to them an unbearable torture.
As they looked forward to the time when I should
exercise command over them, they could not help
feeling the mortification which would be upon them.

I must modify my statement.   They may be prejudiced, and yet gentlemen, and if gentlemen they
will not evade authority even though vested in me.

We go into camp at West Point on the 17th of
June, '76, for ten days.   During all that time I enjoy
all the privileges of first-classmen.   Nothing is done
to make it unpleasant or in any way to discourage
or dishearten me.   We go to Philadelphia.   We visit

the Centennial, and there not only is the same kindness shown me, but I find a number of cadets accost me whenever we meet, on the avenues and streets, on the grounds and in the city.   They ask questions, converse, answer questions.   This occurred several times at the Southern Restaurant, as well as elsewhere.   After the parade on the 4th of July, every kindness was shown me.   Those cadets near me bought lemons, lemonade, etc, and shared with me, and when, on another occasion, I was the purchaser, they freely partook of my "good cheer." What conclusion shall I draw from this ?   That they are unfriendly or prejudiced ?   I fain would drop my pen and burn my manuscript if for even an instant I thought it possible.   And yet how shall I explain away this bit of braggadocio in the words italicized in this article from the Philadelphia *Times ?*

" *The Color Line.*—One of the first-classmen is Mr. Flipper, of Georgia, a young colored man. ' We don't have any thing to do with him off duty,' said one of the cadets yesterday. ' *We don't even speak to him.* Of course we have to eat with him, and drill with him, and go on guard with him, *but that ends it.   Outside of duty, we don't know him.*' ' Is he intelligent ?' ' Yes ; he stands high in his class, and I see no reason to doubt that he will graduate next June. He has the negro features strongly developed, but in color he is rather light.' "

Easily enough, I think.   In the first place the statement is too broad, if made by a cadet, which I very much doubt.   There are some of that "we" who do know me outside of duty.   And if a cadet made the statement he must have been a plebe, one unacquainted with my status in the corps, or one who, strenuously avoiding me himself, supposed all others likewise did so.   The cadet was not a first-classman. There is a want of information in his last answer which could not have been shown by a first-classman.

Again, he says we "go on guard with him." Now that is untrue, as I understand it. The word "with" would imply that we were on guard in the same capacity, viz., as privates. But first-classmen do no guard duty in that capacity, and hence not being himself a first-classman he could not have been on guard "with" me. If he had said "under him," his statement would have been nearer the truth.

After a stay of ten days in Philadelphia, we return to West Point, and still the same respect is shown me. There is but little more of open recognition, if any, than before, and yet that I am respected is shown in many ways. See, for example, the latter part of chapter on "Treatment."

Again, during my first year I many times overheard myself spoken of as "the nigger," "the moke," or "the thing." Now openly, and when my presence was not known, I always hear myself mentioned as Mr. Flipper. There are a few who use both forms of address as best suits their convenience or inclination at the time. But why is it? Why not "nigger," "moke," or "thing" as formerly? Is there, can there be any other reason than that they respect me more now than then? I am most unwilling to believe there could be.

We begin our regular routine of duties, etc. We have practical military engineering, ordnance, artillery, practical astronomy in field and permanent observatories, telegraphy, and guard. We are detailed for these duties. Not the least distinction is made.

8

Not the slightest partiality is shown. Always the same regard for my feelings, the same respect for me! See the case of gabion in the chapter on "Treatment."

At length, in my proper order, I am detailed for officer of the guard. True, the cadets expressed some wonderment, but why? Simply, and reasonably enough too, because I was the first person of color that had ever commanded a guard at the Military Academy of the United States. It is but a natural curiosity. And how am I treated? Is my authority recognized? Indeed it is. My sergeant not only volunteered to make out the guard report for me, but also offered any assistance I might want, aside from the discharge of his own duty as sergeant of the guard. Again, a number of plebes were confined in the guard tents for grossness and carelessness. I took their names, the times of their imprisonment, and obtained permission to release them. I was thanked for my trouble. Again, a cadet's father wishes to see him. He is in arrest. I get permission for him to visit his father at the guard tents. I go to his tent and tell him, and start back to my post of duty. He calls me back and thanks me. Must I call that natural aversion for the negro, or even prejudice? Perhaps it is, but I cannot so comprehend it. It may have that construction, but as long as the other is possible it is generous to accept it. And again, I am ordered to report a cadet. I do it. I am stigmatized, of course, by some of the low ones (see that case under "Treatment"); but my conduct, both in obeying the order and subsequently, is approved by the better portion of the corps.   The commandant said to me : " Your duty was a plain one, and you discharged it properly.   You were entirely right in reporting Mr. ——."   What is the conduct of this cadet himself afterwards ?   If different at all from what it was before, it is, in my presence at least, more cordial, more friendly, more kind.   Still there is no ill-treatment, assuming of course that my own conduct is proper, and not obtrusive or overbearing.   And so in a multitude of ways this fact is proved.   I have noticed many things, little things perhaps they were, but still proofs, in the conduct of all the cadets which remove all doubt from my mind.   And yet with all my observation and careful study of those around me, I have many times been unable to decide what was the feeling of the cadets toward me.   Some have been one thing everywhere and at all times, not unkind or ungenerous, nor even unwilling to hear me and be with me, or near me, or on duty with me, or alone with me.   Some again, while not avoiding me in the presence of others have nevertheless manifested their uneasy dislike of my proximity.   When alone with me they are kind, and all I could wish them to be.   Others have not only strenuously avoided me when with their companions, but have even at times shown a low disposition, a desire to wound my feelings or to chill me with their coldness.   But alone, behold they know how to mimic gentlemen.   The kind of treatment which I was to receive, and have received at the hands of the cadets, has been a matter of little moment to me.   True, it has at times been galling, but its severest effects have been but temporary and have caused me no considerable trouble or inconvenience. I have rigidly overlooked it all.

The officers, on the contrary, as officers and gentlemen, have in a manner been bound to accord me precisely the same privileges and advantages, etc., which they granted the other cadets, and they have ever done so.

I must confess my expectations in this last have been most positively unfulfilled, and I am glad of it. The various reports, rumors, and gossips have thus been proved not only false but malicious, and that proof is of considerable consequence. That they have not been unkind and disposed to ill-treat me may be readily inferred from the number of demerits I have received, and the nature of the offences for which those demerits were given. They have never taken it upon themselves to watch me and report me for trifling offences with a view of giving me a bad record in conduct, and thereby securing my dismissal, for one hundred demerits in six months means dismissal. They have ever acted impartially, and, ignoring my color, have accorded me all immunities and privileges enjoyed by other cadets, whether they were allowed by regulations or were mere acts of personal favor. Of the majority of the cadets I can speak likewise, for they too have power to spy out and report.

As to treatment in the section-room, where there were many opportunities to do me injustice by giving me low marks for all recitations, good or bad, for instance, they have scrupulously maintained their honor, and have treated me there with exact justice and impartiality. This is not a matter of opinion. I can give direct and positive proof of its truthfulness. In the chapter on " Studies," in the record of marks that proof can be found, my marks per recitation, and the average are good. By rank in section is meant the order of my mark—that is, whether best, next, the next, or lowest. Are these marks not good ? In law, for example, once I received the eighth out of nine marks, then the fifth, the first, second, third, first, first, and so on. Surely there was nothing in them to show I was marked low either purposely or otherwise.

My marks in the section for each week, month, and the number of men in each section, afford the means of comparison between the other members of the section and myself. And my marks are not only evidence of the possession on my part of some " good faculties," but also of the honor of my instructors and fellow-members of section.

What manner of treatment the cadets chose to manifest toward me was then of course of no account. But what is of importance, and great importance too, is how they will treat me in the army, when we have all assumed the responsibilities of manhood, coupled with those of a public servant, an army officer. Of course the question cannot now be answered. I feel nevertheless assured that the older officers at least will not stoop to prejudice or caste, but will accord me proper treatment and respect. Men of responsibility are concerned, and it is not presumable that they will disregard the requirements of their professions so far as to ill-treat even myself. There is none of the recklessness of the student in their actions, and they cannot but recognize me as having a just claim upon their good-will and honor.

The year wears away—the last year it is too—and I find myself near graduation, with every prospect of success. And from the beginning to the close my life has been one not of trouble, persecution, or punishment, but one of isolation only. True, to an unaccustomed nature such a life must have had many anxieties and trials and displeasures, and, although it was so with me, I have nothing more than that of which to complain. And if such a life has had its unpleasant features, it has also had its pleasant ones, of which not the least, I think, was the constantly growing prospect of ultimate triumph. Again, those who have watched my course and have seen in its success the falsity of certain reports, cannot have been otherwise than overjoyed at it, at the, though tardy, vindication of truth. I refer especially to certain erroneous ideas which are or were extant concerning the treatment of colored cadets, in which it is claimed that color decides their fate. (See chapter on "Treatment.")

I hope my success has proved that not color of face, but color of character alone can decide such a question. It is character and nothing else that will merit a harsh treatment from gentlemen, and of course it must be a bad character. If a man is a man, *un homme comme il faut,* he need fear no ill-treatment from others of like calibre. Gentlemen avoid persons not gentlemen. Resentment is not a characteristic of gentlemen. A gentlemanly nature must shrink from it. There may be in it a certain

amount of what is vulgarly termed pluck, and perhaps courage.   But what of that?   Everybody
more or less admires pluck.   Everybody worships
courage, if it be of a high order, but who allows that
pluck or even courage is an excuse for passion or its
consequences?   The whites may admire pluck in the
negro, as in other races, but they will never admit un-
warrantable obtrusiveness, or rudeness, or grossness,
or any other ungentlemanly trait, and no more in the
negro than in others.   This is quite just.   A negro
would not allow it even in another.

I did not intend to discuss social equality here,
but as it is not entirely foreign to my subject I may
be pardoned a word or so upon it.

Social equality, as I comprehend it, must be the
natural, and perhaps gradual, outgrowth of a similarity of instincts and qualities in those between
whom it exists.   That is to say, there can be no
social equality between persons who have nothing in
common.   A civilized being would not accept a savage as his equal, his *socius*, his friend.   It would
be repugnant to nature.   A savage is a man, the
image of his Maker as much so as any being.   He
has all the same rights of equality which any other
has, but they are political rights only.   He who
buried his one talent to preserve it was not deemed
worthy to associate with him who increased his five
to ten.   So also in our particular case.   There are
different orders or classes of men in every civilized
community.   The classes are politically equal, equal
in that they are free men and citizens and have all
the rights belonging to such station.   Among the

several classes there can be no social equality, for they have nothing socially in common, although the members of each class in itself may have.

Now in these recent years there has been a great clamor for rights. The clamor has reached West Point, and, if no bad results have come from it materially, West Point has nevertheless received a bad reputation, and I think an undeserved one, as respects her treatment of colored cadets.

A right must depend on the capacity and end or aim of the man. This capacity and end may, and ought to be, moral, and not political only. Equal capacities and a like end must give equal rights, and unequal capacities and unlike ends unequal rights, morally, of course, for the political end of all men is the same. And therefore, since a proper society is a moral institution where a certain uniformity of views, aims, purposes, properties, etc., is the object, there must be also a uniformity or equality of rights, for otherwise there would be no society, no social equality.

This, I apprehend, is precisely the state of affairs in our own country. Among those who, claiming social equality, claim it as a right, there exists the greatest possible diversity of creeds, instincts, and of moral and mental conditions, in which they are widely different from those with whom they claim this equality. They can therefore have no rights socially in common ; or, in other words, the social equality they claim is not a right, and ought not to and cannot exist under present circumstances, and any law that overreaches the moral reason to the contrary must be admitted as unjust if not impolitic.

But it is color, they say, color only, which deter-
mines how the negro must be treated. Color is his
misfortune, and his treatment must be his misfortune
also. Mistaken idea! and one of which we should
speedily rid ourselves. It may be color in some
cases, but in the great majority of instances it is
mental and moral condition. Little or no education, little moral refinement, and all their repulsive
consequences will never be accepted as equals of
education, intellectual or moral. Color is absolutely
nothing in the consideration of the question, unless
we mean by it not color of skin, but color of character, and I fancy we can find considerable color
there.

It has been said that my success at West Point
would be a grand victory in the way of equal rights,
meaning, I apprehend, social rights, social equality,
inasmuch as all have, under existing laws, equal
political rights. Doubtless there is much truth in
the idea. If, however, we consider the two races
generally, we shall see there is no such right, no such
social right, for the very basis of such a right, viz.,
a similarity of tastes, instincts, and of mental and
moral conditions, is wanting. The mental similarity
especially is wanting, and as that shapes and refines
the moral one, that too is wanting.

To illustrate by myself, without any pretensions
to selfishness. I have this right to social equality,
for I and those to whom I claim to be equal are similarly educated. We have much in common, and
this fact alone creates my right to social and equal
recognition.

" But the young gentlemen who boast of holding

only official intercourse with their comrade, should remember that no one of them stands before the country in any different light from him.   . . . Amalgamated by the uniform course of studies and the similarity of discipline, the separating fragments at the end of the student life carry similar qualities into the life before them, and step with almost remarkable social equality into the world where they must find their level."—*Philadelphia North American*, July 7th, 1876.

If we apply this to the people as a unit, the similarity no longer exists. The right, therefore, also ceases to exist.

The step claimed to have been made by my success is one due to education, and not to my position or education *at West Point*, rather than at some other place ; so that it follows if there be education, if the mental and moral condition of the claimants to that right be a proper one, there will necessarily be social equality, and under other circumstances there can be no such equality.

" Remember, dear friend," says a correspondent, " that you carry an unusual responsibility. The nation is interested in what you do. If you win your diploma, your enemies lose and your friends gain one very important point in the great argument for equal rights. When you shall have demonstrated that you have equal powers, then equal rights will come in due time. The work which you have chosen, and from which you cannot now flinch without dishonor, proves far more important than either you or me (Faculty at A. U.) at first conceived. Like all great things its achievement will involve much of trial and hardship.''

Alas ! how true ! What a trial it is to be socially ostracized, to live in the very midst of life and yet be lonely, to pass day after day without saying perhaps a single word other than those used in the section-room during a recitation. How hard it is to live month after month without even speaking to woman, without feeling or knowing the refining influence of her presence ! What a miserable existence !

Oh ! 'tis hard, this lonely living, to be
In the midst of life so solitary,
To sit all the long, long day through and gaze
In the dimness of gloom, all but amazed
At the emptiness of life, and wonder
What keeps sorrow and death asunder.
'Tis the forced seclusion most galls the mind,
And sours all other joy which it may find.
'Tis the sneer, tho' half hid, is bitter still,
And wakes dormant anger to passion's will.
But oh ! 'tis harder yet to bear them all
Unangered and unheedful of the thrall,
To list the jeer, the snarl, and epithet
All too base for knaves, and e'en still forget
Such words were spoken, too manly to let
Such baseness move a nobler intellect.
But not the words nor e'en the dreader disdain
Move me to anger or resenting pain.
'Tis the thought, the thought most disturbs my mind,
That I'm ostracized for no fault of mine,
'Tis that ever-recurring thought awakes
Mine anger—

Such a life was mine, not indeed for four years, but for the earlier part of my stay at the Academy.

But to return to our subject. There are two questions involved in my case. One of them is, Can a negro graduate at West Point, or will one ever graduate there ? And the second, If one never graduate there, will it be because of his color or prejudice ?

My own success answers most conclusively the first question, and changes the nature of the other. Was it, then, color or actual deficiency that caused the dismissal of all former colored cadets ? I shall not venture to reply more than to say my opinion is deducible from what I have said elsewhere in my narrative.

However, my correspondent agrees with me that color is of no consequence in considering the question of equality socially. My friends, he says, gain an important point in the argument for equal rights. It will be in this wise, viz., that want of education, want of the proof of equality of intellect, is the obstacle, and not color. And the only way to get this proof is to get education, and not by "war of races." Equal rights must be a consequence of this proof, and not something existing before it. Equal rights will come in due time, civil rights bill, war of races, or any thing of that kind to the contrary notwithstanding.

And moreover, I don't want equal rights, but identical rights. The whites and blacks may have equal rights, and yet be entirely independent, or estranged from each other. The two races cannot live in the same country, under the same laws as they now do, and yet be absolutely independent of each other. There must, there should, and there will be a mutual dependence, and any thing that tends to create independence, while it is thus so manifestly impossible, can engender strife alone between them. On the other hand, whatever brings them into closer relationship, whatever increases their knowledge and appreciation of fellowship and its positive importance, must necessarily tend to remove all prejudices, and all ill-feelings, and bring the two races, and indeed the world, nearer that degree of perfection to which all things show us it is approaching. Therefore I want identical rights, for equal rights may not be sufficient.

"It is for you, Henry, more than any one I know of, to demonstrate to the world around us, in this part of it at least (the North), the equality of intellect in the races. You win by your uprightness and intelligence, and it cannot be otherwise than that you will gain respect and confidence."

Thus a lady correspondent (Miss M. E. H., Durham Centre, Ct.) encourages, thus she keeps up the desire to graduate, to demonstrate to the world "the equality of intellect in the races," that not color but the want of this proof in this semi-barbarous people is the obstacle to their being recognized as social equals. A tremendous task! Not so much to prove such an equality — for that had already been abundantly demonstrated—but rather to show the absurdity and impracticability of prejudice on account of color; or, in other words, that there is no such prejudice. It is prejudice on account of non-refinement and non-education.

As to how far and how well I have discharged that duty, my readers, and all others who may be in any manner interested in me, must judge from my narrative and my career at West Point. Assuring all that my endeavor has been to act as most becomes a gentleman, and with Christian forbearance to disregard all unfriendliness or prejudice, I leave this subject, this general résumé of my treatment at the hands of the cadets, and my own conduct, with the desire that it be criticised impartially if deemed worthy of criticism at all.

"*Reporter.*—Have you any more colored cadets?

"*Captain H*——.—Only one—Henry O. Flipper, of Georgia. He is a well-built lad, a mulatto, and is bright, intelligent, and studious.

"*Reporter.*—Do the cadets dislike him as much as they did Smith?

"*Captain H.*——.—No, sir; I am told that he is more popular. I have heard of no doubt but that he will get through all right."—*New York Herald,* July, 1874.

CHAPTER XII.

PLEASURES AND PRIVILEGES.

THE privileges allowed cadets during an encampment are different generally for the different classes. These privileges are commonly designated by the rank of the class, such, for instance, as " first-class privileges," " third-class privileges," etc. Privileges which are common receive their designation from some characteristic in their nature or purpose. Thus we have " Saturday afternoon privileges," and " Old Guard privileges."

The cadets are encamped and are not supposed to leave their camp save by permission. This permission is granted by existing orders, or if for any reason it be temporarily denied it can be obtained by " permit " for some specified time. Such permission or privilege obtained by " permit " for a particular class is known as " class privileges," and can be enjoyed only by the class that submits and gets the permit.

" First-class privileges" permit all members of the first class to leave camp at any time between troop and retreat, except when on duty, and to take advantage of the usual " Saturday afternoon privileges," which are allowed all classes and all cadets. These privileges, however, cannot be enjoyed on the Sabbath by any except the first-class officers, without special permission.

The usual form of a permit is as follows :

WEST POINT, N. Y., November 6, 1876.

Cadet A—— B——C—— has permission to walk on public lands between the hours of 8 A.M and 4 P.M.

—— —— ————,
Lieut.-Colonel First Art'y, Comd'g Corps of Cadets.
—— —— ————,
Commanding Company " A."

By " Saturday afternoon privileges" is meant the right or privilege to walk on all public lands within cadet limits on Saturday afternoon. This includes also the privilege of visiting the ruins of old Fort Putnam, which is not on limits. These privileges are allowed throughout the year.

The second class being absent on furlough during the encampment, of course have no privileges. Should any member of the class be present during the encampment, he enjoys " first-class privileges," unless they are expressly denied him.

" Third-class privileges" do not differ from " first-class privileges," except in that they cannot be taken advantage of on the Sabbath by any member of the class.

The fourth class as a class have no privileges.

" Old Guard privileges" are certain privileges by which all members of the " Old Guard " are exempted from all duty on the day they march off guard until one o'clock, and are permitted to enjoy privileges similar to those of Saturday afternoon during the same time. They also have the privilege of bathing at that time.

The baths are designated as " first," " second,"

and " third." The officers and non-commissioned officers have the first baths, and the privates the others.

Cadets who march off guard on Sunday are restricted in the enjoyment of their privileges to exemption from duty on the Sabbath only. They may take advantage of the other privileges on the following Monday during the usual time, but are not excused from any duty. All members of the " Old Guard," to whatever class they may belong, are entitled to " Old Guard privileges."

Besides these there are other privileges which are enjoyed by comparatively few. Such are " Hop managers' privileges." " Hop managers" are persons elected by their classmates from the first and third classes for the management of the hops of the summer. To enable them to discharge the duties of their office, they are permitted to leave camp, whenever necessary, by reporting their departure and return.

Under pleasures, or rather sources of pleasure, may be enumerated hops, Germans, band practice, and those incident to other privileges, such as " spooneying," or " spooning." The hops are the chief source of enjoyment, and take place on Mondays and Fridays, sometimes also on Wednesdays, at the discretion of the Superintendent.

Germans are usually given on Saturday afternoons, and a special permit is necessary for every one. These permits are usually granted, unless there be some duty or other cause to prevent.

Two evenings of every week are devoted to band

practice, Tuesday evening for practice in camp, and Thursday evening for practice in front of the Superintendent's quarters. Of course these entertainments, if I may so term them, have the effect of bringing together the young ladies and cadets usually denied the privilege of leaving camp during the evening. It is quite reasonable to assume that they enjoy themselves. On these evenings " class privileges" permit the first- and third-classmen to be absent from camp till the practice is over. Sometimes a special permit is necessary. It might be well to say here, ere I forget it, that Wednesday evening is devoted to prayer, prayer-meeting being held in the Dialectic Hall. All cadets are allowed to attend by reporting their departure and return. The meeting is under the sole management of the cadets, although they are by no means the sole participants. Other privileges, more or less limited, such as the holding of class meetings for whatever purpose, must be obtained by special permit in each case.

> We have not much longer here to stay,
>   Only a month or two,
> Then we'll bid farewell to cadet gray,
>   And don the army blue.
> Army blue, army blue, we'll don the army blue,
> We'll bid farewell to cadet gray and don the army blue.
>
> To the ladies who come up in June,
>   We'll bid a fond adieu,
> And hoping they will be married soon,
>   We'll don the army blue.
> Army blue, army blue, we'll don the army blue,
> We'll bid farewell to cadet gray and don the army blue.

Addresses to the Graduating Class of the U. S. Military Academy, West Point, N. Y., June 14th, 1877. By PROFESSOR C. O. THOMPSON, MAJOR-GENERAL WINFIELD S. HANCOCK, HONORABLE GEORGE W. MCCRARY, *Secretary of War,* MAJOR-GENERAL JOHN M. SCHOFIELD, *Superintendent U. S. Military Academy.*

ADDRESS BY PROFESSOR C. O. THOMPSON,

President of the Board of Visitors.

YOUNG GENTLEMEN OF THE GRADUATING CLASS : The courtesy of your admirable Superintendent forbids a possible breach in an ancient custom, and lays upon me, as the representative, for the moment, of the Board of Visitors, the pleasant duty of tendering to you their congratulations on the close of your academic career, and your auspicious future.

The people of this country have a heavy stake in the prosperity of this institution. They recognize it as the very fountain of their security in war, and the origin of some of their best methods of education. And upon education in colleges and common schools the pillars of the State assuredly rest.

To participants and to bystanders, this ceremony of graduation is as interesting and as exciting as if this were the first, instead of the seventy-fifth occurrence. Every such occasion is clothed with the splendor of perpetual youth. The secret of your future success lies in the impossibility of your entering into the experience of your predecessors. Every man's life begins with the rising sun. The world would soon become a frozen waste but for the inextinguishable ardor of youth, which believes success still to be possible where every attempt has failed.

That courage which avoids rashness by the restraints of knowledge, and dishonor by the fear of God, is the best hope of the world.

History is not life, but its reflection.

The great armies of modern times which have won immortal victories have been composed of young men who have turned into historic acts the strategy of experienced commanders.

To bystanders, for the same and other reasons, the occasion is profoundly interesting.

For educated men who are true to honor and to righteousness, the world anxiously waits ; but an educated man who is false, the world has good reason to dread. The best thing that can be said of this Academy, with its long roll of heroes in war and in peace, is, that every year the conviction increases among the people of the United States, that its graduates are men who will maintain, at all hazards, the simple virtues of a robust manhood—like Chaucer's young Knight, courteous, lowly, and serviceable.

I welcome you, therefore, to the hardships and perils of a soldier's life in a time of peace. The noise and the necessities of war drive men in upon themselves and keep their faculties awake and alert ; but the seductive influence of peace, when a soldier must spend his time in preparation for the duties of his profession rather than in their practice, this is indeed a peril to which the horrors of warfare are subordinate. It is so much easier for men to fight other men than themselves. So much easier to help govern other men than to wholly govern themselves.

But, young gentlemen, as we have listened to your examination, shared in your festivities, and enjoyed personal acquaintance with you, we strongly hope for you every thing lovely, honorable, and of good report.

You who have chosen the sword, may be helped in some trying hour of your coming lives by recalling the lesson which is concealed in a legend of English history. It is the old lesson of the advantage of knowledge over its more showy counterfeits, and guards against one of the perils of our American society.

A man losing his way on a hillside, strayed into a chamber full of enchanted knights, each lying motionless, in complete armor, with his horse standing motionless beside him. On a rock near the entrance lay a sword and a horn, and the intruder was told that he must choose between these, if he would lead the army. He chose the horn, and blew a loud blast ; whereupon the knights and their horses vanished in a whirlwind, and their visitor was blown back into common air, these words sounding after him upon the wind :

" Cursed be the coward, that ever he was born,
Who did not draw the sword before he blew the horn."

Young gentlemen, the Board of Visitors can have no better wish for our common country than that your future will fulfil the promise of the present.

ADDRESS BY MAJOR-GENERAL W. S. HANCOCK.

To me has been assigned the pleasant duty of welcoming into the service as commissioned officers, the Graduates of the Military Academy of to-day.

Although much time has elapsed since my graduation here, and by contact with the rugged cares of life some of the sharp edges of recollection may have become dulled, yet I have not lived long enough to have forgotten the joy of that bright period. You only experience it to-day as I have felt it before you.

I have had some experience of life since, and it might be worth something to you were I to relate it. But youth is self-confident and impatient, and you may at present doubt the wisdom of listening to sermons which you can learn at a later day.

You each feel that you have the world in a sling, and that it would be wearisome to listen to the croakings of the past, and especially from those into whose shoes you soon expect to step. That is the rule of life. The child growing into manhood, believes that its judgment is better than the knowledge of its parents ; and yet if that experience was duly considered, and its unselfish purposes believed in, many shoals would be avoided, otherwise certain to be met with in the journey of life, by the inexperienced but confident navigator.

You should not forget that there were as bright intellects, and men who possessed equal elements of greatness in past generations as in this, and that deeds have been performed in earlier times which, at best, the men of the present day can only hope to rival. Why then should we not profit by the experiences of the past ; and as our lives are shot at best, instead of following the ruts of our predecessors, start on the road of life where they left off, and not continue to repeat their failures ? I cannot say why, unless it proceeds from the natural buoyancy of youth, self-confidence in its ability to overcome all obstacles, and to carve out futures more dazzling than any successes of the past. In this there is a problem for you to solve. Yet I may do well by acknowledging to you, to-day, that after an active military life of no mean duration, soldiers of my length of service feel convinced that they might have learned wisdom by listening to the experience of those who preceded them. Had they been prepared to assume that experience as a fact at starting, and made departures from it, instead of disregarding it, in the idea that there was nothing worthy of note to be learned from a study of the past, it would be safe to assume that they would have made greater advances in their day.

Were I to give you my views *in extenso,* applicable to the occasion, I could only repeat what has been well and vigorously said here by distinguished persons in the past, in your hearing, on occasions of the graduation of older classes than your own.

You are impatient, doubtless, as I was in your time, and if you have done as my class did before you, you have already thrown your books away, and only await the moment of the conclusion of these ceremonies to don the garb of the officer or the civilian. The shell of the cadet is too contracted to contain your impatient spirits. Nevertheless, if you will listen but for a few minutes to the relation of an old soldier, I will repeat of the lessons of experience a few of those most worthy of your consideration.

There is but one comrade of my class remaining in active service to-day, and I think I might as truly have said the same ten years ago.

In the next thirty years, those of you who live will see that your numbers have become sensibly reduced, if not in similar proportion.

Some will have studied, have kept up with the times, been ready for service at the hour of their country's call, been prepared to accomplish the purposes for which their education was given to them.

Some will have sought the active life of the frontiers, and been also ready to perform their part in the hour of danger.

A few will have seized the passing honors.

It may have depended much upon opportunity among those who were well equipped for the occasion, who gained the greatest distinction ; but it cannot for a moment be doubted that the roll of honor in the future of this class will never again stand as it stands to-day.

It will be a struggle of life to determine who among you will keep their standing in the contest for future honors and distinctions.

You who have been the better students here, and possessed the greater natural qualities, have a start in the race ; but industry, study, perseverance, and other qualities will continue to be important factors in the future, as they have been in the past.

Through continuous mental, moral, and physical development, with progress in the direction of your profession and devotion to duty, lies the road to military glory ; and it may readily come to pass that " the race will not be to the swift, nor the battle to the strong," as you regard your classmates to-day.

It must be admitted, however, that great leaders are born.

A rare combination of natural qualities causes men to develop greatness. Education and training make them greater ; nevertheless, men with fewer natural qualities often succeed, with education and training, when those more richly endowed fail to reach the higher places, and you have doubtless witnessed that in your experience here.

A man in a great place in modern times is not respectable without education. That man must be a God to command modern armies successfully without it ; yet war is a great school ; men learn quickly by experience, and in long wars there will be found men of natural abilities who will appear at the front. It will be found, however, in the long run, that the man who has prepared himself to make the best use of his natural talents will win in the race, if he has the opportunity, while others of equal or greater natural parts may fail from lack of that mental and moral training necessary to win the respect of those they command.

Towards the close of our civil war, men came to the front rank who entered the service as privates. They were men of strong natural qualities. How far the best of them would have proceeded had the war continued, cannot be told ; but it may be safely assumed that if they possessed the moral qualities and the education necessary to command the respect of the armies with which they were associated, they would have won the highest honors ; and yet our war lasted but four years.

Some of them had the moral qualities, some the education ; and I have known of those men who thus came forward, some who would certainly have reached the highest places in a long race, had they had the training given to you.

War gives numerous opportunities for distinction, and especially to those who in peace have demonstrated that they would be available in war ; and soldiers can win distinction in both peace and war if they will but seize their opportunities.

" There is a tide in the affairs of men which, taken at the flood, leads on to victory."

Great responsibilities in time of danger are not given to the ignorant, the slothful, or to those who have impaired their powers of mind or body by the indulgences of life. In times of danger favorites are discarded. When work is to be done, deeds to be performed, men of action have their opportunities and fail not to seize them. It is the interest of commanders that such men should be selected for service, when success or failure may follow, according to the wisdom of the selection, as the instrument may be—sharp or dull, good or bad.

I would say to you, lead active, temperate, studious lives, develop your physical qualities as well as mental. Regard the education acquired here as but rudimentary ; pursue your studies in the line of your profession and as well in such other branches of science or language as may best accord with your inclinations. It will make you greater in your profession and cause you to be independent of it. The latter is but prudent in these practical days.

Study to lead honorable, useful, and respected lives. Even if no opportunity presents for martial glory you will not fail to find your reward.

Avoid the rocks of dissipation, of gambling, of debt ; lead those manly lives which will always find you in health in mind and body, free from entanglements of whatever kind, and you may be assured you will find your opportunities for great services, when otherwise you would have been overlooked or passed by. Such men are known and appreciated in every army and out of it.

Knowledge derived from books may bring great distinction outside of the field of war, as an expert in the lessons of the military profession and in others, but the lessons of hard service are salutary and necessary to give the soldier a practical understanding of the world and its ways as he will encounter them in war. I would advise you to go when young to the plains—to the wilderness—seek active service there, put off the days of indulgence and of ease. Those should follow years.

Take with you to the frontier your dog, your rod and gun ; the pursuit of a life in the open air with such adjuncts will go far to give you health and the vigor to meet the demands to be made upon you in trying campaigns, and to enable you to establish the physical condition necessary to maintain a life of vigor such as a soldier requires. You will by these means, too, avoid many of the temptations incident to an idle life—all calculated to win you from your usefulness in the future, and by no means leave your books behind you.

When I graduated, General Scott, thinking possibly to do me a service, asked me to what regiment I desired to be assigned ; I replied, to the regiment stationed at the most western post in the United States. I was sent to the Indian Territory of to-day. We had not then acquired California or New Mexico, and our western boundary north of Texas was the one hundredth degree of longitude.

I know that that early frontier service and the opportunities for healthy and vigorous out-door exercise were of great advantage to me in many ways, and would have been more so had I followed the advice in reference to study that I have given to you.

There are many " extreme western" posts to-day. It is difficult to say which is the most western in the sense of that day, when the Indian frontiers did not as now, lie in the circumference of an inner circle ; but the Yellowstone will serve your purpose well. And if any of you wish to seek that service your taste will not be difficult to gratify, for the hardest lessons will be certain to be avoided by many. There will be those who in the days of youth will seek the softer places. They may have their appropriate duties there and do their parts well, but it may be considered a safe maxim that the indulgence of the present will have to be paid for in the future A man may not acquire greatness by pursuing religiously the course I have indicated as the best, but it will be safe to assume that when the roll of honor of your class is called after a length of service equal to mine, but few, if any, of your number, will have done their part well in public estimation save of those who shall have pretty closely followed these safe rules of life.

Gentlemen, I bid you welcome.

ADDRESS BY HON. G. W. McCRARY,

Secretary of War.

GENTLEMEN OF THE GRADUATING CLASS : Although not a part of the programme arranged for these exercises, I cannot refuse to say a word by way of greeting, and I would make it as hearty and earnest as possible to you, gentlemen, one and all, upon this occasion, so interesting to you as well as to the entire army, and to the people of the whole country.

There are others here who will speak to you as soldiers, to whom you will listen, and from whom you will receive all counsel and admonition as coming from men who have distinguished themselves in the command of the greatest armies the world has ever seen, and by the achievement of some of the grandest victories recorded upon the pages of history.

I would speak to you as a citizen ; and as such, I desire to assure you that you are to-day the centre of a general interest pervading every part of our entire country. It is not the army alone that is interested in the graduating class of 1877. West Point Military Academy, more than any other institution in the land—far more— is a national institution—one in which we have a national pride.

It is contrary to the policy of this country to keep in time of

9

peace a large standing army We have adopted what I think is a wiser and better policy—that of educating a large number of young men in the science of arms, so that they may be ready when the time of danger comes. You will go forth from this occasion with your commissions as Second Lieutenants in the army ; but I see, and I know that the country sees, that if war should come, and large armies should be organized and marshalled, we have here seventy-six young gentlemen, any one of whom can command not only a company, but a brigade ; and I think I may say a division, or an army corps.

The experience of the past teaches that I do not exaggerate when I say this. At all events, such is the theory upon which our government proceeds, and it is expected that every man who is educated in this institution, whether he remains in the ranks of the army or not, wherever he may be found and called upon, shall come and draw his sword in defence of his country and her flag.

It is a happy coincidence that one hundred years ago to-day, on the 14th of June, 1777, the Continental Congress passed the act which fixed our national emblem as the stars and stripes. It is a happy coincidence that you graduate upon the anniversary of the passage of that act—the centennial birthday of the stars and stripes. I do not know that it will add any thing to your love of the flag and of your country. I doubt whether any thing would add to that ; but I refer to this coincidence with great pleasure.

Gentlemen of the Graduating Class : I am not qualified to instruct you in your duties as soldiers, but these is one thing I may say to you, because it ought to be said to every graduating class, and to all young men about to enter upon the active duties of life, and that is, that the profession does not ennoble the man, but the man ennobles the profession Behind the soldier is the man.

Character, young men, is every thing ; without it, your education is nothing ; without it, your country will be disappointed in you. Go forth into life, then, firmly resolved to be true, not only to the flag of your country, not only to the institutions of the land, not only to the Union which our fathers established, and which the blood of our countrymen has cemented, but to be true to yourselves and the principles of honor, of rectitude, of temperance, of virtue, which have always characterized the great and successful soldier, and must always characterize such a soldier in the future.

ADDRESS BY MAJOR-GENERAL JOHN M. SCHOFIELD,

Superintendent U. S. Military Academy.

GENTLEMEN OF THE GRADUATING CLASS : The agreeable duty now devolves upon me of delivering to you the diplomas which the Academic Board have awarded you as Graduates of the Military Academy.

These diplomas you have fairly won by your ability, your industry, and your obedience to discipline. You receive them, not as favors from any body, but as the just and lawful reward of honest and persistent effort.

You have merited, and are about to receive, the highest honors attainable by young men in our country. You have won these honors by hard work and patient endurance, and you are thus prepared to prize them highly. Unless thus fairly won, honors, like riches, are of little value.

As you learn, with advancing years, to more fully appreciate the value in life of the habits you have acquired of self-reliance, long-sustained effort, obedience to discipline, and respect for lawful authority, a value greater even than that of the scientific knowledge you have gained, you will more and more highly prize the just reward which you are to-day found worthy to receive.

You are now prepared to enter upon an honorable career in the great arena of the world. The West Point Diploma has ever been a passport to public respect, and to the confidence of government. But such respect and confidence imply corresponding responsibilities. The honor of West Point and that of the army are now in your keeping ; and your country is entitled to the best services, intellectual, moral, and physical, which it may be in your power to render.

That you may render such services, do not fail to pursue your scientific studies, that you may know the laws of nature, and make her forces subservient to the public welfare. Study carefully the history, institutions, and laws of your country, that you may be able to see and to defend what is lawful and right in every emergency. Study not only the details of your profession, but the highest principles of the art of war. You may one day be called to the highest responsibility. And, above all, be governed in all things by those great moral principles which have been the guide of great and good men in all ages and in all countries. Without such guide the greatest genius can do only evil to mankind.

One of your number, under temptation which has sometimes proved too great for even much older soldiers, committed a breach of discipline for which he was suspended. The Honorable Secretary of War has been kindly pleased to remit the penalty, so that your classmate may take his place among you according to his academic rank.

You have to regret the absence of one of your number, who has been prevented by extreme illness from pursuing the studies of the last year. But I am glad to say that Mr. Barnett has so far recovered that he will be able to return to the Academy, and take his place in the next class.

Another member of the class has been called away by the death of his father, but he had passed his examination, and will graduate with you. His diploma will be sent to him.

With the single exception, then, above mentioned, I have the satisfaction of informing you that you graduate with the ranks of your class unbroken.

We take leave of you, gentlemen, not only with hope, but with full confidence that you will acquit yourselves well in the honorable career now before you. We give you our parental blessing, with fervent wishes for your prosperity, happiness, and honor.

Loud applause greeted the close of the general's speech, and the graduates were then called up one by one and their diplomas delivered to them. The first to step forward was Mr. William M. Black, of Lancaster, Penn., whose career at the Academy has been remarkable. He has stood at the head of his class for the whole four years, actually distancing all competitors. He is a young man of signal ability, won his appointment in a competitive examination, and has borne himself with singular modesty and good sense. During the past year he has occupied the position of Adjutant of the Corps of Cadets—the highest post which can be held. General Sherman shook hands with the father of the young cadet—a grand-looking old gentleman, and very proud of his son, as he has a right to be—and warmly congratulated him on the brilliant career which was before the young man. The next on the list was Mr. Walter F. Fisk. When Mr. Flipper, the colored cadet, stepped forward, and received the reward of four years of as hard work and unflinching courage and perseverance as any young man could be called upon to go through, the crowd of spectators gave him a round of hearty applause. He deserves it. Any one who knows how quietly and bravely this young man—the first of his despised race to graduate at

West Point—has borne the difficulties of his position ; how for four years he has had to stand apart from his classmates as one with them but not of them ; and to all the severe work of academic official life has had added the yet more severe mental strain which bearing up against a cruel social ostracism puts on any man ; and knowing that he has done this without getting soured, or losing courage for a day —any one, I say, who knows all this would be inclined to say that the young man deserved to be well taken care of by the government he is bound to serve. Everybody here who has watched his course speaks in terms of admiration of the unflinching courage he has shown. No cadet will go away with heartier wishes for his future welfare.

When the last of the diplomas had been given, the line reformed, the band struck up a lively tune, the cadets marched to the front of the barracks, and there Cadet Black, the Adjutant, read the orders of the day, they being the standing of the students in their various classes, the list of new officers, etc. This occupied some time, and at its conclusion Colonel Neil, Commandant of Cadets, spoke a few kind words to the First Class, wished them all success in life, and then formally dismissed them.

At the close of the addresses the Superintendent of the Academy delivered the diplomas to the following cadets, members of the Graduating Class. The names are alphabetically arranged :

Ammon A. Augur,
William H. Baldwin,
Thomas H. Barry,
George W. Baxter,
John Baxter, Jr.,
John Bigelow, Jr.,
William M. Black,
Francis P. Blair,
Augustus P. Blocksom,
Charles A. Bradley,
John J. Brereton,
Oscar J. Brown,
William C. Brown,
Ben. I. Butler,
George N. Chase,
Edward Chynoweth,
Wallis O. Clark,

Charles J. Crane,
Heber M. Creel,
Matthias W. Day,
Millard F. Eggleston,
Robert T. Emmet,
Calvin Esterly,
Walter L. Fisk,
Henry O. Flipper,
Fred. W. Foster,
Daniel A. Frederick,
F. Halverson French,
Jacob G. Galbraith,
William W. Galbraith,
Charles B. Gatewood,
Edwin F. Glenn,
Henry J. Goldman,
William B. Gordon,

John F. Guilfoyle,
John J. Haden,
Harry T. Hammond,
John F. C. Hegewald,
Curtis B. Hoppin,
George K. Hunter,
James B. Jackson,
Henry Kirby,
Samuel H. Loder,
James A. Maney,
James D. Mann,
Frederick Marsh,
Medad C. Martin,
Solon F. Massey,
Ariosto McCrimmon,
David N. McDonald,
John McMartin,
Stephen C. Mills,
Cunliffe H. Murray,
James V. S. Paddock,
Theophilus Parker,

Alexander M. Patch,
Francis J. Patten,
Thomas C. Patterson,
John H. Philbrick,
Edward H. Plummer,
David Price, Jr.,
Robert D. Read, Jr.,
Solomon W. Roessler,
Robert E. Safford,
James C. Shofner,
Adam Slaker,
Howard A. Springett,
Robert R. Stevens,
Monroe P. Thorington,
Albert Todd,
Samuel P. Wayman,
John V. White,
Wilber E. Wilder,
Richard H. Wilson,
William T. Wood,
Charles G. Woodward.

CHAPTER XIII.

FURLOUGH.

OF all privileges or sources of pleasure which tend to remove the monotony of military life, there are none to which the stripling soldier looks forward with more delight than furlough. Indeed it is hard to say which is the stronger emotion that we experience when we first receive information of our appointment to a cadetship, or that which comes upon us when we are apprised that a furlough has been granted us. Possibly the latter is the stronger feeling. It is so with some, with those, at least, who received the former announcement with indifference, as many do, accepting it solely to please a mother, or father, or other friend or relative. With whatever feeling, or for whatever reason the appointment may have been accepted, it is certain that all are equally anxious to take advantage of their furlough when the time comes. This is made evident in a multitude of ways.

A furlough is granted to those only who have been present at two annual examinations at least, and by and with the consent of a parent or guardian if a minor.

Immediately after January next preceding their second annual examination, the furloughmen, as they are called, have class meetings, or rather furlough meetings, to celebrate the "good time coming." They hold them almost weekly, and they are devoted to music, jesting, story-telling, and to general jollification. It can be well imagined with what joy a cadet looks forward to his furlough. It is the only interruption in the monotony of his Academy life, and it is to him for that very reason extremely important. During all this time, and even long before January, the furloughmen are accustomed to record the state of affairs respecting their furlough by covering every available substance that will bear a pencil or chalk mark with numerous inscriptions, giving the observer some such information as this: "100 days to furlough," "75 days to furlough," "only two months before furlough," and thus even to the day before they actually leave.

The crowning moment of all is the moment when the order granting furloughs is published.

I am sure my happiest moment at West Point, save when I grasped my "sheepskin" for the first time, was when I heard my name read in the list. It was a most joyous announcement. To get away from West Point, to get out among friends who were not ashamed nor afraid to be friends, could not be other than gratifying. It was almost like beginning a new life, a new career, and as I looked back from the deck of the little ferryboat my feelings were far different from what they were two years before.

My furlough was something more than an interruption of my ordinary mode of life for the two years previous. It was a complete change from a life of isolation to one precisely opposite. And of course I enjoyed it the more on that account.

The granting of furloughs is entirely discretionary with the Superintendent. It may be denied altogether, but usually is not, except as punishment for some grave offence.

It is customary to detain for one, two, three, or even more days those who have demerits exceeding a given number for a given time. The length of their leave is therefore shortened by just so many days.

There are a number of customs observed by the cadets which I shall describe here.

To disregard these customs is to show—at least it is so construed—a want of pride. To say that this or that "is customary," is quite sufficient to warrant its conception and execution. Among these customs the following may be mentioned :

To begin with the fourth class. Immediately after their first semi-annual examination the class adopts a class crest or motto, which appears on all their stationery, and often on many other things. To have class stationary is a custom that is never overlooked. Each class chooses its own design, which usually bears the year in which the class will graduate.

Class stationary is used throughout the period of one's cadetship.

In the early spring, the first, second, and third classes elect hop managers, each class choosing a given number. This is preparatory to the hop given by the second to the graduating class as a farewell token. This custom is rigorously kept up.

Next to these are customs peculiar to the first class. They are never infringed upon by other classes, nor disregarded even by the first class.

First, prior to graduation it is an invariable custom of the graduating class to adopt and procure, each of them, a class ring. This usually bears the year of graduation, the letters U. S. M. A., or some other military character.

This ring is the signet that binds the class to their Alma Mater, and to each other. It is to be in after years the souvenir that is to recall one's cadet life, and indeed every thing connected with a happy and yet dreary part of one's career.

The class album also is intended for the same purpose. It contains the "smiling shadows" of class-mates, comrades, and scenes perhaps never more to be visited or seen after parting at graduation. Oh! what a feeling of sadness, of weariness of life even, must come upon him who in after years opens his album upon those handsome young faces, and there silently compares their then lives with what succeed-ing years have revealed! Who does not, would not grieve to recall the sad tidings that have come anon and filled one's heart and being with portentous gloom? This, perhaps a chum, an especial favorite, or at any rate a classmate, has fallen under a rude savage warfare while battling for humanity, without the advantages or the glory of civilized war, but sim-ply with the consciousness of duty properly done. That one, perchance, has fallen bravely, dutifully, without a murmur of regret, and this one, alas! where is he? Has he, too, perished, or does he yet remember our gladsome frolics at our beloved Alma Mater. My mind shudders, shrinks from the sweet and yet sad anticipations of the years I have not seen and may perhaps never see. But there is a sweet-ness, a fondness that makes me linger longingly upon the thought of those unborn days.

CHAPTER XIV.

INCIDENT, HUMOR, ETC.

IT may not be inappropriate to give in this place a few—as many as I can recall—of the incidents, more or less humorous, in which I myself have taken part or have noticed at the various times of their occurrence. First, then, an adventure on " Flirtation."

During the encampment of 1873—I think it was in July—Smith and myself had the—for us—rare enjoyment of a visit made us by some friends. We had taken them around the place and shown and explained to them every thing of interest. We at length took seats on " Flirtation," and gave ourselves up to pure enjoyment such as is found in woman's presence only. The day was exceedingly beautiful ; all nature seemed loveliest just at that time, and our lone, peculiar life, with all its trials and cares, was quite forgotten. We chatted merrily, and as ever in such company were really happy. It was so seldom we had visitors—and even then they were mostly males—that we were delighted to have some one with whom we could converse on other topics than official ones and studies. While we sat there not a few strangers, visitors also, passed us, and almost invariably manifested surprise at seeing us.

I do think uncultivated white people are unapproachable in downright rudeness, and yet, alas !

they are our superiors.   Will prejudice ever be obliterated from the minds of the people ?   Will man ever
cease to prejudge his fellow-being for color's sake
alone ?   Grant, O merciful God, that he may !

But *au fait!*   Anon a cadet, whose perfectly
fitting uniform of matchless gray and immaculate
white revealed the symmetry of his form in all its
manly beauty, saunters leisurely by, his head erect,
shoulders back, step quick and elastic, and those
glorious buttons glittering at their brilliant points
like so many orbs of a distant stellar world.   Next a
plebe strolls wearily along, his drooping shoulders,
hanging head, and careless gait bespeaking the need
of more squad drill.   Then a dozen or more "picnicers," all females, laden with baskets, boxes, and
other et ceteras, laughing and playing, unconscious
of our proximity, draw near.   The younger ones trip-
ping playfully in front catch sight of us.   Instantly
they are hushed, and with hands over their mouths
retrace their steps to disclose to those in rear their
astounding discovery.   In a few moments all appear,
and silently and slowly pass by, eyeing us as if we
were the greatest natural wonder in existence.   They
pass on till out of sight, face about and "continue
the motion," passing back and forth as many as five
times.   Wearied at length of this performance, Smith
rose and said, " Come, let's end this farce," or something to that effect.   We arose, left the place, and
were surprised to find a moment after that they
were actually following us.

The " Picnicers," as they are called in the corps,
begin their excursions early in May, and continue

them till near the end of September. They manage to arrive at West Point at all possible hours of the day, and stay as late as they conveniently can. In May and September, when we have battalion drills, they are a great nuisance, a great annoyance to me especially. The vicinity of that flank of the battalion in which I was, was where they "most did congregate." It was always amusing, though most embarrassing, to see them pointing me out to each other, and to hear their verbal accompaniments, "There he is, the first"—or such—"man from the right"—"or left." "Who ?" "The colored cadet." "Haven't you seen him ? Here, I'll show him to you," and so on *ad libitum*.

All through this encampment being "——young ; a novice in the trade," I seldom took advantage of Old Guard privileges, or any other, for the reason that I was not accustomed to such barbarous rudeness, and did not care to be the object of it.

It has always been a wonder to me why people visiting at West Point should gaze at me so persistently for no other reason than curiosity. What there was curious or uncommon about me I never knew. I was not better formed, nor more military in my bearing than all the other cadets. My uniform did not fit better, was not of better material, nor did it cost more than that of the others. Yet for four years, by each and every visitor at West Point who saw me, it was done. I know not why, unless it was because I was in it.

There is an old man at Highland Falls, N. Y.,
who is permitted to peddle newspapers at West
Point. He comes up every Sabbath, and all are
made aware of his presence by his familiar cry,
"Sunday news! Sunday news!" Indeed, he is
generally known and called by the soubriquet, "Sunday News."

He was approaching my tent one Sunday afternoon, but was stopped by a cadet who called out to
him from across the company street, "Don't sell
your papers to them niggers!" This kind advice
was not heeded.

This and subsequent acts of a totally different
character lead me to believe that there is not so much
prejudice in the corps as is at first apparent. A general dislike for the negro had doubtless grown up in
this cadet's mind from causes which are known to
everybody at all acquainted with affairs at West
Point about that time, summer of 1873. On several
occasions during my second and third years I was the
grateful recipient of several kindnesses at the hands
of this same cadet, thus proving most conclusively
that it was rather a cringing disposition, a dread of
what others might say, or this dislike of the negro
which I have mentioned, that caused him to utter
those words, and not a prejudiced dislike of "them
niggers," for verily I had won his esteem.

Just after returning from this encampment to our
winter quarters, I had another adventure with Smith,
my chum, and Williams, which cost me dearly.

It was just after "evening call to quarters." I
knew Smith and Williams were in our room. I had

been out for some purpose, and was returning when it occurred to me to have some fun at their expense. I accordingly walked up to the door—our "house" was at the head of the stairs and on the third floor —and knocked, endeavoring to imitate as much as possible an officer inspecting. They sprang to their feet instantly, assumed the position of the soldier, and quietly awaited my entrance. I entered laughing. They resumed their seats with a promise to repay me, and they did, for alas! I was "hived." Some cadet reported me for "imitating a tactical officer inspecting." For this I was required to walk three tours of extra guard duty on three consecutive Saturdays, and to serve, besides, a week's confinement in my quarters. The "laugh" was thus, of course, turned on me.

During the summer of '74, in my "yearling camp," I made another effort at amusement, which was as complete a failure as the attempt with Smith and Williams. I had been reported by an officer for some trifling offence. It was most unexpected to me, and least of all from this particular officer. I considered the report altogether uncalled for, but was careful to say nothing to that effect. I received for the offence one or two demerits. A short while afterwards, being on guard, I happened to be posted near his tent. Determined on a bit of revenge, and fun too, at half-past eleven o'clock at night I placed myself near his tent, and called off in the loudest tone I could command, "No. ——, half-past eleven o'clock, and all-l-l-l's well-l-l!" It woke him. He arose, came to the front of his tent, and called me back to him. I went, and he ordered me to call the corporal. I did so. When the corporal came he told him to "report the sentinel on No. —— for calling off improperly." If I mistake not, I was also reported for not calling off at 12 P.M. loud enough to be heard by the next sentinel. Thus my bit of revenge recoiled twofold upon myself, and I soon discovered that I had been paying too dear for my whistle.

On another occasion during the same camp I heard a cadet say he would submit to no order or command of, nor permit himself to be marched anywhere by " the nigger," meaning myself. We were in the same company, and it so happened at one time that we were on guard the same day, and that I was the senior member of our company detail. When we marched off the next day the officer of the guard formed the company details to the front, and directed the senior member of each fifteen to march it to its company street and dismiss it. I instantly stepped to front and assumed command. I marched it as far as the color line at " support arms ;" brought them to a " carry" there and saluted the colors. When we were in the company street, I commanded in loud and distinct tone, " Trail arms ! Break ranks ! March !" A cadet in a tent near by recognized my voice, and hurried out into the company street. Meeting the cadet first mentioned above, he thus asked of him :

" Did that nigger march you in ?"

" Yes-es, the nigger marched us in," speaking slowly and drawling it out as if he had quite lost the power of speech.

At the following semi-annual examination (January, '75), the gentleman was put on the "retired list," or rather on the list of "blasted hopes." I took occasion to record the event in the following manner, changing of course the names :

FAILED.

SCENE.—*Hall of Cadet Barracks at West Point. Characters :* RANSOM *and* MARS, *both Cadets.* RANSOM, *who has been "found" at recent semiannual examination, meets his more successful chum,* MARS, *on the stoop. After a moment's conversation, they enter the hall.*

MARS (*as they enter*).
Ah ! how ! what say ? Found ! Art going away ?
Unfortunate rather ! 'm sorry ! but stay !
Who hadst thou ? How didst thou ? Badly, I'm sure.
Hadst done well they had not treated thee so.

RANSOM (*sadly*).
Thou sayest aright. I did do my best,
Which was but poorly I can but confess.
The subject was hard. I could no better
Unless I'd memorized to the letter.

MARS.
Art unfortunate ! but tho' 'twere amiss
Me half thinks e'en that were better than this.
Thou couldst have stood the trial, if no more
Than to come out low. That were better, 'm sure.

RANSOM.
But 'tis too late. 'Twas but an afterthought,
Which now methinks at most is worth me naught :
" Le sort en est jetté," they say, you know ;
'Twere idle to dream and still think of woe.

MARS.
Thou sayest well ! Yield not to one rebuff.
Thou'rt a man, show thyself of manly stuff.
The bugle calls ! I must away ! Adieu !
May Fortune grant, comrade, good luck to you !

(*They shake hands,* MARS *hurries out to answer the bugle call.* RANSOM *prepares for immediate departure for home.*)

"O dear! it is hawid to have this cullud cadet—perfectly dre'fful. I should die to see my Geawge standing next to him." Thus did one of your models of womankind, one of the negro's superiors, who annually visit West Point to flirt, give vent to her opinion of the "cullud cadet," an opinion thought out doubtless with her eyes, and for which she could assign no reason other than that some of her acquaintances, manifestly cadets, concurred in it, having perhaps so stated to her. And the cadets, with their accustomed gallantry, have ever striven to evade "standing next to him." No little amusement—for such it was to me—has been afforded me by the many ruses they have adopted to prevent it. Some of them have been extremely ridiculous, and in many cases highly unbecoming a cadet and a gentleman.

While I was a plebe, I invariably fell in in the rear rank along with the other plebes. This is a necessary and established custom. As soon as I became a third-classman, and had a right to fall in in the front rank whenever necessary or convenient, they became uneasy, and began their plans for keeping me from that rank. The first sergeant of my company did me the honor of visiting me at my quarters and politely requested me—not order me, for he had no possible authority for such an act—to fall in invariably on the right of the rear rank. To keep down trouble and to avoid any show of presumption or forwardness on my part, as I had been advised by an officer, I did as he requested, taking my place on the right of the rear rank at every formation of the company for another whole year. But with all this condescension on my part I was still the object of solicitous care. My falling in there did not preclude the possibility of my own classmates, now also risen to the dignity of third-classmen, falling in next to me. To perfect his plan, then, the first sergeant had the senior plebe in the company call at his " house," and take from the roster an alphabetical list of all the plebes in the company. With this he (the senior plebe) was to keep a special roster, detailing one of his own classmates to fall in next to me. Each one detailed for such duty was to serve one week—from Sunday morning breakfast to Sunday morning breakfast. The keeper of the roster was not of course to be detailed.

It is astonishing how little care was taken to conceal this fact from me. The plan, etc., was formed in my hearing, and there seems to have been no effort or even desire to hide it from me. Returning from supper one evening, I distinctly heard this plebe tell the sergeant that " Mr. —— refused to serve." " You tell him," said the sergeant, " I want to see him at my ' house ' immediately after supper. If he doesn't serve I'll make it so hot for him he'll wish he'd never heard of West Point."

Is it not strange how these models of mankind, these our superiors, strive to thrust upon each other what they do not want themselves ? It is a meanness, a baseness, an unworthiness from which I should shrink. It would be equally astonishing that men ever submit to it, were it not that they are plebes, and therefore thus easily imposed upon. The plebe in this case at length submitted.

When I became a second-classman, no difference

was made by the cadets in their manner of falling in, whether because their scruples were overcome or because no fitting means presented themselves for avoiding it, I know not. If they happened to be near me when it was time to fall in, they fell in next to me.

In the spring of '76, our then first sergeant ordered us to fall in at all formations as nearly according to size as possible. As soon as this order was given, for some unknown reason, the old régime was readopted. If I happened to fall in next to a first-classman, and he discovered it, or if a first-classman fell in next to me, and afterward found it out, he would fall out and go to the rear. The second and third-classmen, for no other reason than that first-classmen did it, "got upon their dignity," and refused to stand next to me. We see here a good illustration of that cringing, "bone - popularity" spirit which I have mentioned elsewhere.

The means of prevention adopted now were somewhat different from those of a year before. A file-closer would watch and follow me closely, and when I fell in would put a plebe on each side of me. It was really amusing sometimes to see his eagerness, and quite as amusing, I may add, to see his dismay when I would deliberately leave the place thus hemmed in by plebes and fall in elsewhere.

We see here again that cringing disposition to which I believe the whole of the ill-treatment of colored cadets has been due. The file-closers are usually second-class sergeants and third-class corporals. By way of "boning popularity" with the upper classmen, they stoop to almost any thing. In

this case they hedged me in between the two plebes
to prevent upper classmen from falling in next to
me.

But it may be asked why I objected to having
plebes next to me. I would answer, for several
reasons. Under existing circumstances of prejudice,
it was of the utmost importance to me to keep them
away from me. First—and by no means the least
important reason—to put them in the front rank
was violating a necessary and established custom.
The plebes are put in the rear rank because of their
inexperience and general ignorance of the principles
of marching, dressing, etc. If they are in the front
rank, it would simply be absurd to expect good
marching of them. A second reason, and by far
the most important, results directly from this one.
Being between two plebes, who would not, could not
keep dressed, it would be impossible for me to do so.
The general alignment of the company would be destroyed. There would be crowding and opening out
of the ranks, and it would all originate in my immediate vicinity. The file-closers, never over-scrupu-
lous when I was concerned, and especially when
they could forward their own " popularity-boning"
interests, would report me for these disorders in the
company. I would get demerits and punishment for
what the plebes next to me were really responsible
for. The plebes would not be reported, because if
they were their inexperience would plead strongly in
their favor, and any reasonable explanation of an
offence would suffice to insure its removal. I was
never overfond of demerits or punishments, and
therefore strenuously opposed any thing that might

give me either ; for instance, having plebes put next to me in ranks.

Toward the end of the year the plebes, having learned more about me and the way the corps looked upon me, became as eager to avoid me as the others. Not, however, all the plebes, for there were some who, when they saw others trying to avoid falling in next to me, would deliberately come and take their places there. These plebes, or rather yearlings now, were better disciplined, and, of course, my own scruples vanished.

During the last few months of the year no distinction was made, save by one or two high-toned ones.

When the next class of plebes were put in the battalion, the old cadets began to thrust them into the front rank next to me. At first I was indignant, but upon second thought I determined to tolerate it until I should be reported for some offence which was really an offence of the plebes. I intended to then explain the case, *à priori*, in my written explanation to the commandant. I knew such a course would cause a discontinuance of the practice, which was plainly malicious and contrary to regulations. Fortunately, however, for all concerned, the affair was noticed by an officer, and by him summarily discontinued. I was glad of this, for the other course would have made the cadets more unfriendly, and would have made my condition even worse than it was. Thereafter I had no further trouble with the plebes.

One day, during my yearling camp, when I happened to be on guard, a photographer, wishing a view

of the guard, obtained permission to make the necessary negative. As the officer of the day desired to
be "took" with the guard, he came down to the
guard tents, and the guard was "turned out" for
him by the sentinel. He did not wish it then, and
accordingly so indicated by saluting. I was sitting
on a camp-stool in the shade reading. A few minutes after the officer of the day came. I heard the
corporal call out, "Fall in the guard." I hurried
for my gun, and passing near and behind the officer
of the day, I heard him say to the corporal:

"Say, can't you get rid of that nigger? We
don't want him in the picture."

The corporal immediately ordered me to fetch a
pail of water. As he had a perfect right to thus
order me, being for the time my senior officer, I proceeded to obey. While taking the pail the officer of
the day approached me and most politely asked:
"Going for water, Mr. Flipper?"

I told him I was.

"That's right," continued he; "do hurry. I'm
nearly dead of thirst."

It is simply astonishing to see how these young
men can stoop when they want any thing. A cadet
of the second class—when I was in the third class—
was once arrested for a certain offence, and, from
the nature of the charge, was likely to be court-
martialed. His friends made preparation for his defence. As I was not ten feet from him at the time
specified in the charge, my evidence would be required in the event of a trial. I was therefore visited
by one of his friends. He brought paper and pencil
and made a memorandum of what I had to say. The
cadet himself had the limits of his arrest extended

and then visited me in person. We conversed quite a while on the subject, and, as my evidence would be in his favor, I promised to give it in case he was tried. He thanked me very cordially, asked how I was getting along in my studies, expressed much regret at my being ostracized, wished me all sorts of success, and again thanking me took his leave.

There is an article in the academic regulations which provides or declares that no citizen who has been a cadet at the Military Academy can receive a commission in the regular army before the class of which he was a member graduates, unless he can get the written consent of his former classmates.

A classmate of mine resigned in the summer of '75, and about a year after endeavored to get a commission. A friend and former classmate drew up the approval, and invited the class to his " house" to sign it. When half a dozen or more had signed it, it was sent to the guard-house, and the corporal of the guard came and notified me it was there for my consideration. I went to the guard-house at once. A number of cadets were sitting or standing around in the room. As soon as I entered they became silent and remained so, expecting, no doubt, I'd refuse to sign it, because of the treatment I had received at their hands. They certainly had little cause to expect that I would add my signature. Nevertheless I read the paper over and signed it without hesitation. Their anxiety was raised to the highest possible pitch, and scarcely had I left the room ere they seized the paper as if they would de-

vour it. I heard some one who came in as I went
out ask, " Did he sign it ?"

Another case of condescension on the part of an
upper classman occurred in the early part of my
third year at the Academy, and this time in the mess
hall. We were then seated at the tables by classes.
Each table had a commandant, who was a cadet
captain, lieutenant or sergeant, and in a few instances
a corporal. At each table there was also a carver,
who was generally a corporal, occasionally a sergeant or private. The other seats were occupied by
privates, and usually in this order: first-classmen had
first and second seats, second-classmen second and
third seats, third-classmen third and fourth seats,
and fourth-classmen fourth and fifth seats, which
were at the foot of the table. I had a first seat,
although a second-classman. For some reason a
first-classman, who had a first seat at another table,
desired to change seats with me. He accordingly
sent a cadet for me. I went over to his room. I
agreed to make the change, provided he himself
obtained permission of the proper authorities. It
was distinctly understood that he was to take my
seat, a first seat, and I was to take his seat, also a
first seat. He obtained permission of the superintendent of the mess hall, and also a written permit
from the commandant. The change was made, but
lo and behold ! instead of a first seat I got a third.
The agreement was thus violated by him, my
superior (?), and I was dissatisfied. The whole affair
was explained to the commandant, not, however, by

10

myself, but by my consent, the permit revoked, and I gained my former first seat. A tactical officer asked me, "Why did you exchange with him ? Has he ever done any thing for you ?"

I told him he had not, and that I did it merely to oblige him. It was immaterial to me at what table I sat, provided I had a seat consistent with the dignity of my class.

The baseness of character displayed by the gentleman, the reflection on myself and class would have evoked a complaint from me had not a classmate anticipated me by doing so himself.

This gentleman (?) was practically "cut" by the whole corps. He was spoken to, and that was about all that made his status in the corps better than mine.

Just after the semiannual examination following this adventure, another, more ridiculous still, occurred, of which I was the innocent cause. The dismissal of a number of deficient plebes and others made necessary a rearrangement of seats. The commandant saw fit to have it made according to class rank. It changed completely the former arrangement, and gave me a third seat. A classmate, who was senior to me, had the second seat. He did not choose to take it, and for two or more weeks refused to do so. I had the second seat during all this time, while he was fed in his quarters by his chum. He had a set of miniature cooking utensils in his own room, and frequently cooked there, using the gas as a source of heat. These were at last "hived," and he was ordered to "turn them in." He went to dinner one day when I was absent on guard. At supper he appeared again. Some one asked him how it was he was there, glancing at the same time at me. He laughed—it was plainly forced—and replied, " I forgot to fall out."

He came to his meals the next day, the next, and every succeeding day regularly. Thus were his scruples overcome. His refusing to go to his meals because he had to sit next to me was strongly disapproved by the corps for two reasons, viz., that he ought to be man enough not to thrust on others what he himself disliked ; and that as others for two years had had seats by me, he ought not to complain because it now fell to his lot to have one there too.

Just after my return, in September, 1875, from a furlough of two months, an incident occurred which, explained, will give some idea of the low, unprincipled manner in which some of the cadets have acted toward me. It was at cavalry drill. I was riding a horse that was by no means a favorite with us. He happened to fall to my lot that day, and I rather liked him. His greatest faults were a propensity for kicking and slight inequality in the length of his legs. We were marching in a column of fours, and at a slow walk. I turned my head for some purpose, and almost simultaneously my horse plunged headlong into the fours in front of me. It was with difficulty that I retained my seat. I supposed that when I turned my head I had accidentally spurred him, thus causing him to plunge forward. I regained my proper place in ranks.

None of this was seen by the instructor, who was riding at the head of the column. Shortly after this

I noticed that those near me were laughing. I turned my head to observe the cause and caught the trooper on my left in the act of spurring my horse. I looked at him long and fiercely, while he desisted and hung his head. Not long afterwards the same thing was repeated, and this time was seen by the instructor, who happened to wheel about as my horse rushed forward. He immediately halted the column, and, approaching, asked me, " What is the matter with that horse, Mr. F. ?" To which I replied, " The trooper on my left persists in kicking and spurring him, so that I can do nothing with him."

He then caused another trooper in another set of fours to change places with me, and thereafter all went well.

Notwithstanding the secrecy of hazing, and the great care which those who practised it took to prevent being " hived," they sometimes overreached themselves and were severely punished. Cases have occurred where cadets have been dismissed for hazing, while others have been less severely punished.

Sometimes, also, the joke, if I may so call it, has been turned upon the perpetrators to their utter discomfort. I will cite an instance.

Quite often in camp two robust plebes are selected and ordered to report at a specified tent just after the battalion returns from supper. When they report each is provided with a pillow. They take their places in the middle of the company street, and at a given signal commence pounding each other. A crowd assembles from all parts of camp to witness the " pillow fight," as it is called. Sometimes, also,

after fighting awhile, the combatants are permitted
to rest, and another set continues the fight.

On one of these occasions, after fighting quite a
while, a pillow bursted, and one of the antagonists
was literally buried in feathers. At this a shout of
laughter arose and the fun was complete. But alas
for such pleasures ! An officer in his tent, disturbed
by the noise, came out to find its cause. He saw it
at a glance, aided no doubt by vivid recollections of
his own experience in his plebe camp. He called an
orderly and sent for the cadet captain of the company. When he came he was ordered to send the
plebes—he said new cadets—to their tents, and order
them to remain there till permission was given to
leave them. He then had every man, not a plebe,
who had been present at the pillow fight turned out.
When this was done he ordered them to pick up
every feather within half an hour, and the captain to
inspect at the end of that time and to see that the
order was obeyed. Thus, therefore, the plebes got
the better part of the joke.

It was rumored in camp one day that the superintendent and commandant were both absent from
the post, and that the senior tactical officer was therefore acting superintendent. A plebe sentinel on
Post No. 1, seeing him approaching camp, and not
knowing under the circumstances how to act, or
rather, perhaps, I should say, not knowing whether
the report was true or not, called a corporal, and
asked if he should salute this officer with " present
arms." To this question that dignitary replied with
righteous horror, " Salute him with present arms !

No, sir! You stand at attention, and when he gets
on your post shout, ' Hosannah to the supe !' '' This
rather startled the plebe, who found himself more
confused than ever. When it was about time for the
sentinel to do something the corporal told him what
to do, and returned to the guard tents. The officer
was at the time the commanding officer of the camp.

While walking down Sixth Avenue, New York,
with a young lady, on a beautiful Sabbath afternoon
in the summer of 1875, I was paid a high compliment
by an old colored soldier. He had lost one leg and
had been otherwise maimed for life in the great
struggle of 1861–65 for the preservation of the Union.
As soon as he saw me approaching he moved to the
outside of the pavement and assumed as well as possible the position of the soldier. When I was about
six paces from him he brought his crutch to the
position of " present arms," in a soldierly manner,
in salute to me. I raised my cap as I passed, endeavoring to be as polite as possible, both in return
for his salute and because of his age. He took the
position of " carry arms," saying as he did so,
" That's right ! that's right ! Makes me glad to see
it."

We passed on, while he, too, resumed his course,
ejaculating something about " good-breeding," etc.,
all of which we did not hear.

Upon inquiry I learned, as stated, that he had
served in the Federal army. He had given his time
and energy, even at the risk of his life, to his country. He had lost one limb, and been maimed other-

wise for life.   I considered the salute for that reason a greater honor.

During the summer of 1873 a number of cadets, who were on furlough, visited Mammoth Cave. While there they noticed on the wall, written in pencil, the name of an officer who was an instructor in Spanish at West Point.   One of them took occasion to add to the inscription the following bit of information :

"Known at the U. S. Military Academy as the 'Spanish Inquisition.' "

A number of cadets accosted a plebe, who had just reported in May, 1874, and the following conversation ensued :

"Well, mister, what's your name ?"

"John Walden."

"Sir !" yelled rather than spoken.

"John Walden."

"Well, sir, I want to see you put a 'sir' on it," with another yell.

"Sir John Walden," was the unconcerned rejoinder.

Now it was not expected that the " sir" would be put before the name after the manner of a title, but this impenetrable plebe put it there, and in so solemn and " don't-care" a manner that the cadets turned away in a roar of laughter.

Ever afterward he was known in the corps as " Sir John."

Another incident, even more laughable perhaps than the preceding, occurred between a cadet and plebe, which doubtless saved the plebe from further hazing. Approaching him with a look of utter contempt on his face, the cadet asked him :

"Well, thing, what's your name ?"

".Wilreni, sir," meekly responded he.

"Wilreni, sir !" repeated the cadet slowly, and bowing his head he seemed for a moment buried in profoundest thought. Suddenly brightening up, he rejoined in the most unconcerned manner possible : "Oh! yes, yes, I remember now. You are Will Reni, the son of old man Bill Reni," put particular stress on "Will" and "Bill."

I think, though, the most laughable incident that has come under my notice was that of a certain plebe who made himself famous for gourmandizing.

Each night throughout the summer encampment, the guard is supplied from the mess hall with an abundance of sandwiches. The old cadets rarely eat them, but to the plebes, as yet unaccustomed to guard duty, they are quite a treat.

On one occasion when the sandwiches were unusually well prepared, and therefore unusually inviting, it was desirable to preserve them till late in the night, till after the guard had been turned out and inspected by the officer of the day. They were accordingly—to conceal them from the plebes—transferred, with the vessel containing them, to one of the chests of a caisson of the light battery, just in front of camp in park. Here they were supposed to be safe. But alas for such safety ! At an hour not far advanced into the night, two plebes, led by an unerring ins.inctiveness, discovered the hiding-place of the sandwiches and devoured them all.

Now when the hour of feasting was come, a corporal was dispatched for the dainty dish, when, lo and behold ! it had vanished. The plebes—for who else could thus have secretly devoured them—were brought to account and the guilty ones discovered. They were severely censured in that contemptuous manner in which only a cadet, an upper classman, can censure a plebe, and threatened with hazing and all sorts of unpleasantness.

Next morning they were called forth and marched ingloriously to the presence of the commandant. Upon learning the object of the visit he turned to the chief criminal—the finder of the sandwiches—and asked him, " Why did you eat all the sandwiches, Mr. S—— ?"

" I didn't eat them all up, sir. I ate only fifteen," was his ready reply.

The gravity of the occasion, coupled with the enormity of the feast, was too much, and the commandant turned away his head to conceal the laughter he could not withhold. The plebe himself was rather short and fleshy, and the picture of mirth. Indeed to see him walking even along the company street was enough to call forth laughter either at him as he waddled along or at the humorous remarks the act called forth from onlooking cadets.

He was confined to one of the guard tents by order of the commandant, and directed by him to submit a written explanation for eating all the sandwiches of the guard. The explanation was unsatisfactory, and the gentleman received some other light punishment, the nature of which has at this late day escaped my memory.

The other plebe, being only a *particeps criminis*, was not so severely punished. A reprimand, I think, was the extent of his punishment.

The two gentlemen have long since gone where the "woodbine twineth"—that is, been found deficient in studies and dismissed.

There was a cadet in the corps who had a wonderful propensity for using the word "mighty."

With him every thing was "mighty." I honestly do not believe I ever heard him conversing when he did not use "mighty."

Speaking of me one day, and unconscious of my presence, he said, "I tell you he does 'mighty' well."

During drill at the siege battery on the 25th of April, 1876, an accident occurred which came near proving fatal to one of us. I had myself just fired an 8-inch howitzer, and gone to the rear to observe the effect of the other shots. One piece had been fired, and the command for the next to fire had been given. I was watching intently the target when I was startled by the cry of some one near me, "Look out! look out!" I turned my eyes instinctively toward the piece just fired, but saw only smoke. I then looked up and saw a huge black body of some kind moving rapidly over our heads. It was not until the smoke had nearly disappeared that I knew what was the cause of the disturbance. A number of cannoneers and our instructor were vociferously asking, " Anybody hurt ? Anybody hurt ?" We all moved up to the piece, and, finding no one was injured, examined it. The piece, a 4½-inch rifle, mounted on a siege carriage, had broken obliquely from the trunnions downward and to the rear. The re-enforce thus severed from the chase broke into three parts, the nob of the cascabel, and the other portion split in the direction of the bore. The right half of the re-enforce, together with the nob of the cascabel, were projected into the air, describing a curve over our heads, and falling at about twenty feet from the right of the battery, having passed over a horizontal distance of about sixty or seventy feet. The left half was thrown obliquely to the ground, tearing away in its passage the left cheek of the carriage, and breaking the left trunnion plate. A cannoneer was standing on the platform of the next piece on the left with the lanyard in his hand. His feet were on two adjacent deck planks, his heels being on line with the edge of the platform. These two planks were struck upon their ends, and moved bodily, with the cadet upon them, three or four inches from their proper place. The bolts that held them and the adjacent planks together were broken, while not the slightest injury was done the cadet.

It was hardly to be believed, and was not until two or three of the other cannoneers had examined him and found him really uninjured. It was simply miraculous. The instructor sent the cannoneers to the rear, and fired the next gun himself.

After securing the pieces and replacing equipments, we were permitted to again examine the bursted gun, after which the battery was dismissed.

There had been some difficulty in loading the piece, especially in getting the projectile home. It was supposed that this not being done properly caused the bursting.

I was one summer day enjoying a walk on " Flirtation." I was alone, and, if I remember aright, " on Old Guard privileges." Walking leisurely along I soon observed in front of me a number of young ladies, a servant girl, and several small children.

They were all busily occupied in gathering wild flowers, a kind of moss and ferns which grow here in abundance. I was first seen by one of the children, a little girl. She instantly fixed her eyes upon me, and began vociferating in a most joyous manner, " The colored cadet ! the colored cadet ! I'm going to tell mamma I've seen the colored cadet."

The servant girl endeavored to quiet her, but she continued as gayly as ever :

" It's the colored cadet ! I'm going to tell mamma. I'm going to tell mamma I've seen the colored cadet."

All the others stopped gathering flowers, and watched me till I was out of sight.

A similar display of astonishment has occurred at every annual examination since I became a cadet, and on these occasions the ladies more than anybody else have been the ones to show it.

Whenever I took my place on the floor to receive my enunciation or to be questioned, I have observed whisperings, often audible, and gestures of surprise among the lady visitors. I have frequently heard such exclamations as this : " Oh ! there's the colored cadet ! there's the colored cadet !''

All of this naturally tended to confuse me, and it was only by determined effort that I maintained any degree of coolness. Of course they did not intend to confuse me. Nothing was, I dare say, further from their thoughts. But they were women ; and it never occurs to a woman to think before she speaks.

It was rather laughable to hear a cadet, who was expounding the theory of twilight, say, pointing to his figure on the blackboard : " If a spectator should cross this limit of the crepuscular zone he would enter into *final darkness*."

Now " final darkness," as we usually understand it, refers to something having no resemblance whatever to the characteristics of the crepuscular zone.

The solemn manner in which he spoke it, together with their true significations, made the circumstance quite laughable.

The most ludicrous case of hazing I know of is, I think, the following :

For an unusual display of grossness a number of plebes were ordered by the cadet lieutenant on duty over them to report at his "house" at a specified hour. They duly reported their presence, and were directed to assume the position of the soldier, facing the wall until released. After silently watching them for a considerable time, the lieutenant, who had a remarkable *penchant* for joking, called two of them into the middle of the room. He caused them to stand *dos à dos*, at a distance of about one foot from each other, and then bursting into a laugh, which he vainly endeavored to suppress, he commanded, " Second, exercise !"

Now to execute this movement the hands are extended vertically over the head and the hands joined. At the command " Two !" given when this is done, the arms are brought briskly forward and downward until the hands touch if possible the ground or floor. The plebes having gone through the first motion, the lieutenant thus cautioned them :

" When I say ' Two !' I want to see you men come down with life, and touch the floor. Two !"

At the command they both quickly, and " with life," brought their bodies forward and their arms downward ; nay, they but attempted, for scarcely had they left the vertical ere their bodies collided, and they were each hurled impetuously, by the inevitable reaction in opposite directions, over a distance of several feet.

Their bodies being in an inclined position when struck, and the blow being of great force, they were necessarily forced still further from the erect attitude, and were with much difficulty able to keep themselves from falling outright on the floor. Of course all present, save those concerned, enjoyed it immensely. Indeed it was enjoyable. Even the plebes themselves had a hearty laugh over it when they were dismissed.

Again a cadet lieutenant, who was on duty at the time over the " Seps," ordered a number of them to report at his " house" at a given hour. They had been unusually gross, and he intended to punish them by keeping them standing in his quarters. They reported, and were put in position to serve their punishment.   For some reason the lieutenant left the room, when one of the "Seps" faced to the others and thus spoke to them :

"Say, boys, let's kick up the devil. P—— has gone out."

Now it so happened that P——'s chum was present, but in his alcove, and this was not known to the Seps.   When the Sep had finished speaking, this chum came forth and "went for" him.   He made the Sep assume the soldier's position, and then commanded, "Second, exercise !" which command the Sep proceeded to obey.

Another cadet coming in found him vigorously at it, and queried, "Well, mister, what's all that for ?"

"Eccentricity of Mr. M——, sir," he promptly replied.

The word eccentricity was not interpreted by the cadet, of course, as the Sep meant it should be, but in the sense we use it when we speak of the eccentricity of an orbit for instance.

Hence it was that Mr. M—— asked, "Well, sir, what's the expression for my eccentricity ?"

There is another incident remotely connected with my first tour of guard duty which may be mentioned here.

At about eleven o'clock A.M., in obedience to a then recent order, my junior reported at the observatory to make the necessary observations for finding the error of the Tower clock.   After an elaborate ex-

planation by an officer then present upon the graduation of the vernier and the manner of reading it,
the cadet set the finders so as to read the north polar
distance of the sun for that day at West Point apparent noon.   When it was about time for the sun's
limb to begin its transit of the wires, the cadet took
position to observe it.   The instructor was standing
ready to record the times of transit over each wire.
Time was rapidly passing, and not yet had the cadet
called out " Ready."   The anxious instructor cautiously queried :

" Do you see any light, Mr. P—— ?"

" No, sir."

" Can you see the wires ?"

" No, sir, not yet."

" Any light yet, Mr. P—— ?"

" Yes, sir, it is *getting brighter.*"

" Can you see the wires at all ?"

" No, sir ; it *keeps getting brighter, but I can't
see the wires yet.*"

Fearing he might be unable to make his observations that day unless the difficulty was speedily removed, the instructor himself took position at the
transit, and made the ridiculous discovery that the
*cap had not been removed from the farther end of
the telescope*, and yet it kept getting brighter.

One day in the early summer of 1875, a cadet
was showing a young lady the various sights and
wonders at West Point, when they came across an
old French cannon bearing this inscription, viz.,
" Charles de Bourbon, Compte d'Eu, ultima ratio
regum."

She was the first to notice it, and astonished the cadet with the following rendition of it :

" I suppose that means Charles Bourbon made the gun, and the Spanish (?) that the artilleryman must have his rations."

What innocence ! Or shall I say, what ignorance ?

" The authorities of West Point have entered an interdict against the cadets loaning their sashes and other military adornments to young ladies, and great is the force of feminine indignation." Summer of 1873.

COME KISS ME, LOVE.

A young lieutenant at the Academy and his *fiancée* were seen by an old maid at the hotel to kiss each other. At the first opportunity she reproved the fair damsel for, to .her, such unmaidenly conduct. With righteous indignation she repelled the reproof as follows :

" Not let S——- kiss me ! Why, I should die !"
Then lovingly,

> " Come kiss me, love, list not what they say,
> Their passions are cold, wasted away.
> They know not how two hearts like ours are
> Long to mingle i' the sweetness o' the kiss,
> That like the soft light of a heavenly star,
> As it wanders from its world to this,
> Diffuses itself through ev'ry vein
> And meets on the lips to melt again."

CHAPTER XV.

GRADUATION—IN THE ARMY.

" Patience is bitter, but its fruit is sweet."

MY four years were drawing to a close. They had been years of patient endurance and hard and persistent work, interspersed with bright oases of happiness and gladness and joy, as well as weary barren wastes of loneliness, isolation, unhappiness, and melancholy. I believe I have discharged—I know I have tried to do so—every duty faithfully and conscientiously. It had been a sort of bitter-sweet experience, this experimental life of mine at West Point. It was almost over, and whatever of pure sweetness, whatever of happiness, or whatever reward fortune had in store for me, was soon to become known.

" Speaking of the Military Academy, we understand that the only colored cadet now at West Point will not only graduate at the coming June commencement, but that his character, acquirements, and standing on the merit roll are such as will insure his graduation among the highest of his class."—*Harper's Weekly, April 28th*, 1877.

All recitations of the graduating class were discontinued on the last scholar day of May. On June 1st examination began. The class was first examined in mineralogy and geology. In this particular sub-

Henry O. Flipper
2d Lieut 10" Cavy

ject I "maxed it," made a thorough recitation. I was required to discuss the subject of "Mesozoic Time." After I had been examined in this subject Bishop Quintard, of Tennessee, a member of the Board of Visitors, sent for me, and personally congratulated me on my recitation of that day, as well as for my conduct during the whole four years. My hopes never were higher ; I knew I would graduate. I felt it, and I made one last effort for rank. I wanted to graduate as high up as possible. I was not without success, as will subsequently appear. The New York *Herald* was pleased to speak as follows of my recitation in mineralogy and geology :

"To-day the examination of the first class in mineralogy and geology was completed, and the first section was partially examined in engineering. In the former studies the class acquitted themselves in a highly creditable manner, and several members have shown themselves possessed of abilities far above the average. The class has in its ranks a son of General B. F. Butler, Hon. John Bigelow's son, and sons of two ex-Confederate officers. Flipper, the colored cadet, was examined to-day, and produced a highly favorable impression upon the board not less by his ready and intelligent recitation than by his modest, unassuming, and gentlemanly manner. There is no doubt that he will pass, and he is said to have already ordered a cavalry uniform, showing that he has a predilection for that branch of the service."

The class was next examined in law. In this, also, I exceeded my most sanguine expectations, again "maxing it" on a thorough recitation. My subject was "Domicile." Senator Maxey, of the Board of Visitors, questioned me closely. The Bishop of Tennessee left his seat in the board, came outside when the section was dismissed, and shook my hand in hearty congratulation. These were the proudest moments of my life. Even some of my own classmates congratulated me on this recitation. All that loneliness, dreariness, and melancholy of the four years gone was forgotten. I lived only in the time being and was happy. I was succeeding, and was meeting with that success which humble effort never fails to attain.

The New York *Tribune* joins in with its good words as follows :

LIEUTENANT FLIPPER, THE COLORED GRADUATE OF WEST POINT.

" The examination of the first class in law will be completed to-morrow. The sections thus far called up have done very well. The colored cadet, Flipper, passed uncommonly well this morning, showing a practical knowledge of the subject very satisfactory to Senator Maxey, who questioned him closely, and to the rest of the board. He has a good command of plain and precise English, and his voice is full and pleasant. Mr. Flipper will be graduated next week with the respect of his instructors, and not the less of his fellows, who have carefully avoided intercourse with him. The quiet dignity which he has shown during this long isolation of four years has been really remarkable. Until another of his race, now in one of the lower classes, arrived, Flipper scarcely heard the sound of his own voice except in recitation, and it is to be feared that unless he is detailed at Howard University, which has been mentioned as possible, his trials have only begun.''

The class was next examined in civil and military engineering. In this also I did as well as in either of the other studies. I made a thorough recitation. I was required to explain what is meant by an " order of battle," and to illustrate by the battles of Zama, Pharsalia, and Leuctra.

THE COLORED CADET.

" Flipper, the colored cadet from South Carolina, was up this afternoon and acquitted himself remarkably well. Some time since he was recommended for a higher grade than the one he holds, and his performance to-day gained him a still higher standing in the class."

In ordnance and gunnery the class was next examined. In this I was less successful. I was to assume one of Captain Didion's equations of the trajectory in air, and determine the angle of projection represented by ϕ, and the range represented by x in the following equation :

$$y = x \, tan. \, \phi - \frac{g \, x^2}{2 \, V^2} \, B,$$

and to explain the construction and use of certain tables used in connection with it. I made a fair recitation, but one by no means ¯satisfactory to myself. I lost four files on it at least. A good recitation in ordnance and gunnery would have brought me out forty-five or six instead of fifty. I did not make it, and it was too late to better it. This was the last of our examination. It ended on the 11th day of June. On the 14th we were graduated and received our diplomas.

During the examination I received letters of congratulation in every mail. Some of them may not be uninteresting. I give a few of them :

POST-OFFICE DEPARTMENT, ROOM 48, }
WASHINGTON, D. C., June 3, 1877. }

MY DEAR MR. FLIPPER : It has been four years since I last addressed you. Then you had just entered the Academy with other young colored men, who have since dropped by the way. I was at that time the editor of the *Era* in this city, and wrote an article on West Point and snobocracy, which you may remember reading.

I felt a thrill of pleasure here the other day when I read your name as the first graduate from the Academy. I take this opportunity of writing you again to extend my hearty congratulations, and trust your future career may be as successful as your academic one. " My boy," Whittaker, has, I am told, been rooming with you, and I trust has been getting much benefit from the association.

> I am, your friend and well-wisher,
> RICHARD T. GREENER.

> 42 BROAD STREET, NEW YORK, June 4, 1877.

CADET HENRY O. FLIPPER,
> *West Point, N. Y. :*

DEAR SIR : I have been much pleased reading the complimentary references to your approaching graduation which have appeared in the New York papers the past week. I beg to congratulate you most heartily, and I sincerely trust that the same intelligence and pluck which has enabled you to successfully complete your academic course may be shown in a still higher degree in the new sphere of duty soon to be entered upon.

I inclose an editorial from to-day's *Tribune.*

> Respectfully,

> ————.

> DEPARTMENT OF THE INTERIOR,
> UNITED STATES PATENT OFFICE,
> WASHINGTON, D. C., June 5, 1877. }

HENRY O. FLIPPER, ESQ.,
> *U. S. Military Academy, West Point, N. Y. :*

DEAR SIR : Having noticed in the daily papers of this city an account of the successful termination of your course at the Military Academy, we hasten to tender you our sincere congratulations.

We are prompted to this act by an experimental knowledge of the social ostracism and treacherous duplicity to which you must have been made the unhappy victim during the long years of faithful study through which you have just passed.

We congratulate you upon the moral courage and untiring energy which must have been yours, to enable you to successfully battle against the immeasurable influence of the prejudice shown to all of us at both of our *national* schools. We hail your success as a national acknowledgment, in a new way, of the mental and moral worth of our race ; and we feel amply repaid for the many privations we have undergone in the naval branch of our service, in noting the fact that *one* of us has been permitted to successfully stand the trying ordeal.

Trusting that the same firmness of purpose and untiring energy, which have characterized your stay there, may ever be true of your future career on the field and at the hearth side,

We remain, very truly yours,

——,

——.

POST-OFFICE, NEW YORK CITY,' N. Y. ⎫
OFFICE OF THE POSTMASTER, ⎬
Wednesday, June 7, 1877. ⎭

MY DEAR FRIEND : Let me extend to you my full gratitude upon your success at West Point. I was overjoyed when I saw it. My friends are delighted with you, and they desire to see you when you come down. Let me know when you think you will leave West Point, and I will look out for you.

Very truly yours,

——.

HENRY O. FLIPPER, ESQ.,
West Point Military Academy.

WASHINGTON, D. C., June 13, 1877.

HENRY O. FLIPPER, ESQ.,
West Point, N. Y. :

MY DEAR FRIEND : I wish to congratulate you upon passing successfully your final examination, and salute you as the first young colored man who has had the manhood and courage to struggle through and overcome every obstacle. So many of our young men had failed that I wondered if you would be able to withstand all the opposition you met with, whether you could endure the kind of life they mete out to our young men at our national Military Academy. I rejoice to know that you have won this important victory over prejudice and caste. This will serve you in good stead through many a conflict in life. Your path will not be all strewn with roses ; something of that caste and prejudice will still pursue you as you enter the broader arena of military life, but you must make up your mind to live it down, and your first victory will greatly aid you in this direction. One thing, allow me to impress upon you : you are not fighting your own battle, but you are fighting the battle of a struggling people ; and for this reason, my dear Flipper, resolve now in your deepest soul that come what may you will *never* surrender ; that you will *never* succumb.   Others may leave the service for more lucrative pursuits ; your duty to your people and to yourself demand that you remain.

Be assured that whatever you do, wherever you may go, you always have my deepest sympathy and best wishes.

I return to Europe in a few weeks.

Cordially yours,

———.

Even the cadets and other persons connected with the Academy congratulated me.   Oh how happy I was !   I prized these good words of the cadets above all others.   They knew me thoroughly.   They meant what they said, and I felt I was in some sense deserving of all I received from them by way of congratulation.   Several visited my quarters.   They did not hesitate to speak to me or shake hands with me before each other or any one else.   All signs of ostracism were gone.   All felt as if I was worthy of some regard, and did not fail to extend it to me.

At length, on June 14th, I received the reward of my labors, my " sheepskin," the United States Military Academy Diploma, that glorious passport to honor and distinction, if the bearer do never disgrace it.

Here is the manner of ceremony we had on that day, as reported in the New York *Times :*

" The concluding ceremony in the graduation exercises at the West Point Academy took place this morning, when the diplomas were awa led to the graduates.   The ceremony took place in the open air under the shadow of the maple trees, which form almost a grove in front of the Academy building.   Seats had been arranged here for the spectators, so as to leave a hollow square, on one side of which, behind a long table, sat the various dignitaries who were to take part in the proceedings.   In front of them, seats were arranged for the

graduating class. The cadets formed line in front of the barracks
at 10.30, and, preceded by the band playing a stirring air, marched
to the front of the Academy building. The first class came without
their arms ; the other classes formed a sort of escort of honor to
them. The graduating class having taken their seats, the other
classes stacked arms and remained standing in line around the
square. The proceedings were opened by an address from Professor
Thompson, of the School of Technology, Worcester Mass., who is
the Chairman of the Board of Visitors.''

And thus after four years of constant work amid
many difficulties did I obtain my reward.

"Lieutenant H. O. Flipper was the only cadet who received the
cheers of the assembled multitude at West Point upon receiving his
parchment. How the fellows felt who couldn't associate with him
we do not know ; but as the old Christian woman said, they
' couldn't a been on the mountain top.' ''—*Christian Recorder.*

Victor Hugo says somewhere in his works that he
who drains a marsh must necessarily expect to hear
the frogs croak. I had graduated, and of course the
newspapers had to have a say about it. Some of the
articles are really amusing. I couldn't help laughing at them when I read them. Here is something
from the New York *Herald* which is literally true :

"MR. BLAINE AND THE COLORED CADET.

" Senator James G. Blaine, with his wife and daughter and Miss
Dodge (' Gail Hamilton ') left at noon yesterday in anticipation of
the rush. Before going the Senator did a very gracious and kindly
deed in an unostentatious way. Sending for Flipper, the colored
cadet, he said :

" 'I don't know that you have any political friends in your own
State, Mr. Flipper, and you may find it necessary to have an inter-
mediary in Congress to help you out of your difficulties. I want you
to consider me your friend, and call upon me for aid when you need
it.'

" With that he shook the lad's hand and bade him good-by.

11

"Bishop Quintard, of Tennessee, and Senator Maxey, of Texas, also complimented the pioneer graduate of the colored race upon his conduct throughout the four years of his training, and proffered their sympathy and assistance. With these encouragements from prominent men of both political parties the young man seemed deeply touched, and thanking them suitably he returned with a light heart to his quarters."

It was so very kind of the distinguished senators and bishop. I valued these congratulations almost as much as my diploma. They were worth working and enduring for.

The New York *Herald* again speaks, and that about not hearing my voice, etc., made me " larf." Here is the article :

"THE COLORED CADET'S EXPERIENCE AND PROSPECTS.

"Flipper, the colored cadet, who graduates pretty well up in his class, said to me to-day that he is determined to get into either the Ninth or Tenth colored cavalry regiment if possible. He seems to be very happy in view of the honorable close of his academic career, and entertains little doubt that he can procure the appointment he wishes. When asked whether he was not aware that there was a law providing that even colored troops must be officered by white men, he replied that he had heard something of that years ago, but did not think it was true. 'If there is such a law,' he said emphatically, but with good humor, 'it is unconstitutional and cannot be enforced.' He added that several weeks ago he wrote to a prominent gentleman in Alabama to inquire what the existing law on the subject was, and had not yet received an answer. I questioned him about his experience in the Academy, and he said that he had suffered but little on account of his race. The first year was very hard, as the class all made their dislike manifest in a variety of ways. 'That,' he said, 'was in a great measure caused by the bad conduct of Smith, the colored cadet who preceded me. When the class found out that I was not like him, they treated me well. The professors act toward me in every respect as toward the others, and the cadets, I think, do not dislike me. But they don't associate with me. I don't care for that. If they don't want to speak to me I don't want them to, I'm sure.' Save in the recitation-room Flipper never heard the sound of his own voice for months and months at a time ; but he was kept so hard at work all the time that he did not mind it. If he should join a regiment, however, he would be more alone even than he has been here, for the association with other officers in the line of duty would not be so close as it has been with the cadets. He would be isolated—ostracized—and he would feel it more keenly, because he would have more leisure for social intercourse, and his mind would not be so occupied as it has been here with studies.

" Senator Blaine, in the course of a conversation last night, thought the career of Flipper would be to go South and become a leader of his race. He could in that way become famous, and could accomplish much good for the country." . . . .

When I entered the Academy I saw in a paper something about colored officers being put in white regiments, etc. It purported to be a conversation with the then Secretary of War, who said there was such a law, and that it would be enforced. The then Secretary of War has since told me he was sure there was such a law, until to satisfy himself he searched the Revised Statutes, when he found he was mistaken.

I have mentioned elsewhere the untruthfulness of the statement that I never heard my own voice except in the recitation-room. Every one must know that could not be true. The statement is hardly worth a passing remark.

" If he should join a regiment, however," etc. Ah ! well, I have joined my regiment long ago. Let me say, before I go further, I am putting this manuscript in shape for the press, and doing it in my quarters at Fort Sill, I. T. These remarks are inserted *apropos* of this article. From the moment I reached Sill I haven't experienced any thing but happiness. I am not isolated. I am not ostracized by

a single officer.   I do not " feel it more keenly," because what the *Herald* said is not true.   The
Herald, like other papers, forgets that the army is
officered by men who are presumably officers and
gentlemen.   Those who are will treat me as become
gentlemen, as they do, and those who are not I
will thank if they will " ostracize" me, for if they
don't I will certainly " ostracize" them.

> " But to get into a cavalry regiment is the highest ambition of most
> cadets, and failing in that it is almost a toss-up between the infantry
> and the artillery.   Flipper, the South Carolina colored cadet, wants
> to get into the cavalry, and as there is a black regiment of that char-
> acter he will, it is thought, be assigned to that.   There is in existence
> a law specifying that even black regiments shall be officered by white
> men, and it is thought there will be some trouble in assigning Flip-
> per.   As any such law is in opposition to the constitutional amend-
> ments, of course it will be easily rescinded.   From the disposition
> shown by most of the enlisted men with whom I have conversed at
> odd times upon this subject, I fancy that if Flipper were appointed to
> the command of white soldiers they would be restive, and would, if
> out upon a scout, take the first opportunity to shoot him ; and this
> feeling exists even among men here who have learned to respect him
> for what he is."

Now that is laughable, isn't it ?   What he says
about the soldiers at West Point is all " bosh."   No-
body will believe it.   I don't.   I wish the *Herald*
reporter who wrote the above would visit Fort Sill
and ask some of the white soldiers there what they
think of me.   I am afraid the *Herald* didn't get its
" gift of prophecy" from the right place.   Such
blunders are wholly inexcusable.   The *Herald* reporter deserves an " extra" (*vide* Cant Terms, etc.)
for that.   I wish he could get one at any rate.   Perhaps, however, the following will excuse him.   It is
true.

" He is spoken of by all the officers as a hard student and a gentleman. To a very great extent he has conquered the prejudices of his
fellows, and although they still decline to associate with him it is
evident that they respect him. Said one of his class this morning :
' Flipper has certainly shown pluck and gentlemanly qualities, and I
shall certainly shake his " flipper" when we say " Good-by." We
have no feeling against him at all, but we could not associate with
him. You see we are so crowded together here that we are just like
one family, possessing every thing in common and borrowing every
thing, even to a pair of white trousers, and we could not hold such
intimate fellowship with him. It may be prejudice, but we could
not do it ; so we simply let him alone, and he has lived to himself,
except when we drill with him. Feel bad about it ? Well, I suppose he did at first, but he has got used to it now. The boys were
rather afraid that when he should come to hold the position as officer
of the guard that he would swagger over them, but he showed good
sense and taste, merely assuming the rank formally and leaving his
junior to carry out the duty.' "

That glorious day of graduation marked a new
epoch in my military life. Then my fellow-cadets
and myself forgot the past. Then they atoned for
past conduct and welcomed me as one of them as
well as one among them.

I must revert to that *Herald's* article just to
show how absurd it is to say I never heard the sound
of my own voice except in the section-room. I heard
it at reveille, at breakfast, dinner, and supper roll-
calls, at the table, at taps, and at every parade I attended during the day—in all no less than ten or
twelve times every single day during the four years.
Of course I heard it in other places, as I have explained elsewhere. I always had somebody to talk
to every single day I was at the Academy. Why, I
was the happiest man in the institution, except when
I'd get brooding over my loneliness, etc. Such
moments would come, when it would seem nothing

would interest me. When they were gone I was
again as cheerful and as happy as ever. I learned
to hate holidays. At those times the other cadets
would go off skating, rowing, or visiting. I had no
where to go except to walk around the grounds,
which I sometimes did. I more often remained in
my quarters. At these times barracks would be
deserted and I would get so lonely and melancholy I
wouldn't know what to do. It was on an occasion
like this — Thanksgiving Day—I wrote the words
given in another place, beginning,

> " Oh ! 'tis hard this lonely living, to be
>   In the midst of life so solitary," etc.

Here is something from *Harper's Weekly.* The
northern press generally speak in the same tenor of
my graduation.

" Inman Edward Page, a colored student at Brown University, has
succeeded in every respect better than his brother Flipper at West
Point. While a rigid non-intercourse law was for four years maintained
between Flipper and the nascent warriors at the Military Academy,
Page has lived in the largest-leaved clover at Brown, and in the
Senior year just closed was chosen Class-day Orator—a position so
much coveted among students ambitious for class honors that it is
ranked by many even higher than the Salutatory or the Valedictory.
Page has throughout been treated by his classmates as one of themselves. He is a good writer and speaker, though not noticeably better than some of his classmates. His conduct has been uniformly
modest but self-respectful, and he had won the esteem of professors
as well as students. The deportment of his class toward him is in
high and honorable contrast with that pursued by the less manly students supported by the government at West Point, who may have
already learned that the ' plain people ' of the country are with Flipper."

Here is something of a slightly different kind
from a Georgia paper — Augusta *Chronicle and*

Constitutionalist. Its tone betrays the locality of its birth.

"Benjamin F. Butler, Jr., who graduated at West Point last summer in the same class with the colored cadet from Georgia, Flipper, has been assigned for duty to the Ninth Cavalry, the same regiment to which Flipper is attached. The enlisted men in this regiment are all negroes. Ben, senior, doubtless engineered the assignment in order to make himself solid with the colored voters of the South. Ben, like old Joe Bagstock, is devilish sly."

It is in error as to my assignment. Lieutenant Butler (whose name, by the way, is not Benjamin F., Jr.) was assigned to the Ninth Cavalry. Here is the truth about my assignment, given in the Sing Sing (N. Y.) *Republican:*

"Cadet Flipper has been appointed to the Tenth U. S. Cavalry (colored), now in Texas. Secretary of State Bigelow's son has also been assigned to the same regiment. We wonder if the non-intercourse between the two at West Point will be continued in the army. Both have the same rank and are entitled to the same privileges. Possibly a campaign among the Indians, or a brush with the 'Greasers' on the Rio Grande, will equalize the complexion of the two."

The *National Monitor,* of Brooklyn (N. Y.), has this much to say. It may be worth some study by the cadets now at the Academy.

"Lieutenant Flipper, colored, a recent graduate from West Point, is a modest gentleman, and no grumbler. He says that privately he was treated by fellow-cadets with proper consideration, but reluctantly admits that he was publicly slighted. He can afford to be untroubled and magnanimous. How is it with his fellows? Will not shame ere long mantle their cheeks at the recollection of this lack of moral courage on their part? A quality far more to be desired than any amount of physical heroism they may ever exhibit."

Here is something extra good from the *Hudson River Chronicle,* of Sing Sing. To all who want to

know the truth about me physically, I refer them
to this article. I refer particularly to the editor of a
certain New Orleans paper, who described me as a
" little bow-legged *grif* of the most darkly coppery
hue."

"For a few days past Lieutenant Henry O. Flipper, the colored
cadet who graduated from West Point Academy last week, has been
the guest of Professor John W. Hoffman, of this place. Lieutenant
Flipper is a native of Atlanta, Georgia, whence General Sherman
commenced that glorious march to the sea which proved what a hollow shell the Southern Confederacy really was. The lieutenant evidently has a large strain of white blood in his veins, and could probably, if so disposed, trace descent from the F. F's. He stands six feet,
is well proportioned, has a keen, quick eye, a gentlemanly address,
and a soldierly bearing. He goes from here to his home in Georgia,
on a leave of absence which extends to the first of November, when
he will join the Tenth Cavalry, to which he has been assigned as Second Lieutenant. This assignment shows that Lieutenant Flipper stood
above the average of the graduating class, as the cavalry is the next
to the highest grade in the service—only the Engineer Corps taking
precedence of the cavalry arm.

"For four long years Cadet Flipper has led an isolated life at the
Point—without one social companion, being absolutely ostracized by
his white classmates. As much as any mortal, he can say :

> "' In the crowd
> They would not deem me one of such ; I stood
> Among them, but not of them ;-in a shroud
> Of thoughts which were not their thoughts.'

"There must have been much of inherent manhood in a boy that
could stand that long ordeal, and so bear himself at the close that,
when his name was pronounced among the graduates, the fair women
and brave men who had gathered to witness the going out into the
world of the nation's wards, with one accord greeted the lone student
with a round of applause that welcomed none others of the class, and
that could call from Speaker Blaine the strong assurance that if he
ever needed a friend he might trustingly call on him.

"' The path of glory leads but to the grave,' but we venture the
prediction that Lieutenant Flipper will tread that path as fearlessly
and as promptly as any of his comrades of the ' Class of '77.' "

Here is an editorial article from the New York *Tribune*. It needs no comment, nor do the two following, which were clipped from the *Christian Union*.

LIEUTENANT FLIPPER.

" Among the West Point graduates this year is young Flipper, a lad of color and of African descent. It is stated that he acquitted himself very respectably in his examination by the Board of Visitors, that he will pass creditably, and that he will go into the cavalry, which is rather an aristocratic branch, we believe, of the service. Mr. Flipper must have had rather a hard time of it during his undergraduate career, if, as we find it stated, most if not all his white fellow-students have declined to associate with him. He has behaved so well under these anomalous circumstances, that he has won the respect of those who, so far as the discipline of the school would permit, ignored his existence. ' We have no feeling against him,' said one of the students, ' but still we *could not* associate with him. It may be prejudice, but still we *couldn't* do it.' Impossibilities should be required of no one, and if the white West Pointers could not treat Mr. Flipper as if he were one of themselves, why of course that is an end of the matter. So long as they kept within the rules of the service, and were guilty of no conduct ' unbecoming an officer and a gentleman,' it was not for their commanders to interfere. But when they tell us that they couldn't possibly associate with Mr. Flipper, who is allowed to have ' shown pluck and gentlemanly qualities,' we may at least inquire whether they have tried to do so. Conquering prejudices implies a fight with prejudices—have these young gentlemen had any such fight ? Have they too ' shown pluck and gentlemanly qualities ? '

" We are not disposed to speak harshly of these fastidious young fellows, who will not be long out of the school before they will be rather sorry that they didn't treat Mr. Flipper a little more cordially. But a much more important matter is that he has, in spite of his color, made a good record every way, has kept up with his class, has not been dropped or dismissed, but emerges a full-blown Second Lieutenant of Cavalry. He has thus achieved a victory not only for himself but for his race. He has made matters easier for future colored cadets ; and twenty years hence, if not sooner, the young white gentlemen of West Point will read of the fastidiousness of their pre-

decessors with incredulous wonder. Time and patience will settle
every thing."

CADET FLIPPER.

"The most striking illustration of class prejudice this year has
been afforded, not by Mississippi or Louisiana, but by West Point.
In 1873 Cadet Flipper entered the Military Academy. God had
given him a black skin, a warm heart, an active brain, and a patriotic
ambition. He was guilty of no other crime than that of being a
negro, and bent on obtaining a good education. He represented a
race which had done as good fighting for the flag as any done by the
fair-skinned Anglo Saxon or Celt. Congress had recognized his right
and the right of his race to education.

"But his classmates decided that it should be denied him. If they
had possessed the brutal courage of the murderers of Chisholm they
would have shot him, or whipped him, or hung him ; but they were
not brave enough for that, and they invented instead a punishment
worse than the State has inflicted upon its most brutal criminals.
They condemned him to four years of solitude and silence. For four
years not a classmate spoke to Cadet Flipper ; for three years he did
not hear his own voice, except in the recitation-room, on leave of
absence, or in chance conversation with a stray visitor. Then
another negro entered West Point, and he had one companion. The
prison walls of a Sing Sing cell are more sympathetic than human
prejudice. And in all that class of '77 there were not to be found a
dozen men brave enough to break through this wall of silence and
give the imprisoned victim his liberty. At least two thirds of the
class are Republican appointees ; and not one champion of equal
rights. In all that class but one hero—and he a negro. Seventy-
five braves against one ! And the one was victorious. He fought
out the four years' campaign, conquered and graduated. Honor to
the African ; shame to the Anglo-Saxon."

CADET FLIPPER AGAIN.

"We have received several letters on the subject of Cadet Flipper,
to whose treatment at West Point we recently called the attention of
our readers. One of them is from a former instructor, who bears a
high testimony to Lieutenant Flipper's character. He writes :

"'I want to thank you for your editorial in the *Christian Union* about Cadet
Flipper. He was one of our boys ; was with us in school from the beginning of his
education till Freshman year in college, when he received his appointment to West

Point. He was always obedient, faithful, modest, and in every way manly. We were sorry to have him leave us ; but now rejoice in his victory, and take pride in him.

" ' During all these years, in his correspondence with his friends, he has not, so far as I can learn, uttered a single complaint about his treatment.'

" A second is from a Canadian reader, who objects to our condemnation of the Anglo-Saxon race, and insists that we should have reserved it for the Yankees.   In Canada, he assures us, the color line is unknown, and that negroes and Anglo-Saxons mingle in the same school and in the same sports without prejudice.   Strange to say the white men are not colored by the intercourse.

" The third letter comes indirectly from Lieutenant Flipper himself.   In it the writer gives us the benefit of information derived from the lieutenant.   We quote (the italics are ours) :

" ' Mr. Flipper is highly respected here, and has been received by his former teachers and friends with pleasure and pride. His deportment and character have won respect and confidence for himself and his race. As to his treatment at West Point, he assures me that the " papers" are far astray. There was no ostracism on the part of his fellow-cadets, *except in the matter of personal public association.* He was invariably spoken to and treated courteously and respectfully both as a cadet and officer.'

" We are glad to be assured that it was not as bad as we had been informed by what we considered as good authority ; and we are still more glad to know that Lieutenant Flipper, instead of making much of his social martyrdom, has the good sense to make as light of it as he conscientiously can.   But if it is true that there were cadets who did not sympathize with the action of the class, and were brave enough to speak to their colored comrade in private, it was a pity that they were not able to screw their courage up to a little higher point, and put the mark of a public condemnation on so petty and cruel a persecution.''

The people at large seem to be laboring under a delusion about West Point, at least the West Point that I knew.   I know nothing of what West Point was, or of what was done there before I entered the Academy.   I have heard a great deal and read a great deal, and I am compelled to admit I have doubts about much of it.   At the hands of the officers of the institution my treatment didn't differ from that of the other cadets at all, and at the hands of the cadets themselves it differed solely "in the matter of personal public association." I was never persecuted, or abused, or called by approbrious epithets in my hearing after my first year. I am told it has been done, but in my presence there has never been any thing but proper respect shown me. I have mentioned a number of things done to me by cadets, and I have known the same things to be done to white cadets. For instance, I was reported for speaking to a sergeant about the discharge of his duty. (See Chapter X., latter part, on that subject.) The same thing occurred to several members of the class of '74. They were ordered into the rear rank by a sergeant of the second class, when they were first-classmen. They were white. The result was they were all, three in number, I think, put in arrest.

Some New England paper contributes the following articles to this discussion, parts of which I quote :

THE BIGOT AND THE SNOB.

"The Hilton-Seligman controversy is one of those incidents which illustrate some of the features of our social life. The facts can briefly be stated. A Jewish gentleman, of wealth and position, applies for rooms at the Grand Union Hotel, Saratoga, and is flatly refused admission because he is a Jew. The public indignation is so great that the manager of the hotel is obliged to defend the act, and puts in the plea that a man has the right to manage his property as he pleases.

"But before our anger cools, let us remember the case of the colored cadet at West Point. During his course he met with constant rebuffs. He was systematically cut by his fellow-schoolmates. Instead of extending to him a generous sympathy in his noble ambition, they met him with sneers. All the feelings which should guide a chivalric soldier and lead him to honor real heroism, were quenched by the intense prejudice against color. Mean and despicable as is the spirit which prompted the manager of the Grand Union Hotel to refuse to entertain the rich Jewish banker, that which influenced the young men at West Point is still more deserving scorn and contempt. It was meaner and more contemptible than cowardice."

PREJUDICE AGAINST COLOR.

"Within the last thirty years there has been a great change in public sentiment relating to colored persons. That it has become wholly just and kind cannot be shown ; but it is far less unjust and cruel than it used to be. In most of the old free States, at least, tidy, intelligent, and courteous American citizens of African descent are treated with increasing respect for their rights and feelings. In public conveyances we find them enjoying all the consideration and comforts of other passengers. At our public schools they have cordial welcome and fair play. We often see them walking along the street with white schoolmates who have evidently lost sight of the difference in complexions. Colored boys march in the ranks of our school battalions without receiving the slightest insult. Colored men have been United States senators and representatives. Frederick Douglass is Marshal of the District of Columbia.

"There is one conspicuous place, however, where caste-feeling seems to have survived the institution of slavery, and that is West Point. There the old prejudice is as strong, active, and mean as ever. Of this there has been a recent and striking instance in the case of young Flipper who has just graduated. It appears that during his whole course this worthy young man was subjected to the most relentless ' snubbing.' All his fellow-students avoided him habitually. In the recitation-room and upon the parade ground, by day and by night, he was made to feel that he belonged to an inferior and despised race, and that no excellence of deportment, diligence in study, or rank in his class could entitle him to the recognition accorded to every white dunce and rowdy. Yet with rare strength of character he persevered, and when, having maintained the standing of No. fifty in a class of seventy-six, he received his well-earned diploma, there was a round of tardy applause.

"If West Point is to continue to be a school characterized by aristocracy based upon creed, race, or color, so undemocratic and unrepublican as to be out of harmony with our laws and institutions, it will do more harm than good, and, like other nuisances, it should be abated. If our rulers are sincere in their professions, and faithful to their duties, a better state of things may be brought about. Military arts must be acquired somewhere ; but if the present Academy cannot be freed from plantation manners, it may be well to establish a new one without pro-slavery traditions, or, as has been suggested by the Providence *Journal*, to endow military departments in the good colleges where character and not color is the test of worth and manhood.''

(From the New York Sun.)

COLORED CADET FLIPPER.

TWO HUNDRED OF HIS NEW YORK ADMIRERS HONORING HIM WITH A RECEPTION.

" A reception was given last evening by Mr. James W. Moore, in the rooms of the Lincoln Literary Musical Association, 132 West Twenty-seventh Street, to Lieutenant H. O. Flipper, of Georgia, the colored cadet who has just graduated at West Point. Mr. Moore has had charge of the sick room of Commodore Garrison since his illness. The chandeliers were decorated with small flags. On a table on the platform rested a large basket of flowers, bearing the card of Barrett H. Van Auken, a grandson of Commodore Garrison. Among the pictures on the wall were many relating to Lincoln and the emancipation proclamation. Cheerful music was furnished from a harp and violin.

" The guests began to arrive about nine o'clock, the ladies in large numbers, and the room was soon abreeze with a buzz of conversation and the rustle of gayly-colored dresses and bright ribbons.

" The grand entree was at a quarter before ten. Lieutenant Flipper entered the room in full uniform. A heavy yellow horse-hair plume fell down over his cavalry helmet. His coat was new and bright, and glittered with its gold buttons and tasselled aigulets. By his side hung a long cavalry sabre in a gilt scabbard. His appearance was the signal for a buzz of admiration. He is very tall and well made. Beside him was Mr. James W. Moore. Behind him, as he walked through the thronged rooms, were the Rev. Dr. Henry Highland Garnett, and Mrs. Garnett ; the Rev. E. W. S. Peck of the Thirty-fifth Street Methodist Church ; Mr. Charles Remond Douglass, son of Fred Douglass, and United States Consul in San Domingo ; the Rev. J. S. Atwell, of St. Philip's Episcopal Church ; the Rev. John Peterson ; Professor Charles L. Reason, of the Forty-first Street Grammar School ; John J. Zuilille ; Richard Robinson, and others.

" The Lieutenant was led upon the stage by Mr. Garnett and seated at the extreme left, while Dr. Garnett took a seat at the extreme right. Next to the Lieutenant sat Miss Martha J. Moore and Miss Fanny McDonough, Mr. P. S. Porter, Dr. Ray, Mr. Atwell, and Professor Reason completed the semicircle, of which Lieutenant Flipper and Dr. Garnett formed the extremities. The Rev. Mr. Atwell sat in the middle.

"After all were seated, Dr. Garnett called Mr. Douglass forward to a vacant seat on the platform. In introducing Lieutenant Flipper, Dr. Garnett said he had honored himself and his race by his good scholarship and pluck. Nowhere else was there, he thought, such iron-bound and copper-covered aristocracy as in West Point. Who could have thought that any one wearing the ' shadowed livery of the burnished sun ' would ever dare to be an applicant? Young Smith's high personal courage had led him to resent a blow with a blow, and his career in the Academy was cut short. Lieutenant Flipper had encountered the same cold glances, but he had triumphed, and appeared before his friends in the beautiful uniform of the national army. (Applause.) The Doctor believed he would never disgrace it. (Applause, and waving of handkerchiefs by the ladies.)

" At the close of his address, Dr. Garnett said : ' Ladies and gentlemen, I take great pleasure in introducing to you Lieutenant H. O. Flipper.' The Lieutenant rose and bowed low, his hands resting on the hilt of his sabre. He said nothing. Mr. Douglass was introduced, but excused himself from speaking.

"Then Mr. James Crosby was called on. He said when the regiment in which he was orderly sergeant had marched to Port Hudson, General —— met it, and said to Colonel Nelson : ' Colonel, what do you call these? ' ' I call them soldiers,' answered Colonel Nelson. ' Well, if these are soldiers, and if I've got to command niggers, the government is welcome to my commission. Take them down to the right to General Payne. He likes niggers.' ' Soon afterward,' added Mr. Crosby, ' occurred that terrible slaughter of the colored troops which you all remember so well. This year Lieutenant Flipper and a nephew of General —— graduated in the same class, and the colored man rated the highest.'

"After the addresses Lieutenant Flipper descended to the floor, and without formal introductions shook hands with all. He had taken off his cavalry helmet while sitting on the stage. Lemonade and ice-cream were served to the guests. About two hundred persons, all colored, were present. The Lieutenant will start for his home in Georgia on Monday. He will join his regiment, the Tenth Cavalry, on the Rio Grande in November."

(*From the Atlanta (Ga.) Constitution.*)

FLIPPER AGAIN.

" Flipper has flopped up again, and seems to be decidedly in luck. He has been transferred to the Tenth Cavalry, which is alluded to by a New Orleans paper as the ' Tenth Nubian Light Foot.' This, it seems to us, is a dark hint as to the color of this gallant corps, but as the State of Texas lies somewhere between New Orleans and the Rio Grande, we suppose the matter will be allowed to pass. But as to Flipper, Flipper has got his regiment and he has had a reception at the hands of his colored friends and acquaintances in New York. Common people are generally embarrassed at receptions given to themselves, but not so with Flipper. The reception was exceedingly high-toned, as well as highly colored, and took place in the rooms of the ' Lincoln Literary Musical Association.' Flipper, rigged out in full uniform, with a yellow horse-hair plume flowing felicitously over his cavalry helmet, sailed in, according to accounts, just as chipper and as pert as you please. There was no lager beer handed around, but the familiar sound of the band, which was composed of a harp and a violin, made its absence painfully apparent. There were few speeches, but the affair was decidedly formal. When every thing was ready for business, a party of the name of Garnett rose and introduced Flipper, and in the course of his remarks took occasion to attack the newly-made lieutenant by accusing him of wearing ' the sha-dowed livery of the burnished sun.' Whereupon Flipper got up, placed his hands on the hilt of his bloody sabre, and bowed. The crowd then shook hands all around, the music played, and lemonade and ice-cream were brought out from their hiding-places, and all went merry as the milkman's bell. As we said before, Flipper is in luck. He is a distinguished young man. He will reach home during the present week, and it is to be hoped that his friends here are ready to give him an ice-cream lunch, or something of that kind."

(*From the Christian Recorder.*)

LIEUTENANT FLIPPER IN NEW YORK—HIS RECEPTION—CALLS ON BELKNAP.

" Lieutenant Flipper has, by his manly conduct and noble bearing, his superior intellectual powers shown his fellow-cadets and tutors that all the colored student wants is a ' chance.' His term of four years, his graduation, his appointment, will all mark a new era in American history. That the ' feat ' he has accomplished is appreciated has been shown in too many ways to mention. His advent into New York City was marked by many courtesies. His friends, not unmindful of his new field and position, tendered him a grand reception at Lincoln Literary Hall on the 30th of June. It was the writer's good fortune to arrive at New York just in time to be present and pay him similar honors with others. The hall was tastefully and beautifully decorated with flowers and flags, representing the different States in the Union. At the appointed hour the distinguished guests were seen gathering, filling the hall to its utmost capacity. Among the number we noticed especially Dr. H. H. Garnett and Professor Reason. A few and appropriate remarks were made by Dr. Garnett as an introduction, after him others followed. After these formal exercises were over, Mr. Flipper came down from the rostrum and welcomed his friends by a hearty shake of the hand, then all supplied the wants of the inner man by partaking of cream, cake, and lemonade, which were so bountifully supplied. The evening was certainly a pleasant one, as delightful as one could wish, and I presume there was no one present who did not enjoy himself. In addition to what has already been mentioned the occasion was still more enlivened by the strains of sweet music. The exercises of the evening being concluded, the distinguished guests departed each one for his home. Lieutenant Flipper spent some days in New York, and during this visit, as he tells me, ex-Secretary Belknap sent him a written invitation to call on him. This he did, and was received very cordially and congratulated on the victory achieved. He spoke of the pros and cons, and seemed anxious that success might attend his footsteps in all the avenues of army life. That Belknap is interested in the young soldier and desires his success I do not deny ; but whether the ex-Secretary would have given him any assistance when in his power is a question I shall not presume to answer."

(*From the Atlanta* (*Ga.*) *Constitution.*)

FLYING AROUND FLIPPER.

HIS RECEPTION UPON HIS RETURN HOME—EAGERNESS TO SHAKE
THE HAND OF THE "BAD MAN WID DE GUB'MENT STROPS ON !"
—A SOCIAL RECEPTION ON MONDAY NIGHT.

" ' Flip's done come home ! ' was the familiar, and yet admiring manner in which the young negroes about town yesterday spread the information that Second Lieutenant Henry O. Flipper, of the Tenth Cavalry, and the first colored graduate of the United States Military

Academy at West Point, had arrived. His coming has created quite a sensation in colored circles, and when he appeared upon the streets, last evening, taking a drive with his delighted father, he was the cynosure of all the colored people and the object of curious glances from the whites. The young man had ' been there before,' however, and took all the ogling with patience and seeming indifference. Once in awhile he would recognize an old acquaintance and greet him with a smile and a bow.

" The last number of *Frank Leslie's Illustrated Newspaper* contains an excellent likeness of Flipper, dressed in his cadet uniform. His features betray his intelligence, and indicate the culture which he has acquired by hard study. His arrival here was the occasion of a buzz about the Union depot. His parents and a number of intimate friends were present to receive him, and the scene was an interesting one to all concerned.

" ' Dat's him ! ' said a dozen of the curious darkeys who stood off and hadn't the honor of the youth's acquaintance. They seemed to feel lonesome.

" ' He's one ob de United States Gazettes ! ' shouted a young darkey, in reply to a query from a strange negro who has moved here since Flipper went away.

" But the young officer was speedily spirited out of the crowd and taken home to his little bed for a rest.

" On the streets he was greeted by many of our citizens who knew him, and who have watched his career with interest. His success was complimented, and he was urged to pursue his course in the same spirit hereafter. Among his colored friends he was a lion, and they could not speak their praises in language strong enough.

" A darkey would approach the young man, cautiously, feel of his buttons and clothes, and enthusiastically remark : " ' Bad man wid de gub'ment strops on ! '

" These were the expressions of admiration that best suited the ideas of his delighted acquaintances. They will give him a reception on Monday night next, at which all his friends will be present, and some of our leading white citizens will be invited to be present.

" We will try and give the young man's views and experiences in to-morrow's issue."

This paper is noted for its constant prevarication. Whatever it says about negroes is scarcely worth noticing, for be it in their favor or not it is almost certainly untrue. My "delighted father" was not within three hundred miles of Atlanta when I reached that place. I did not appear on the streets in uniform for several days after my arrival, and then only at the request of many friends and an officer of the Second Infantry then at McPherson Barracks.

(*From the Atlanta (Ga.) Republican.*)

" Lieutenant Flipper arrived in our city last week on a visit to his friends. His father lives in Thomasville, but he was educated in this city. His intelligence and manly course has won for him the praise of even the Bourbons."

(*From the Atlanta (Ga.) Republican.*)

" We acknowledge the courtesy of an invitation to a reception given to Lieutenant H. O. Flipper of the Tenth Cavalry, by his colored friends in Atlanta. Circumstances beyond our control prevented our attending.

" We are informed it was a pleasant affair, and that Lieutenant Flipper embraced the opportunity to give something of his four years' experience at West Point, and to correct some of the misstatements of the Atlanta *Constitution* concerning the treatment he received while a cadet at the Military Academy. An article alluding to this subject has been crowded out this week, but will appear in our next issue.

(*From the Augusta (Ga.) Chronicle and Constitutionalist.*)

A FALSEHOOD.

" The Cincinnati *Gazette* says : ' Lieutenant Flipper, the young colored man who is guilty of having been graduated with credit from West Point, continues to be the butt of Georgia Democratic journals.' We would like to know where the *Gazette* gets its information. Flipper has been treated with nothing but kindness in Georgia. Wherever he has reviewed the colored military, accounts of the reviews have been published, but we have yet to see a single word in a Georgia paper in disparagement or ridicule of the colored graduate."

Witness the following from the Atlanta *Constitution :*

FLIPPER AS A FRAUD.

FREEMAN'S PROTEGE ON SOUTHERN CIVILIZATION—HE TALKS AT THE
RECEPTION AND MAKES OF HIMSELF AN ASS—THE ANOMALOUS
CREATURE ON EXHIBITION—HE SHOWS THE CLOVEN FOOT.

" Last night the colored people of the city gave a ' reception ' to
Flipper, of the United States Army. They did this from a feeling of
pride over the fact that one of their color, a townsman, had succeeded in attaining his rank. They doubtless, little suspected that he
would make such use of the occasion as he did. More than one of
them so expressed their feeling before the evening ended. The relations between the races in this city have for years been such as to
make remarks like those in which Flipper indulged not only uncalled
for, but really distasteful. They are not to be blamed for his conduct.

" The crowd that gathered in the hall on the corner of Mitchell and
Broad Streets was large. It was composed almost entirely of well-
dressed and orderly colored people. There were present several of
the white male and female teachers of the negro schools ; also,
some of our white citizens occupying back seats, who were drawn
thither by mere curiosity.

" Flipper was dressed lavishly in regimentals and gold cord, and
sat upon the stage with his immense and ponderous cavalry sabre
tightly buckled around him. He had the attitude of Wellington or
Grant at a council of war. He was introduced to the audience by J.
O. Wimbish, a high-toned negro politician (as was) of this city, who
bespattered the young warrior with an eulogy such as no school-mas-
ter would have written for less than $5 C. O. D. It was real slushy
in its copiousness and diffusiveness.

FRIP FIRES OFF.

" He arose with martial mien, and his left hand resting on his
sabre hilt. He said :

" ' Some weeks ago he had been called upon at a reception in New
York to make a speech, but he had reminded the gentleman who
called upon him that he had been taught to be a soldier and not an
orator. While upon this occasion he still maintained that he was not
an orator, yet he would tell them something of his career at West

Point. He referred to his colored predecessors in the Academy and their fates, particularly of Smith, whose last year there was his (F.'s) first. During that year, on Smith's account, he had received his worst treatment at the Academy. Prejudice against us was strong there at that time. During his first encampment he had a better time than almost any man in his class. In 1874 Smith left, and a rumor prevailed that he (F) was afraid to stay and was going to resign. Colonel Upton, the commandant, sent for him to his house, told him not to do so, but to stick it out. Of course he had no intention of resigning, and he followed this superfluous advice. So far as the cadets were concerned they always treated me fairly, would speak to me, and some came to my room and talked with me, but the only thing they did that was wrong, perhaps, was that they would not associate with me openly. The officers always treated me as well as they did any other cadet. All these reports about my bad treatment there, especially in Southern newspapers, are absolutely false.

" 'I will read and comment upon some of these articles. In *The Constitution* of last Saturday it said I had the hardest four years of any cadet who ever passed through the Academy. That is in some respects true, but not wholly so. Speaking of Ben Butler's son, I am proud to say that among the three hundred cadets I hadn't a better friend than the son of the Massachusetts statesman. (Applause.) As to Mr Bigelow's son, mentioned here, I know him well, and his whole family—his father, the distinguished ex-Secretary of State, his mother and his two sisters, and have met them at their home. Mrs. Bigelow, recognizing my position, and thinking to assure my feelings, sent me a nice box of fruit with her compliments.'

" He then commented on articles from Beecher's *Christian Union*, the New York *Tribune, Harper's Weekly*, and the New York *Telegram*, characterizing many of their statements about himself as false.

SOCIAL EQUALITY IN THE ARMY.

" The article last named was about social equality in the army. Flipper said that he was cordially met by the army officers in Chattanooga. In return he paid his respects to the commandant and was introduced and shown through the barracks. He was treated with every courtesy.

" 'How it is here you have all seen as I walked about the city. I have walked with the officers of the garrison here several times today, even up and down Whitehall Street, and one of them invited me into Schumann's drug store, and had a glass of soda together. I know it is not a usual thing to sell to colored people, but we got it. (Laughter and applause.) And to-night as Mr. J. O. Wimbish and myself were coming to the hall, we met with one of the officers at the corner, and went into Schumann's again. We called for soda-water, and got it again ! (Applause.) And I called at the barracks, through military courtesy, and paid my respects to the commandant. I understand that the officers there have had my case under consideration, and have unanimously agreed that I am a graduate of the national Academy, and hold a commission similar to their own, and am entitled to the same courtesy as any other officer. I have been invited to visit them at their quarters to-morrow. These things show you something of social equality in the army, and when this happens with officers who have lived in the South, and had opportunity to be tainted with Southern feeling, I expect still less trouble from this source when I reach my regiment and among officers who have not lived in the South and had occasion to be tainted in this way. The gentlemen of the army are generally better educated than the people of the South.'

" He spoke of his graduation and of the applause with which he was greeted. He closed by thanking his audience.

FLOURISHING HIS FLIPPER.

" Then Flipper was escorted upon the floor, and the announcement was made that all who desired could now be introduced to the youth.

" The first man to receive this distinguished honor was George Thomas, the Assistant United States Attorney. He was followed closely by several Northern school-marms and teachers, and a host of the colored people.]

" After shaking, the crowd took ice-cream and cake and adjourned. *Sic transit!*"

I pass over the preceding article with the silent contempt it deserves. Some of the papers commented upon it. I give two such articles :

(*From the Atlanta (Ga.) Republican.*)

" The Atlanta *Constitution*, true to principle, comes out in a slanderous attack upon Lieutenant Flipper. In its issue of Tuesday, July 10th, it calls him a fraud. Would to heaven we had ten thousand such frauds in Georgia for the good of the State and progress in general !

"It takes exception, too, to the manner in which the colored lieutenant appeared at the reception given by the colored people in his honor. He was 'lavishly dressed in full regimentals,' it says, ' with gold cord. He sat upon the stage with his massive and ponderous sword, looking like Wellington or Grant in war council. He made remarks uncalled for and distasteful.' Oh dear ! Oh !

"Now we (that is I, this individual, Mr. Editor, for I would not assume your grand editorial pronoun) should like to know how the *Constitution* would have the young officer dress. Surely it was entirely proper and becoming that he should appear in full regimental cap, coat, boots, spurs, and all, full fledged, just as he issued forth from West Point.

"In the first place it was a novel sight for the colored people. Surely the *Constitution* would not rob us of the privilege and pleasure of seeing in full military costume the first and only one of our race who has been permitted to pass through West Point with honor.

"In regard to the ostentatious manner in which the lieutenant conducted himself on that evening, nothing could be further from the truth. In fact, the general comment of the evening by both black and white was on the modesty of his bearing.

"It is not strange, however, that the *Constitution*, whose judgment and sense of right and justice have been perverted through years of persistent sinning, should see things in a different light.

"The ' uncalled for and distasteful ' remarks were doubtless those made in regard to the fact that Northern people coming into contact with Southern prejudice are tainted by it, and that West Pointers are generally better educated than the Southern people. Of course this would stir up the wrath of the *Constitution ;* for what could be more hateful in its sight than truth ?

" Justitia."

(*From the New York World.*)

"Lieutenant Flipper would have shown better sense if he had not made any speech at Atlanta. But if he was to make any speech at all upon the subject of his treatment at West Point, it could scarcely be expected that he should make one more modest, manly and sensible than that which is reported in our news columns."

Here are two other articles of the abusive order from the Southern press :

"J. C. Freeman, the only white man in Georgia that ever disgraced the military of the United States, was in the city yesterday. It will be remembered that this individual at one time misrepresented this district in Congress, and during that time he appointed one negro by color, and Flipper by name, to West Point. But then, nevertheless, the negro is as good as he is, and better too, and we have no doubt but what Freeman thinks he did a big thing, but the good people of the State think different. This notice is not paid for."

"The following is the way the Southerners solidify their section — that is, it is one way—the other, being the masked Kuklux. What it says, however, about the North, is just about so :

"'Lieutenant Flipper, the colored cadet, is in Macon, and the darkies there think him a bigger man that General Grant. They'll want him to be President after awhile, and the Northern people will then be the first to say no.'"

The article of social equality referred to was clipped from the New York *Evening Telegram*. It is as follows :

NEGRO EQUALITY IN THE ARMY.

"There is no danger of negro equality, oh no ! But it will be so delightful for the white soldier to be commanded to pace the greensward before the tent of Lieutenant Flipper, the negro graduate of West Point, and the white soldier will probably indulge in a strange train of thought while doing it. And when promotion comes, and the negro becomes Majah Flippah, or Colonel Flippah, the prospects of the white captains and lieutenants will be so cheerful, particularly if they have families and are stationed at some post in the far West, where any neglect in the social courtesies toward their superior officer would probably go hard with them and their families."

To go back to the article "Flying Around Flipper," I want to say the white people of Georgia can claim no credit for any part of my education. The Storrs school was not a public school at the time I went to school there. It did not become such until I went to West Point. The Atlanta University receives $8000 per annum from the State of Georgia in lieu of the share of the agricultural land scrip due to the colored people for educational purposes. Efforts have been made to take even this from the university, but all have been failures.

(*From the Macon (Ga.) Telegram and Messenger.*)

BATTALION PARADE.

" On Monday evening the colored companies of the city had a battalion parade and review.

" The three companies, viz., the Lincoln Guards, the Bibb County Blues, and the Central City Light Infantry, formed on Fourth Street, and to martial music marched up Mulberry to First, down First to Walnut, up Walnut to Spring Street, and there formed for dress parade and inspection.

" On the right of the line were the Light Infantry under Captain W. H. DeLyons. The Blues bore the colors, and were commanded by Spencer Moses, Captain, and the Guards supported the extreme left. T. N. M. Sellers, Captain of the Lincoln Guards, acted as major. After some preliminary movements the troops were inspected by Lieutenant Flipper, the colored graduate of West Point. The troops then marched around the inspecting officer.

" The line was again formed, and the major addressed Lieutenant Flipper in a short speech, in which was expressed gratitude to the government and thanks to the inspecting officer.

" Lieutenant Flipper replied in a few very sensible and appropriate remarks : That he wished all success, honor, and thanks to the companies for their kindness and courtesy. Hoped they would all make soldiers and fight for their country. That he was a soldier rather than a speaker. That he had tried to do his duty at West Point, and that he expected to continue to try to do his duty, and ' again thanking you for your hospitality, kindness, and attention to myself, I renew my wish for your future success.'

" After the speaking there was a general hand-shaking. The entire parade was very creditable indeed, showing considerable profi-

12

ciency in the tactics, and was witnessed by a large crowd of about twelve hundred of whites and blacks.

"This is the first review ever held by the colored troops in the city of Macon. About eighty men rank and file were out. The colors used was the United States flag. The uniforms were tasty and well gotten up."

There was a very scurrilous article in one of the Charleston (S. C.) papers. I have not been able to get it. I am informed that after commenting on my graduation, assignment, etc., it indulged in much speculation as to my future. It told how I would live, be treated, etc., how I would marry, beget "little Flippers," and rear them up to "don the army blue," and even went far enough to predict their career. It was a dirty piece of literature, and I am not very sorry I couldn't obtain it.

(*From the Atlanta (Ga.) Republican.*)

SUCCESSFUL COLORED YOUNG MEN.

"At length a colored youth has overcome the difficulties that surrounded him as a student at the West Point Military Academy, and has graduated, with the respect of his white associates who were at first very much opposed to him. Mr. Flipper, the successful young man is a Georgia boy, and was appointed a cadet to West Point from the Fifth Congressional District—the Atlanta District—by Congressman Freeman, we believe. He was raised by Rev. Frank Quarles, of this city, and is regarded by him almost as a son.

"John F. Quarles, Esq., the son of Rev. Frank Quarles, is spending a few days with his father. Mr. J. F. Quarles was educated in Pennsylvania since the war, and returned to Georgia in 1870. He read law and was admitted to the Augusta bar after a careful examination before three of the ablest lawyers at that bar, which is noted for its talent. He passed a very creditable examination, and is, we believe, the only colored man who has been admitted to the Georgia bar. He was soon after appointed consul to Port Mahon, in the Mediterranean Sea, and served with credit until he was legislated out of office by the Democratic Congress.   President Hayes recently appointed him consul to Malaga, Spain.

"Rev. Mr. Quarles is justly proud of two such boys."

Here, too, is a venerable colored man claiming the honor of having raised me. Why, I never was away from my mother and father ten consecutive hours in my life until I went to West Point. It is possible, nay, very probable, that he jumped me on his knee, or boxed me soundly for some of my childish pranks, but as to raising me, that honor is my mother's, not his.

Before leaving West Point the following communications were sent me from the head-quarters of the Liberia Exodus Association, 10 Mary Street, Charleston, S. C. I replied in very courteous terms that I was opposed to the whole scheme, and declined to have any thing to do with it. I was in Charleston later in the year, and while there I was besieged by some of the officers of the association, who had not yet despaired of making me "Generalissimo of Liberia's Army," as one of them expressed himself. Wearied of their importunities, and having no sympathy with the movement, I published the following in the Charleston *News and Courier :*

FLIPPER ON LIBERIA.

"Lieutenant Flipper, of the Tenth United States Cavalry, the newly-fledged colored West Pointer, has something to say on the question of the Liberian Exodus, which will be interesting to the people of his race. The lieutenant, by his creditable career as a cadet at the Military Academy, has certainly earned the right to be heard by the colored population with at least as much respect and attention as has been given to the very best of the self-constituted apostles of the Exodus. Here is his letter :

To the Editor of The News and Courier :

" ' SIR : A rumor has come to me from various sources, to the effect that I have promised to resign my commission in the army after serving the two years required by law, and to then accept another as General Commander-in-Chief of the Liberian Army.

" ' It has also come to my notice that many, particularly in the counties adjoining Georgia, are being persuaded, and intend going to Liberia because I have made this promise.

" ' I shall consider it no small favor if you will state that there is no law requiring me to serve *two* years, that I never authorized any such statement as here made, that I have no sympathy whatever for the "Liberian Exodus" movement, that I give it neither countenance nor support, but will oppose it whenever I feel that the occasion requires it. I am not at all disposed to flee from one shadow to grasp at another—from the supposed error of Hayes's Southern policy to the prospective glory of commanding Liberia's army.

" ' Very respectfully, your obedient servant,

" ' HENRY O. FLIPPER,

" ' *Second Lieutenant Tenth U. S. Cavalry.*

" ' CHARLESTON, S. C., October 19, 1877.' "

THE LETTERS FROM CHARLESTON.

ROOMS OF THE LIBERIAN AFRICAN ASSOCIATION,
10 MARY STREET, CHARLESTON, S. C.,
June 22, 1877.

To HENRY O. FLIPPER, ESQ.,

U. S. Military Academy, West Point, N. Y. :

DEAR FRIEND AND BROTHER : Your future, as foreshadowed by the press of this country, looks dismal enough. We have conned its remarks with mingled feelings of sympathy and exultation. Exultation ! because we believe fate has something higher and better in store for you than they or you ever dreamed. Inclosed please find copy of a letter to the Honorable the Secretary of State. We have not yet received a reply. Also, inclosed, a number of the *Missionary Record* containing the call referred to. We have mentioned you in our note to His Excellency Anthony Gardner, President of Liberia. Please communicate with us and say if this letter and inclosures do not open up a bright vista in the future to your imagination and reasonable aspirations ? *We* picture to ourselves our efforts to obtain a line of steamers crowned with success ; and behold you as commander-in-chief organizing and marshalling Liberia's military forces in the interests of humanity at large, and the especial development of a *grand* African nationality that shall command the respect of the nations :

So Afric shall resume her seat in the
    Hall of Nations vast ;
And strike upon her restrung lyre
    The requiem of the past :
And sing a song of thanks to God,
    For his great mercy shown,
In leading, with an outstretched arm,
    The benighted wanderer home.   Selah !

Provide yourself at once with maps, etc., master the chorography of Africa in general, and the topography of Liberia in particular, that is to say, the whole range of the Kong mountains, including its eastern slope on to the Niger, our natural boundary ! for the next thirty years ! after that, onward ! Cultivate especially the artillery branch of the service ; this is the arm with which we can most surely overawe all thought of opposition among the native tribes ; whilst military engineering will dot out settlements with forts, against which, they will see, 'twould be madness to hurl themselves. We desire to absorb and cultivate them. The great obstacle to this is their refusal to have their *girls* educated. This results from their institution of polygamy. Slavery is the same the world over—it demands the utter ignorance of its victims. We must compel their enlightenment. Have we not said enough ? Does not your intelligence grasp, and your ambition spring to the great work ? Let us hear from you. You can be a great power in assisting to carry out our Exodus. If you desire we will elect you a member of our council and keep you advised of our proceedings. We forward you by this mail some of our numbers and the Charleston *News* of the 20th. See the article on yourself, and let it nerve you to thoughts and deeds of greatness. Let us know something about Baker and McClennan. Are they at Annapolis ? Cadets ? (We will require a navy as well as an army.) Also something about yourself. What part of the State are you from ? Hon. R. H. Cain is not here, or probably he could inform us.

Affectionately yours. By our President,

B. F. PORTER,
Pastor of Morris Brown Chapel.

GEO. CURTIS, *Corresponding Secretary.*

P. S.—We have received a reply from the Secretary of State— very courteous in its tone—but " regrets" to say that he has " no special means of forming an opinion upon the subject. The measure referred to would require an Act of Congress, in respect to whose future proceedings it would not be prudent to venture a prediction."

The answer is all we expected. We have made ourselves known to, and are recognized by, the Executive ; our next step is to address Senators Morton and Blaine—Hon. R. H. Cain will see to it, that the question is pushed in the House.   G. C.

COPY.

ROOMS OF THE LIBERIA EXODUS ASSOCIATION,)
10 MARY STREET, CHARLESTON, S. C.   }
June 14, 1877.   )

HON. WM. J. EVARTS,
        Secretary of State, Washington, D. C. :

SIR : Inclosed please find a call on our people to prepare to organize for an exodus to Liberia.

We think it explains itself, but any further explanation called for we will gladly supply.

In the event of a sufficient response to our call, please inform us if there is any probability of our government placing one or more steamers on the route between here, or Port Royal, and Liberia for our transportation ; and if so, then the charge for passage ; and if, to those unable to pay ready money, time will be given, and the payment received in produce ?

Tens of thousands are now eager to go from this State alone, but we want a complete exodus, if possible, from the whole United States ; thus leaving *you* a homogeneous people, opening up an immense market for your products, giving a much required impetus to your trade, commerce, and manufactures ; and for *ourselves* attaining a position where, removed from under the shade of a " superior race," we will have full opportunity for developing whatever capacity of soul growth our Creator has endowed us with.

That Africa *will be* developed, and chiefly through the instrumentality of its five millions of descendants in America, is certain. Now the question is, who shall have the chief handling and consequent benefit of this grand instrument, next to itself, of course, for we are treating of a sentient instrumentality. We beseech you that you do not send us, Columbus-like, from court to court offering the development of a new world to incredulous ears. We are asking the President of Liberia, the American Colonization Society, and all friends of the measure, for their aid, advice, and co-operation.

We desire to carry our first shipment of emigrants not later than September or October proximo.

We have the honor to be, Sir, in all respect and loyalty, yours to command.

The Council of the L. E. A.   By our President,

B. F. PORTER,

Pastor Morris Brown A. M. E. Church.

GEO. CURTIS, *Corresponding Secretary.*

Here is an article from some paper in New Orleans. Contempt is all it deserves. I am sure all my readers will treat it as I do. Frogs will croak, won't they?

LIEUTENANT FLIPPER.

" With the successful examination of the colored cadet Flipper, at West Point, and his appearance in the gazette as a full-fledged lieutenant of cavalry, the long vexed question has been settled just as it ceased to be a question of any practical import. Out of three or four experiments Flipper is the one success. As the whole South has now passed into Democratic control, and the prospect for Southern Republican congressmen is small, the experiments will hardly be repeated, and he must stand for those that might have been.

"It would be interesting to know how Flipper is to occupy his time. The usual employments of young lieutenants are of a social nature, such as leading the German at Narraganset Pier and officiating in select private theatricals in the great haunts of Fashion. Flipper is described as a little bow-legged *grif* of the most darkly coppery hue, and of a general pattern that even the most enthusiastic would find it hard to adopt. Flipper is not destined to uphold the virtues and graces of his color in the salons of Boston and New York, then, nor can he hope to escape the disagreeably conspicuous solitude he now inhabits among his fellow-officers through any of those agencies of usage and familiarity which would result if other Flippers were to follow him into the army and help to dull the edge of the innovation. Just what Flipper is to do with himself does not seem altogether clear. Even the excitement of leading his men among the redskins will be denied him, now that Spotted Tail has pacified the malcontents and Sitting Bull has retired to the Canadas. It is to be presumed that those persons who patronized Flipper and had him sent to West Point are gratified at the conclusion, and there is a sort of reason for believing that Flipper himself is contented with the lot

he has accepted ; but whether the experiment is worth all the annoyance it occasions is a problem not so easily disposed of.

" His prospects don't appear to be very brilliant as regards social
delights or domestic enjoyments, but of course that is Flipper's business—not ours. It merely struck us that things had happened a little unfortunately for him, to become the lonesome representative of
h:s race in the midst of associations that object to him and at a time
when the supply of colored officers is permanently cut off. Personally we are not interested in Flipper."

I am indebted to a Houston Texas, paper for the
following :

THE COLORED WEST POINTER.

" We had a call yesterday from Lieutenant H. O. Flipper, of the
United States Army. Mr. Flipper, it will be remembered, is the colored cadet who graduated at the Military Academy at West Point
last session, occupying in his class a position that secured his appointment to the cavalry service, a mark of distinction. He was
gazetted as second lieutenant in the Tenth Cavalry, and he enjoys
the honor of being the first colored man who has passed by all the
regular channels into an official station in the army.

" This young officer is a bright mulatto, tall and soldierly, with a
quiet unobtrusive manner, and the bearing of a gentleman. As the
forerunner of his race in the position he occupies, he is placed in a
delicate and trying situation, a fact which he realizes. He remarked
that he knew it was one of the requirements of an officer of the army
to be a gentleman, a man of honor and integrity under all circumstances, and he hoped to be equal to his duties in this regard. He
goes on to Fort Concho to join his regiment, which is likely to have
work to do soon, if there is any thing in the signs of the times.

" We bespeak for this young officer the just consideration to
which the difficulties of his position entitle him."

I was originally ordered to Fort Concho, but at
Houston, Texas I met my lieutenant-colonel, who
informed me that my company was *en route* to Fort
Sill. My orders were then changed, and I proceeded
to Sill.

Here is another article from a paper in the same place :

THE DIFFERENCE.

"The *Age* yesterday had a call from Henry O. Flipper second lieutenant Tenth United States Cavalry, who is on his way under orders to join his regiment at Fort Concho. So far there is nothing very unusual in this item, but interest will be given to it when we add that Lieutenant Flipper is the first colored graduate of West Point. He went to the institution from Georgia, and graduated last June, fifty-fifth in a class of seventy-six. There is a preponderance of white blood in his veins, and in general appearance, except for color, he is a perfect image of Senator Plumb of Kansas. He reports that since he has struck the South he has been treated like a gentleman, *which is something different from his experience in the North.* He made the acquaintance of Senator Maxey at West Point—the Senator himself being a graduate of the Academy—and regards him as a very pleasant gentleman. During the ten minutes he spent in the *Age* editorial rooms several prominent democrats of the city called to see and shake hands with him, partly out of curiosity to see the colored cadet who was *so bitterly persecuted by Northern students at West Point,* and partly to bid him a welcome to the South such as none of his political party friends would have thought of giving him in the North. *Before many years he will be, as all intelligent colored men will be, a democrat.*"

Wherever I have travelled in the South it has been thrown into my face that the Southern people had, would, and did treat me better than the Northern people. This is wholly untrue. It is true that the men generally speak kindly and treat me with due courtesy, but never in a single instance has a Southern man introduced me to his wife or even invited me to his house. It was done North in every place I stopped. In many cases, when invited to visit gentlemen's residences, they have told me they wanted their wives to meet me. A distinguished New York lady, whose name has occurred in print several times with mine, gave me with her own hands a handsome floral tribute, just after receiving my diploma. During five months' stay in the South, after my graduation, not a single Southern white woman spoke to me. I mistake. I did buy some articles from one who kept a book-store in a country town in Georgia. This is the only exception. This is the way Southern people treated me better than Northern people. The white people (men) of Houston, Texas, showed me every possible courtesy while I was there. My treatment there was in high and honorable contrast to that I received in Atlanta.

Here are two articles that have a few words to say about me. I adopt and quote them at length :

(From the New York Tribune.)

WEST POINT.

" The examinations of the boys in the national school have become an object of national interest this year more than any other, simply because there is a stagnation of other news. While the public is waiting for an outbreak from Kars or the new party, it has leisure to look into the condition of these incipient officers. Hence reporters have crowded to West Point, the Board of Visitors and cadets have both been quickened to unwonted zeal by the consciousness of the blaze of notoriety upon them, and the country has read with satisfaction each morning of searching examinations and sweeping cavalry charges, giving a shrug, however, at the enthusiastic recommendation of certain members of the board that the number of yearly appointments should be doubled or quadrupled. In this cold ague of economy with which the nation is attacked just now, and which leaves old army officers unpaid for a disagreeably long time, the chances of any addition to the flock in the nest are exceedingly small. In fact, while the average American in war time recognized the utility of a trained band of tacticians, he is apt to grumble at their drain upon his pocket in piping times of peace. Only last year he relieved himself in Congress and elsewhere by a good deal of portentous talking as to the expediency of doing away with the naval and military free schools altogether. He has, in short, pretty much the opinion of the army officer that Hodge has of his parish priest, ' useful enough for Sundays and funerals, but too consumedly expensive a luxury for week days.'

" This opinion, no doubt, appears simply ludicrous and vulgar to the gallant young fellows who are being trained for their country's service up the Hudson, and who already look upon themselves as its supports and bulwarks, but there is a substratum of common-sense in it which we commend to their consideration, because, if for no other reason, that the average American is the man who pays their bills and to whom they owe their education and future livelihood. If they do not accept his idea of the conduct and motives of action by which they may properly repay him the debt they owe, it certainly is fitting that their own idea should be indisputably a higher one. We begin to doubt whether it is not much lower. The country, in establishing this school, simply proposed to train a band of men skilled to serve it when needed as tacticians, engineers, or disciplinarians ; the more these men founded their conduct on the bases of good sense, honor, and republican principles, the better and higher would be their service. The idea of the boys themselves, however, within later years, seems to be that they constitute an aristocratic class (moved by any thing but republican principles) entitled to lay down their own laws of good-breeding and honor. Accounts which reach us of their hazing, etc., and notably their treatment of the colored cadets, show that these notions are quite different from those accepted elsewhere. Now such ideas would be natural in pupils of the great French or Austrian military schools, where admission testifies to high rank by birth or to long, patient achievement on the part of the student. But really our boys at West Point must remember that they belong to a nation made up of working and trades men ; that they are the sons of just such people ; that the colored laborer helps to pay for their support as well as that of the representative of his race who sits beside them. Furthermore, they have done nothing as yet to entitle them to assume authority in such matters. They have recited certain lessons, learned to drill and ride, and to wear their clothes with precision ; but something more is needed. The knight of old was skilled in gentleness and fine courtesy to the weak and unfortunate as well as in horsemanship. It was his manners, not his trousers, which were beyond reproach.

" It is not as trifling a matter as it seems that these young fellows should thus imbibe mistaken ideas of their own position or the requirements of real manliness and good-breeding. The greatest mistakes in the war were in consequence of just such defects in some of our leading officers, and the slaughter of the Indians in the South-West upon two occasions proceeded from their inability to recognize the rights of men of a different color from themselves. Even in trifles, however, such matters follow the rule of inexorable justice—as, for instance, in this case of Cadet Flipper, who under ordinary circumstances might have passed without notice, but is now known from one end of the country to the other as a credit to his profession in scholarship, pluck, and real dignity ; while his classmates are scarcely mentioned, though higher in rank, except in relation to their cruel and foolish conduct toward him."

(*From the New York World.*)

" WEST POINT, August 29.—In my earnest desire to do justice to the grand ball last night I neglected to mention the arrival of the new colored candidate for admission into the United States, Military Academy, although I saw him get off at the steamboat landing and was a witness to the supreme indifference with which he was treated, save by a few personal friends. Minnie passed the physical examination easily, for he is a healthy mulatto. Whether this stern Alma Mater will matriculate him is still a question. It is really astonishing, and perhaps alarming, in view of the enthusiastic endeavors of the Republican party to confer upon the colored race all the rights and privileges of citizens of the United States, to see with what lofty contempt every candidate for academic honors who is in the slightest degree ' off color,' is received. As you are aware, there is at present a colored, or partly colored, cadet in the Freshman Class—Whittaker by name. This poor young mulatto is completely ostracized not only by West Point society, but most thoroughly by the corps of cadets itself. Flipper got through all right, and, strange to say, the cadets seem to have a certain kind of respect for him, although he was the darkest ' African ' that has yet been seen among the West Point cadets. Flipper had remarkable pluck and nerve, and was accorded his parchment—well up on the list, too—at last graduation day. He is made of sterner staff than poor Whittaker.

" A most surprising fact is that not one of the cadets—and I think I might safely include the professors—tries to dissemble his animosity for the black, mulatto, or octoroon candidate. When I asked a cadet to-day some questions concerning the treatment of Cadet Whittaker by the corps, he said : ' Oh, we get along very well, sir. The cadets simply ignore him, and he understands very well that we do not intend to associate with him.' This cadet and several others were asked whether Minnie, if admitted, would also be ostracized socially. Their only answer was : ' Certainly ; that is well understood by all. We don't associate with these men, but they have all the rights that we have nevertheless.' I asked if he knew whether Whittaker attended the ball last night. The cadet said he didn't see him at the ball, but that he might have been looking on from the front stoop ! ' How does this young man Whittaker usually amuse himself when the rest of the boys are at play ? ' I asked. ' Well, we don't get much play, and I think that Whittaker has as much as he can do to attend to his studies. He managed to pull through at last examination, but I doubt if he ever graduates,' was the reply. Meeting another cadet to whom I had been introduced I asked what he had heard of the prospects of the new colored candidate, Minnie. ' I haven't heard any thing, but I hope he won't get through,' said the cadet. Another cadet who stood near said that the case of Flipper, who graduated so successfully, was an exceptional one. Flipper didn't care for any thing except to graduate, but he was confident that these other colored cadets would fail. So far as I have been able to ascertain, the Faculty have never attempted to prevent the colored cadets from having an equal chance with their white fellows. In fact under the present management it would be next to impossible for them to do so.''

I can't let this article pass without quoting a few words from a letter I have from Whittaker, now at West Point. He says :

" I have been treated bully since I came in from camp (of summer of '77). Got only one ' skin ' last month (Deccember, '77). I am still under ' —— ' (tactical officer), and he treats me bully ; he wanted to have a man court-martialled, when we were in camp, for refusing to close up on me. One day a corporal put me in the rear rank when there were plebes in the front rank, and —— told him if any such act ever occurred again he would have him and the file confined to the guard-house. He has never ' skinned ' me since you left. He is O.K. towards me, and the others are afraid of him. . . . . As I am sitting in my room on third floor, sixth ' div,' a kind of

sadness creeps over me, for I am all alone. Minnie went home on last
Friday. He was weighed in the 'math' scale and found wanting. The poor fellow did not study his 'math' and could not help
being 'found.' He was treated *fairly and squarely*, but he did not
study. I did all I could to help and encourage him, but it was all in
vain. He did not like —— (an instructor) very much, and a carelessness seized him, which resulted in his dismissal. I was sorry to see
him go away, and he himself regretted it very much. He saw his
great error only when it was too late. On the day he left he told me
that he did not really study a 'math' lesson since he entered ; and
was then willing to give any thing to remain and redeem himself.
He had a very simple subject on examination, and when he came
back *he told me that he had not seen* the subject for some two or three
weeks before, and he, consequently, did not know what to put on the
board. All he had on it was wrong, and he could not make his de-
monstration."

The *World* reporter seems to be as ignorant as
some of the others. I was by no means the " darkest ' African ' that has yet been seen among the West
Point cadets." Howard, who reported in 1870 with
Smith, was unadulterated, as also were Werle and
White, who reported in 1874. There were others who
were also darker than I am : Gibbs and Napier, as I
am informed. I never saw the last two.

The Brooklyn *Eagle* is more generous in its
views. It proposes to utilize me. See what it says :

" Probably Lieutenant Flipper could be made much more usefu
than as a target for Indian bullets, if our government would withdraw him from the army and place him in some colored college, where
he could teach the pupils engineering, so that when they reach Africa
they could build bridges, railroads, etc."

This article was signed by " H. W. B." It is not
difficult to guess who that is.

I have had considerable correspondence with an
army officer, a stranger to me, on this subject of

being detailed at some college. He is of opinion it would be best for me. I could not agree with him. After I joined my company an effort (unknown to me) was made by the Texas Mechanical and Agricultural College to have me detailed there. It was published in the papers that I had been so detailed. I made some inquiries, learned of the above statements, and that the effort had completely failed. Personally I'd rather remain with my company. I have no taste and no tact for teaching. I would decline any such appointment.

(*From the Thomasville (Ga.) Times.*)

"Wm. Flipper, the colored cadet, has graduated at West Point and been commissioned as a second lieutenant of cavalry in the United States Army. He is the first colored individual who ever held a commission in the army, and it remains to be seen how the thing will work. Flipper's father resides here, and is a first-class boot and shoe maker. A short time back he stated that he had no idea his son would be allowed to graduate, but he will be glad to know that he was mistaken."

Of course everybody knows my name is not William.

(*From the Thomasville (Ga.) Enterprise.*)

"Lieutenant Henry O. Flipper of the United States Army is spending a few days here with his father's family, he has been on the streets very little, spending most of his time at home. He wears an undress uniform and deports himself, so far as we have heard, with perfect propriety. This we believe he has done since his graduation, with the exception of his unnecessary and uncalled-for criticisms on the Southern people in his Atlanta speech. He made a mistake there ; one which his sense and education ought to teach him not to repeat. Not that it would affect our people, or that they care about it, but for his own good."*

---

* In all the places I visited after graduation I was treated with the utmost respect and courtesy except in Atlanta. The white people, with one exception, didn't notice me at all. All foreigners treated me with all due consideration. One young

That " undress uniform" was a " cit " suit of blue Cheviot. The people there, like those in Atlanta, don't seem to know a black button from a brass one, or a civilian suit from a military uniform.

(*From the Charleston (S. C.) News and Courier.*)

THE COLORED WESTPOINTER.

" Lieutenant H. O. Flipper, the colored graduate of West Point, was entertained in style at Tully's, King Street, Tuesday night. The hosts were a colored organization called the Amateur Literary and Fraternal Association, which determined that the lieutenant who will leave this city to-day to join his regiment, the Tenth Cavalry, now in Texas, should not do so without some evidence of their appreciation of him personally, and of the fact that he had reflected credit on their race by passing through the National Academy. Over forty persons were at the entertainment, to whom the lieutenant was presented by A. J. Ransier, the colored ex-member of Congress. The lieutenant responded briefly, as he has invariably done, and expressed his warm thanks for the courtesy shown by the association. A number of sentiments were offered and speeches made, and the evening passed off very agreeably to all, especially so to the recipient of the hospitality.

" Lieutenant Flipper expects to start to-day for Texas. While he has been in this city he has made friends with whites and blacks by he sensible course he has pursued."

---

man, whom I knew many years, who has sold me many an article, and awaited my convenience for his pay, and who met me in New York, and walked and talked with me, hung his head and turned away from me, just as I was about to address him on a street in Atlanta. Again and again have I passed and repassed acquaintances on the streets without any sign of recognition, even when I have addressed them. Whenever I have entered any of their stores for any purpose, they have almost invariably " gotten off " some stuff about attempts on the part of the authorities at West Point to "freeze me out," or about better treatment from Southern boys than from those of the North. That is how they treated me in Atlanta, although I had lived there over fourteen years, and was known by nearly every one in the city. In Thomasville, Southwest, Ga., where I was born, and which I had not seen for eighteen years, I was received and treated by the whites almost as one of themselves.

(*From the Charleston (S. C.) Commercial.*)

LIEUTENANT FLIPPER'S ENTERTAINMENT.

" The Amateur Literary and Fraternal Association, of which A. J. Ransier is the President, learning that Lieutenant Flipper, of the United States Cavalry, was preparing to depart to the position assigned him on duty on the plains in Texas, at once determined to give him a reception, and for this purpose the following committee was appointed to arrange the details and programme for an entertainment : J. N. Gregg, W. H. Birny, A. J. Ransier, C. C. Leslie, and George A. Gibson.

" The arrangements were made, and the members of the association and invited guests to the number of some forty, of the most respectable colored people of Charleston, met last night at Tully's Hall, King Street, where a bounteous feast was prepared for the occasion. The guest, Lieutenant Flipper, soon arrived, and was introduced to the party, and, in the course of time, all sat down at the table, upon which was spread the most palatable dishes which the king caterer of Charleston could prepare. This was vigorously attacked by all.

" Wines were then brought on, and speech-making introduced as a set off. A. J. Ransier, in one of his usual pleasant speeches, introduced Lieutenant Flipper, paying him a deserved tribute for his success in the attainment of the first commission issued to a colored graduate of West Point.

" Lieutenant Flipper, in a brief and courteous speech, acknowledged the compliment, and thanked the association for the kind attention paid him, promising them that in his future career in the army of his country he would ever strive to maintain a position which would do credit to his race.

" W. H. Birney next responded in eloquent terms to the toast, ' The State of South Carolina.' J. N. Gregg was called upon, and responded in a wise and discreet manner to the toast of ' The Future of the Colored Man in this Country.' ' The Press,' and ' Woman' were next respectively toasted, and responded to by Ransier and F. A. Carmand. Other speeches were made by C. C. Leslie, J. J. Connor, and others, and at a late hour the party retired, after a most pleasant evening's enjoyment. Lieutenant Flipper leaves for Texas to-morrow."

Before closing my narrative I desire to perform a very pleasant duty. I sincerely believe that all my

success at West Point is due not so much to my perseverance and general conduct there as to the early
moral and mental training I received at the hands of
those philanthropic men and women who left their
pleasant homes in the North to educate and elevate
the black portion of America's citizens, and that,
too, to their own discomfort and disadvantage. How
they have borne the sneers of the Southern press, the
ostracism from society in the South, the dangers of
Kuklux in remote counties, to raise up a downtrod-
den race, not for personal aggrandizement, but for
the building up and glory of His kingdom who is no
respecter of persons, is surely worthy our deepest
gratitude, our heartfelt thanks, and our prayers and
blessing.   Under the training of a good Christian old
lady, too old for the work, but determined to give
her mite of instruction, I learned to read and to
cipher—this in 1866.   From her I was placed under
control of a younger person, a man.   From him I
passed to the control of another lady at the famous
"Storr's School."   I remained under her for two
years more or less, when I passed to the control of
another lady in what was called a Normal School.
From here I went to the Atlanta University, and
prepared for the college course, which in due time I
took up.   This course of training was the foundation
of all my after-success.   The discipline, which I
learned to heed, because it was good, has been of in-
calculable benefit to me.   It has restrained and
shaped my temper on many an occasion when to
have yielded to it would have been ruin.   It has
regulated my acts when to have committed them as
I contemplated would have been base unmanliness.

And it has made my conduct in all cases towards others generous, courteous, and Christian, when it might otherwise have been mean, base, and degrading. It taught me to be meek, considerate, and kind, and I have verily been benefited by it.

The mind-training has been no less useful. Its thoroughness, its completeness, and its variety made me more than prepared to enter on the curriculum of studies prescribed at West Point. A less thorough, complete, or varied training would never have led to the success I achieved. I was not prepared expressly for West Point. This very thoroughness made me competent to enter any college in the land.

How my heart looks back and swells with gratitude to these trainers of my youth! My gratitude is deeply felt, but my ability to express it is poor. May Heaven reward them with long years of happiness and usefulness here, and when this life is over, and its battles won, may they enter the bright portals of heaven, and at His feet and from His own hands receive crowns of immortal glory.

CHAPTER XVII.

JAMES WEBSTER SMITH, a native of South Carolina, was appointed to a cadetship at the United States Military Academy at West Point, New York, in 1870, by the Hon. S. L. Hoge. He reported, as instructed, at the Military Academy in the early summer of 1870, and succeeded in passing the physical and intellectual examination prescribed, and was received as a "conditional cadet." At the same time one Howard reported, but unfortunately did not succeed in "getting in."

In complexion Smith was rather light, possibly an octoroon. Howard, on the contrary, was black. Howard had been a student at Howard University, as also had been Smith. Smith, before entering the Academy, had graduated at the Hartford High School, and was well prepared to enter upon the new course of studies at West Point.

In studies he went through the first year's course without any difficulty, but unfortunately an *affaire d'honneur*—a "dipper fight"—caused him to be put back one year in his studies In going over this course again he stood very high in his class, but when it was finished he began going down gradually until he became a member of the last section of his class, an "immortal," as we say, and in constant danger of being "found."

He continued his course in this part of his class

till the end of his second class year, when he was declared deficient in natural and experimental philosophy, and dismissed. At this time he had been in the Academy four years, but had been over only a three-years' course, and would not have graduated until the end of the next year, June, 1875.

As to his trials and experiences while a cadet, I shall permit him to speak. The following articles embrace a series of letters written by him, after his dismissal, to the *New National Era and Citizen*, the political organ of the colored people, published at Washington, D. C. :

THE COLORED CADET AGAIN.

PERTINENT OR IMPERTINENT CARD FROM CADET SMITH.

" COLUMBIA, S. C., July 27, 1874.

To the Editor of the National Republican :

" SIR : I saw an article yesterday in one of our local papers, copied from the Brooklyn *Argus*, concerning my dismissal from the Military Academy. The article referred to closes as follows : ' Though he has written letters to his friends, and is quite sanguine about returning and finally graduating, the professors and cadets say there is not the slightest chance. Said a professor to a friend, the other day : " It will be a long time before any one belonging to the colored race can graduate at West Point." '

" Now, Sir, I would like to ask a few questions through the columns of your paper concerning these statements, and would be glad to have them answered by some of the knowing ones.

" In the first place, what do the professors and cadets know of my chances for getting back, and if they know any thing, how did they find it out ? At an interview which I had with the Secretary of War, on the 17th instant, he stated that he went to West Point this year for a purpose, and that he was there both before and after my examination, and conversed with some of the professors concerning me. Now, did that visit and those conversations have any thing to do with

the finding of the Academic Board ? Did they have any thing to do
with that wonderful wisdom and foresight displayed by the professors
and cadets in commenting upon my chances for getting back ? Why
should the Secretary of War go to West Point this year ' for a purpose,' and converse with the professors about me both *before* and *after*
the examination ? Besides, he spoke of an interview he had had with
Colonel Ruger, Superintendent of the Academy, in New York, on Sunday, the 12th instant, in reference to me ; during which Colonel Ruger
had said that the Academic Board would not recommend me to return.
Is it very wonderful that the Academic Board should refuse such recommendation after those very interesting conversations which were
held ' both *before* and *after* the recommendation ? ' Why was the
secretary away from West Point *at the time of* the examination.

"In the next place, by what divine power does that learned oracle,
a professor, prophesy that it will be a long time before any one belonging to the colored race can graduate at West Point? It seems
that he must have a wonderful knowledge of the negro that he can
tell the abilities of all the colored boys in America. But it is possible
that he is one of the younger professors, perhaps the professor of philosophy, and therefore expects to live and preside over that department for a long time, though to the unsophisticated mind it looks
very much as though he would examine a colored cadet on the color
of his face.

"I think he could express himself better and come much nearer the
truth by substituting *shall* for *can* in that sentence. Of course, while
affairs remain at West Point as they have always been, and are now,
no colored boy will graduate there ; but there are some of us who are
sanguine about seeing a change, even if we can't get back.

" J. W. SMITH,
" <i>Late Cadet U. S. M. A.</i>"</div>

THE DIPPER DIFFICULTY.

" COLUMBIA, S. C., July 30, 1874.

To the Editor of the New National Era :

"As I told you in my last communication, I shall now proceed to
give you an account of my four years' stay at West Point.

"I reported there on the 31st of May, 1870, and had not been there
an hour before I had been reminded by several thoughtful cadets that
I was ' nothing but a d—d nigger.' Another colored boy, Howard,
of Mississippi, reported on the same day, and we were put in the same

room, where we stayed until the preliminary examination was over, and Howard was sent away, as he failed to pass.

" While we were there we could not meet a cadet anywhere with. out having the most opprobrious epithets applied to us ; but after complaining two or three times, we concluded to pay no attention to such things, for, as we did not know these cadets, we could get no satisfaction.

" One night about twelve o'clock some one came into our room, and threw the contents of his slop-pail over us while we were asleep. We got to our door just in time to hear the ' gentleman ' go into his room on the floor above us.   This affair reported itself the next morning at ' Police Inspection,' and the inspector ordered us to search among the tobacco quids, and other rubbish on the floor, for something by which we might identify the perpetrator of the affair.   The search resulted in the finding of an old en-velope, addressed to one McCord, of Kentucky.   That young ' gen-tleman ' was questioned in reference, but succeeded in convincing the authorities that he had nothing to do with the affair and knew nothing of it.

" A few days after that, Howard was struck in the face by that young ' gentleman,' ' because,' as he says, ' the d—d nigger didn't get out of the way when I was going into the boot-black's shop.' For that offence Mr. McCord was confined to his room, but was never punished, as in a few days thereafter he failed at the pre-liminary examination, and was sent away with all the other unfortu-nates, including Howard.

" On the 28th of June, 1870, those of us who had succeeded in pass-ing the preliminary examination were taken in ' plebe camp,' and there I got my taste of ' military discipline,' as the petty persecu-tions of about two hundred cadets were called.   Left alone as I was, by Howard's failure, I had to take every insult that was offered, with-out saying anything, for I had complained several times to the Com-mandant of Cadets, and, after ' investigating the matter,' he invari-ably came to the conclusion, ' from the evidence deduced,' that I was in the wrong, and I was cautioned that I had better be very par-ticular about any statements that I might make, as the regulations were very strict on the subject of veracity.

" Whenever the ' plebes ' (new cadets) were turned out to ' police ' camp, as they were each day at 5 A.M. and 4 P.M., certain cadets would come into the company street and spit out quids of tobacco which they would call for me to pick up.   I would get a broom and shovel for the purpose, but they would immediately begin swearing at and abusing 'me for not using my fingers, and then the corporal of police would order me to put down that broom and shovel, 'and not to try to play the gentleman here,' for my fingers were 'made for that purpose.' Finding there was no redress to be had there, I wrote my friend Mr. David Clark, of Hartford, Ct., to do something for me. He had my letter published, and that drew the attention of Congress to the matter, and a board was sent to West Point to inquire into the matter and report thereon. That board found out that several cadets were guilty of conduct unbecoming a cadet and a gentleman and recommended that they be court-martialled, but the Secretary of War thought a reprimand would be sufficient. Among those reprimanded were Q. O'M. Gillmore, son of General Gillmore ; Alex. B. Dyer, son of General Dyer ; and James H. Reid, nephew of the Secretary of War (it is said). I was also reprimanded for writing letters for publication.

"Instead of doing good, these reprimands seemed only to increase the enmity of the cadets, and they redoubled their energies to get me into difficulty, and they went on from bad to worse, until from words they came to blows, and then occurred that 'little onpleasantness' known as the 'dipper fight.' On the 13th of August, 1870, I, being on guard, was sent to the tank for a pail of water. I had to go a distance of about one hundred and fifty yards, fill the pail by drawing water from the faucet in a dipper (the faucet was too low to permit the pail to stand under it), and return to the guard tent in ten minutes. When I reached the tank, one of my classmates, J. W. Wilson, was standing in front of the faucet drinking water from a dipper. He didn't seem inclined to move, so I asked him to stand aside as I wanted to get water for the guard. He said : 'I'd like to see any d—d nigger get water before I get through.' I said : 'I'm on duty, and I've got no time to fool with you,' and I pushed the pail toward the faucet. He kicked the pail over, and I set it up and stooped down to draw the water, and then he struck at me with his dipper, but hit the brass plate on the front of my hat and broke his dipper. I was stooping down at the time, but I stood up and struck him in the face with my left fist ; but in getting up I did not think of a tent fly that was spread over the tank, and that pulled my hat down over my eyes. He then struck me in the face with the handle of his dipper (he broke his dipper at the first blow), and then I struck him two or three times with my dipper, battering it, and cutting him very severely on the left side of his head near the temple. He bled very profusely, and fell on the ground near the tank.

"The alarm soon spread through the camp, and all the cadets came running to the tank and swearing vengeance on the 'd—d nigger.'

"An officer who was in his tent near by came out and ordered me to be put under guard in one of the guard tents, where I was kept until next morning, when I was put 'in arrest.' Wilson was taken to the hospital, where he stayed two or three weeks, and as soon as he returned to duty he was also placed in arrest. This was made the subject for a court-martial, and that court-martial will form the subject of my next communication.

" Yours respectfully,
" J. W. SMITH,
" <i>Late Cadet U. S. M. A.</i>"</div>

THE INJUSTICE AT WEST POINT.

" COLUMBIA, S. C., August 7, 1874.

To the Editor of the New National Era :

"SIR : In my last communication I related the circumstances of the 'dipper fight,' and now we come to the court-martial which resulted therefrom.

"But there was another charge upon which I was tried at the same time, the circumstances of which I will detail.

"On the 15th of August, 1870, just two days after the 'dipper fight,' Cadet Corporal Beacom made a report against me for 'replying in a disrespectful manner to a file-closer when spoken to at drill, P.M.' For this alleged offence I wrote an explanation denying the charge ; but Cadet Beacom found three cadets who swore that they heard me make a disrespectful reply in ranks when Cadet Beacom, as a file-closer on duty, spoke to me, and the Commandant of Cadets, Lieutenant Colonel Upton, preferred charges against me for making false statements.

"The court to try me sat in September, with General O. O. Howard as President. I plead 'not guilty' to the charge of assault on Cadet Wilson, and also to the charge of making false statements.

"The court found both Cadet Wilson and myself 'guilty' of assault, and sentenced us to be confined for two or three weeks, with some other light punishment in the form of 'extra duty.'

"The finding of the court was approved by President Grant in the

13

case of Cadet Wilson, but disapproved in my case, on the ground that
the punishment was not severe enough. Therefore, Cadet W.
served his punishment and I did not serve mine, as there was no authority vested in the President to increase it.

"On the second charge I was acquitted, for I proved, by means of
the order book of the Academy that there was no *company* drill on
that day—the 15th of August—that there was *skirmish* drill, and by
the guard reports of the same date, that Cadet Beacom and two of his
three witnesses were on guard that day, and could not have been at
drill, even if there had been one. To some it might appear that the
slight inconsistencies existing between the sworn testimony of those
cadets and the official record of the Academy, savored somewhat of
perjury, but they succeeded in explaining the matter by saying that
' Cadet Beacom only made a mistake in date.' Of course he did ; how
could it be otherwise ? It was necessary to explain it in some way so
that I might be proved a liar to the corps of cadets, even if they
failed to accomplish that object to the satisfaction of the court.

"I was released in November, after the proceedings and findings
of the court had been returned from Washington, where they had been
sent for the approval of the President, having been in arrest for three
months. But I was not destined to enjoy my liberty for any length of
time, for on the 13th of December, same year, I was in the ranks of
the guard, and was stepped on two or three times by Cadet Anderson,
one of my classmates, who was marching beside me

"As I had had some trouble with the same cadet some time before,
on account of the same thing, I believed that he was doing it intention-
ally, and as it was very annoying, I spoke to him about it, saying :
' I wish you would not tread on my toes.' He answered : ' Keep
your d—d toes out of the way.' Cadet Birney, who was standing
near by, then made some invidious remarks about me, to which I did
not condescend to reply. One of the Cadet Corporals, Bailey, reported me for ' inattention in ranks,' and in my written explanation
of the offence, I detailed the circumstances, but both Birney and Anderson denied them, and the Commandant of Cadets took their statement in preference to mine, and preferred charges against me for
falsehood.

"I was court martialled in January, 1871, Captain Piper, Third
Artillery, being President of the court. By this court I was found
' guilty,' as I had no witnesses, and had nothing to expect from the
testimony of the witnesses for the prosecution. Cadet Corporal Bailey, who made the report, Cadets Birney and Anderson were the

witnesses who convicted me ; in fact they were the *only* witnesses summoned to testify in the case. The sentence of the court was that I should be dismissed, but it was changed to one year's suspension, or, since the year was almost gone before the finding of the court was returned from Washington, where it was sent for the approval of President Grant, I was put back one year.

" I had no counsel at this trial, as I knew it would be useless, considering the one-sided condition of affairs. I was allowed to make the following written statement of the affair to be placed among the records of the proceedings of the court :

" ' May it please the court : I stand here to day charged with a most disgraceful act—one which not only affects my character, but will, if I am found guilty, affect it during my whole life—and I shall attempt, in as few words as possible, to show that I am as innocent as any person in this room. I was reported on the 18th of December, 1870, for a very trivial offence. For this offence I submitted an explanation to the Commandant of Cadets. In explanation I stated the real cause of committing the offence for which I was reported. But this cause, as stated, involved another cadet, who, finding himself charged with an act for which he was liable to punishment, denies all knowledge of it. He tries to establish his denial by giving evidence which I shall attempt to prove absurd. On the morning of the 13th of December, 1870, at guard-mounting, after the new guard had marched past the old guard, and the command of " Twos left, halt !" had been given, the new guard was about two or three yards to the front and right of the old guard. Then the command of " Left backward, dress," was given to the new guard, " Order arms, in place rest." I then turned around to Cadet Anderson, and said to him, " I wish you would not tread on my toes." This was said in a moderate tone, quite loud enough for him to hear. He replied, as I understood, " Keep your d—d toes out of the way." I said nothing more, and he said nothing more. I then heard Cadet Birney say to another cadet —I don't know who it was—standing by his side, " It (or the thing) is speaking to Mr. Anderson. If he were to speak to me I would knock him down." I heard him distinctly, but as I knew that he was interfering in an affair that did not concern him, I took no further notice of him, but turned around to my original position in the ranks. What was said subsequently I do not know, for I paid no further attention to either party. I heard nothing said at any time about taking my eyes away, or of Cadet Anderson compromising his dignity. Having thus reviewed the circumstances which gave rise to the charge, may it please the court, I wish to say a word as to the witnesses. Each of these cadets testifies to the fact that they have discussed the case in every particular, both with each other and with other cadets. That is, they have found out each other's views and feelings in respect to it, compared the evidence which each should give, the probable result of the trial ; and one has even testified that he has expressed a desire as to the result. Think you that Cadet Birney, with such a desire in his breast, influencing his every thought and word, with such an end in view, could give evidence unbiassed, unprejudiced, and free from that desire that " Cadet Smith might be sent away and proved a liar ?" Think you that he could give evidence which should be " the truth, the whole truth, and nothing but the truth, so help me God ?" It seems impossible for me to have justice done me by the evidence of such witnesses, but I will leave that for the court to decide. There is another question here which must be answered by the finding of the court. It is this : " Shall Cadet Smith be allowed to complain to the Commandant of Cadets when he considers himself unjustly dealt with ?" When the court takes notice of the fact that this charge and these specifications are the result of a complaint made by me, it will agree with me as to the importance its findings will have in answering that question. As to what the finding will be, I can say nothing ; but if the court is convinced that I have lied, then I shall expect a finding and sentence in accordance with such conviction. A lie is as disgraceful to one man as another, be he white or black, and I say here, as I said to the Commandant of Cadets, " If I were guilty of falsehood, I should merit and expect the same punishment as any other cadet ;" but, as I said before, I am as innocent of this charge as any person in this room. The verdict of an infallible judge—conscience—is, " Not guilty," and that is the finding I ask of this court.

    " ' Respectfully submitted.

(Signed)   " ' J. W. SMITH,
" ' *Cadet U. S. M. A.'*

    " Thus ended my second and last court-martial.

" Yours respectfully,
" J. W. SMITH.
" *Late Cadet U. S. M. A.*"

THE HONOR OF A CADET AND GENTLEMAN.

"COLUMBIA, S. C., August 13, 1874.

To the Editor of the New National Era :

"SIR : In relating the events of my first year at West Point, I omitted one little affair which took place, and I will now relate the circumstances. One Sunday, at dinner, I helped myself to some soup, and one cadet, Clark, of Kentucky, who sat opposite me at table, asked me what I meant by taking soup before he had done so. I told him that I took it because I wished it, and that there was a plenty left. He seemed to be insulted at that, and asked : 'Do you think I would eat after a d—d nigger?' I replied : 'I have not thought at all on the subject, and, moreover, I don't quite understand you, as I can't find that last word in the dictionary.' He then took up a glass and said he would knock my head off. I told him to throw as soon as he pleased, and as soon as he got through I would throw mine. The commandant of the table here interfered and ordered us to stop creating a disturbance at the table, and gave me to understand that thereafter *I should not touch any thing on that table until the white cadets were served.*

"When we came back from dinner, as I was going into my room, Cadet Clark struck at me from behind. He hit me on the back of my neck, causing me to get into my room with a little more haste than I anticipated, but he did not knock me down. He came into my room, following up his advantage, and attempted to take me by the throat, but he only succeeded in scratching me a little with his nails, as I defended myself as well as possible until I succeeded in getting near my bayonet, which I snatched from the scabbard and then tried to put it through him. But being much larger and stronger than I, he kept me off until he got to the door, but then he couldn't get out, for *some one was holding the door on the outside,* for the purpose, I suppose, of preventing my escape, as no doubt they thought I would try to get out. There were a great many cadets outside on the stoop, looking through the window, and cheering their champion, with cries of 'That's right, Clark ; kill the d—d nigger,' 'Choke him,' 'Put a head on him,' etc., but when they saw him giving way before the bayonet, they cried, 'Open the door, boys,' and the door was opened, and Mr. Clark went forth to rejoice in the bosom of his friends as the hero of the day. The cadet officer of the day 'happened around' just *after* Clark had *left,* and wanted to know what did I mean by making all that noise in and around my quarters. I told him what the trouble was about, and soon after I was sent for by the 'officer in charge,' and questioned in reference to the affair. Charges were preferred against Clark for entering my room and assaulting me, but before they were brought to trial he sent two of his friends to me asking if I would withdraw the charges providing he made a written apology. I told these cadets that I would think of the matter and give them a definite answer the next evening.

"I was perfectly well satisfied that he would be convicted by any court that tried him ; but the cadets could easily prove (according to their way of giving evidence) that I provoked the assault, and I, besides, was utterly disgusted with so much wrangling, so when the cadets called that evening I told them that if his written apology was satisfactory I would sign it, submit it to the approval of the Commandant of Cadets, and have the charges withdrawn.

"They then showed me the written apology offered by Clark, in which he stated that his offence was caused by passion, because he thought that when I passed him on the steps in going to my room I tried to brush against him. He also expressed his regret for what he had done, and asked forgiveness. I was satisfied with his apology, and signed it, asking that the charges be withdrawn, which was done, of course, and Clark was released from arrest. I will, in justice to Cadet Clark, state that I never had any further trouble with him, for, while he kept aloof from me, as the other cadets did, he alway thereafter acted perfectly fair by me whenever I had any official relations with him.

"A few days after the settlement of our dispute I found, on my return from fencing one day, that some one had entered my room and had thrown all my clothes and other property around the floor, and had thrown the water out of my water-pail upon my bed. I immediately went to the guard-house and reported the affair to the officer of the day, who, with the 'officer in charge,' came to my room to see what had been done. The officer of the day said that he had inspected my quarters soon after I went to the Fencing Academy and found everything in order, and that it must have been done within a half hour. The Commandant of the Cadets made an investigation of the matter, but could not find out what young 'gentleman' did it, for every cadet stated that he knew nothing of it, although the corps of cadets has the reputation of being a truthful set of young men.

"'Upon my honor as a cadet and a gentleman,'" is a favorite expression with the West Point cadet ; but what kind of honor is that by which a young man can quiet his conscience while telling a base falsehood for the purpose of shielding a fellow-student from punishmen for a disgraceful act ? They boast of the *esprit de corps* existing among the cadets ; but it is merely a cloak for the purpose of covering up their iniquities and silencing those (for there are some) who would, if allowed to act according to the dictates of their own consciences, be above such disgraceful acts. Some persons might attribute to me the same motives that actuated the fox in crying ' sour grapes,' and to such I will say that I never asked for *social equality* at West Point. I never visited the quarters of any professor, official, or cadet except on duty, for I did not wish any one to think that I was in any way desirous of social recognition by those who felt themselves superior to me on account of color. As I was never recognized as ' a cadet and a gentleman,' I could not enjoy that blessed privilege of swearing ' upon my honor,' boasting of my share in the *esprit de corps,* nor of concealing my sins by taking advantage of them. Still, I hope that what I lost (?) by being deprived of these little benefits will be compensated for the ' still small voice,' which tells me that I have done *my* best.

> " Yours respectfully,
>
> > " J. W. SMITH,
> > " *Late Cadet U. S. M. A.*"

> " COLUMBIA, S. C., August 19, 1874.

To the Editor of the New National Era :

" SIR : My communications, thus far, have brought me to the end of my first year at the Academy, and now we come to the events of the second. In June of 1871, the proverbial silver lining, which the darkest cloud is said to have, began to shine very faintly in the West Point firmament, and I thought that at last the darkness of my cadet life was to be dispelled by the appearance above the horizon of another colored cadet. And, indeed, I was not disappointed, for, one day, I was greeted by the familiar face and voice of Mr. H. A. Napier, a former fellow-student at Howard University. Soon after his arrival, and admittance, the corps of cadets, accompanied by the ' plebes,' took up quarters in camp—' plebe camp ' to the latter, and ' yearling camp ' to us who had entered the previous year.

" During the cadet encampment there are certain dances given three times each week, known as ' Cadet Hops.' These ' hops ' are attended by the members of the first and third classes, and their lady friends, and no ' plebe ' ever has the assurance of dreaming of

attending the ' hops ' until he shall have risen to the dignity of a
' yearling '—third-classman. So long as I was a ' plebe,' no one
anticipated any such dire calamity as that I would attend the ' hops,'
but as soon as I became a ' yearling,' and had a perfect right to go,
if I wished, there was a great hue and cry raised that the sanctity of
the ' hop ' room was to be violated by the colored cadet.

"Meetings were held by the different classes, and resolutions passed to the effect that as soon as the colored cadet entered the ' hop '
room, the ' hop ' managers were to declare the ' hop ' ended, and
dismiss the musicians. But the ' hops ' went on undisturbed by the
presence of the colored cadet for two or three weeks, and all began to
get quiet again, when one day my brother and sister, with a couple
of lady friends whom they had come to visit, came to camp to see
me.

" This started afresh the old report about the ' hops,' and every one
was on the *qui vive* to get a glimpse of ' nigger Jim and the nigger
wenches who are going to the hops,' as was remarked by a cadet
who went up from the guard tent to spread the alarm through camp.

"In a few minutes thereafter the ' gentlemen ' had all taken position at the end of the ' company street,' and, with their opera-glasses,
were taking observations upon those who, as they thought, had come
to desecrate the ' hop ' room. I was on guard that day, but not being on post at that time, I was sitting in rear of the guard tents with
my friends—that place being provided with camp-stools for the ac-
commodation of visitors—when a cadet corporal, Tyler, of Kentucky,
came and ordered me to go and fasten down the corner of the first
guard tent, which stood a few paces from where we were sitting.

" I went to do so, when he came there also, and immediately began
to rail at me for being so slow, saying he wished me to know that
when he ordered me to do anything, I must ' step out ' about it, and
not try to shirk it. I said nothing, but fastened down the corner of
the tent, and went back to where my friends were.

" In a few minutes afterwards he came back, and wanted to know
why I hadn't fastened down that tent wall. I told him that I had.

" He said it was not fastened then, and that he did not wish any
prevarication on my part.

" I then told him that he had no authority to charge me with prevarication, and that if he believed that I had not fastened down the
tent wall, the only thing he could do was to report me. I went back
to the tent and found that either Cadet Tyler or some other cadet had
unfastened the tent wall, so I fastened it down again. Nothing now

was said to me by Cadet Tyler, and I went back to where my friends were ; but we had been sitting there only about a half hour, when a private soldier came to us and said, ' It is near time for parade, and you will have to go away from here.' I never was more surprised in my life, and I asked the soldier what he meant, for I surely thought he was either drunk or crazy, but he said that the superintendent had given him orders to allow no colored persons near the visitors' seats during parade.

"I asked him if he recognized me as a cadet. He said he did. I then told him that those were my friends ; that I had invited them there to see the parade, and that they were going to stay. He said he had nothing to do with me, of course, but that he had to obey the orders of the superintendent. I then went to the officer of the guard, who was standing near by, and stated the circumstances to him, re-questing him to protect us from such insults. He spoke to the soldier, saying that he had best not try to enforce that order, as the order was intended to apply to servants, and then the soldier went off and left us.

" Soon after that the drum sounded for parade, and I was compelled to leave my friends for the purpose of falling in ranks, but promising to return as soon as the parade was over, little thinking that I should not be able to redeem that promise ; but such was the case, as I shall now proceed to show.

" Just as the companies were marching off the parade ground, and before the guard was dismissed, the ' officer in charge,' Lieutenant Charles King, Fifth Cavalry, came to the guard tent and ordered me to step out of ranks three paces to the front, which I did.

" He then ordered me to take off my accoutrements and place them with my musket on the gun rack. That being done, he ordered me to take my place in the centre of the guard as a prisoner, and there I stood until the ranks were broken, when I was put in the guard tent. Of course my friends felt very bad about it, as they thought that they were the cause of it, while I could not speak a word to them, as they went away ; and even if I could have spoken to them, I could not have explained the matter, for I did not know myself why I had been put there—at least I did not know what charge had been trumped up against me, though I knew well enough that I had been put there for the purpose of keeping me from the ' hop,' as they expected I would go. The next morning I was put ' in arrest ' for ' disobedience of orders in not fastening down tent wall when ordered,' and ' replying in a disrespectful manner to a cadet corporal,' etc. ; and thus the simplest thing was magnified into a very serious offence, for the purpose of satisfying the desires of a few narrow-minded cadets. That an officer of the United States Army would allow his prejudices to carry him so far as to act in that way to a subordinate, without giving him a chance to speak a word in his defence —nay, without allowing him to know what charge had been made against him, and that he should be upheld in such action by the ' powers that be,' are sufficient proof to my mind of the feelings which the officers themselves maintained towards us. While I was in ranks, during parade, and my friends were quietly sitting down looking at the parade, another model ' officer and gentleman,' Captain Alexander Piper, Third Artillery—he was president of my second court-martial—came up, in company with a lady, and ordered my brother and sister to get up and let him have their camp-stools, and he actually took away the camp-stools and left them standing, while a different kind of a gentleman—an ' obscure citizen,' with no aristocratic West Point dignity to boast of—kindly tendered his camp-stool to my sister.

" I only wish I knew the name of that gentleman ; but I could not see him then, or I should certainly have found it out, though in answer to my brother's question as to his name, he simply replied, ' I am an obscure citizen.' What a commentary on our ' obscure citizens,' who know what it is to be gentlemen in something else besides the name—gentlemen in practice, not only in theory—and who can say with Burns that ' a man's a man for a' that,' whether his face be as black as midnight or as white as the driven snow.

" There is something in such a man which elevates him above many others who, having nothing- else to boast of, can only say, ' I am a white man, and am therefore your superior,' or ' I am a West Point graduate, and therefore an officer and a gentleman.'

" After the usual ' investigation ' by the Commandant of Cadets, I was sentenced to be confined to the ' company street ' until the 15th of August, about five weeks, so that I could not get out to see my brother and sister after that, except when I was at drill, and then I could not speak to them. I tried to get permission to see them in the ' Visitors' Tent ' the day before they left the ' Point ' on their return home, but my permit was not granted, and they left without having the privilege of saying ' Good-by.'

" I must say a word in reference to the commandant's method of making ' investigations.' After sending for Cadet Corporal Tyler and other white cadets, and hearing their side of the story in reference to the tent wall and the disrespectful reply, he sent for me to hear what I had to say, and after I had given my version of the affair, he told me that I must surely be mistaken, as my statement did not coincide with those of the other cadets, who were unanimous in saying that I used not only disrespectful, but also profane language while addressing the cadet corporal. I told him that new Cadet Napier and my brother were both there and heard the conversation, and they would substantiate my statement if allowed to testify. He said he was convinced that I was in the wrong, and he did *not* send for either of them. What sort of justice is that which can be meted out to one without allowing him to defend himself, and even denying him the privilege of calling his evidence ? What a model Chief Justice the Commandant of Cadets would make, since he can decide upon the merits of the case as soon as he has heard one side. Surely he has missed his calling by entering the army, or else the American people cannot appreciate true ability, for that ' officer and gentleman ' ought now to be wearing the judicial robe so lately laid down by the lamented Chase.

" In reply to my complaint about the actions of the soldier in ordering my friends away from the visitors' seats, he said that the soldier had misunderstood his orders, as the superintendent had told him to keep the colored servants on the ' Point ' from coming in front of the battalion at parade, and that it was not meant ¦to apply to my friends, who could come there whenever they wished.

" It seems, though, very strange to me that the soldier could misunderstand his orders, when he saw me sitting there in company with them, for it is one of the regulations of the Academy which forbids any cadet to associate with a servant, and if I had been seen doing such a thing I would have been court-martialled for ' conduct unbecoming a cadet and a gentleman. ''

" The cadets were, of course, very much rejoiced at my being ' in arrest,' and after my sentence had been published at parade, they had quite a jubilee over it, and boasted of ' the *skill* and *tact* which Cadet Tyler had shown in putting the nigger out of the temptation of taking those black wenches to the hops.' They thought, no doubt, that their getting me into trouble frightened me out of any thoughts I might have had of attending the ' hops ;' but if I had any idea of going to the ' hops,' I should have been only more determined to go, and should have done so as soon as my term of confinement was ended   I have never thought of going to the ' hops,' for it would be very little pleasure to go by myself, and I should most assuredly not have asked a lady to subject herself to the insults consequent upon going there. Besides, as I said before, I did not go to West Point for the purpose of advocating social equality, for there are many cadets in the corps with whom I think it no honor for any one to associate, although they are among the high-toned aristocrats, and will, no doubt, soon be numbered among the ' officers and gentlemen ' of the United States Army.

" Yours respectfully,

" J. W. SMITH. '
" <i>Late Cadet U. S. M. A.</i>"</div>

REPLY TO THE " WASHINGTON CHRONICLE."

" COLUMBIA, S. C., August 25, 1874.

To the Editor of the New National Era :

" SIR : The following article appeared in the <i>Washington Chronicle</i> of the 14th inst., and as I feel somewhat interested in the statements therein contained, I desire to say a few words in reference to them. The article referred to reads as follows :

" ' The recent attack of the colored ex-Cadet Smith upon the Board of Visitors at West Point has attracted the attention of the officers of the War Department. They say that the Secretary of War was extremely liberal in his interpretation of the regulations on behalf of Cadet Smith, and that he did for him what had never been done for a white boy in like circumstances. The officers also say that Smith was manifestly incompetent, that he had a fair examination, and that the Congressional Board of Visitors unanimously testified to his incompetency.'

" Now, sir, I am at a loss to know what are ' the recent attacks of the colored ex-Cadet Smith upon the Board of Visitors,' for I am not aware that I have said any thing, either directly or indirectly, concerning the Board of Visitors. My remarks thus far have been confined to the <i>Academic Board</i> and Secretary of War.

" As the members of the Board of Visitors were simply spectators, and as they were not present when I was examined, I had no reason to make any ' attack ' upon them, and, therefore, as I said before, confined my remarks (or ' attacks,' if that word is more acceptable to the <i>Chronicle</i>) to those who acted so unjustly toward me.

" As to the extreme liberality of the Secretary of War, in his interpretation of the regulations on behalf of Cadet Smith, and that he did for him what he had never ' done for a white boy in like circumstances,' I hardly know what to say ; for such absurd cant seems intended to excite the laughter of all who know the circumstances of the case. What devoted servants those officers of the War Department must be, that they can see in their chief so much liberality !

"But in what respect was the Secretary of War so 'liberal in his interpretation of the regulations ? '

"Was it in dismissing me, and turning back to a lower class two white cadets who had been unable to complete successfully the first year of the course with everything in their favor, while I had completed three years of the same course in spite of all the opposition which the whole corps of cadets, backed by the 'powers that be,' could throw in my way? Or was it his decision that 'I *can* give Mr. Smith a re-examination, but I *won't* ? ' The *Chronicle* is perfectly correct in saying 'that he did for him what had never been done for a white boy in like circumstances,' for, in the first place, I don't think there ever was 'a white boy in like circumstances,' certainly not while I was at the Academy, and if there ever were a white boy so placed, we are pretty safe in concluding, from the general treatment of white boys, that the secretary was not so frank in his remarks nor so decided in his action.

"'I want another cadet to represent your district at West Point, and I have already sent to Mr. Elliott to appoint one,' means something more than fair dealing (or, as the *Chronicle* would imply, partiality) toward the colored cadet. It means that the gentleman was pleasing himself in the choice of a cadet from the Third Congressional District of South Carolina, and that he did not recognize the rights of the people of that district to choose for themselves. 'You are out of the service and will stay out,' for 'the Academic Board will not recommend you to come back under any circumstances,' shows that it is the Academic Board that must choose our representative, and not we ourselves, and that our wishes are only secondary in comparison with those of the service and the Academic Board. We are no longer free citizens of a sovereign State, and of the United States, with the right to choose for ourselves those who shall represent us ; but we must be subordinate to the Secretary of War and the Academic Board, and must make our wishes subservient to those of the above-named powers, and unless we do that we are pronounced to be 'naturally bad '—as remarked the Adjutant of the Academy, Captain R. H. Hall, to a *Sun* reporter—and must have done for us 'what had never been done for a white boy in like circumstances.' Now, sir, let us see what has 'been done for a white boy in like circumstances.' In July, 1870, the President was in Hartford, Ct., and in a conversation with my friend the Hon. David Clark, in reference to

my treatment at West Point, he said : ' Don't take him away now ;
the battle might just as well be fought now as at any other time,'
and gave him to understand that he would see me protected in my
rights ; while his son Fred, who was then a cadet, said to the same
gentleman, and *in the presence of his father*, that ' the time had not
come to send colored boys to West Point.' Mr. Clark said if the
time had come for them to be in the United States Senate, it had
surely come for them to be at West Point, and that he would do all
in his power to have me protected. Fred Grant then said : ' Well,
no d—d nigger will ever graduate from West Point.' This same
young gentleman, with other members of his class, entered the rooms
of three cadets, members of the fourth class, on the night of January
3, 1871, took those cadets out, and drove them away from the
' Point,' with nothing on but the light summer suits that they wore
when they reported there the previous summer. Here was a most
outrageous example of Lynch law, disgraceful alike to the first
class, who were the executors of it, the corps of cadets, who were
the abettors of it, and the authorities of the Academy, who were
afraid to punish the perpetrators because the President's son was implicated, or, at least, one of the prime movers of the affair. Congress
took the matter in hand, and instructed the Secretary of War to dismiss all the members of the class who were implicated, but the latter
gentleman ' was extremely liberal in his interpretation of the regulations,' and declined to be influenced by the action of Congress, and
let the matter drop.

  " Again, when a Court of Inquiry, appointed by Congress to investigate complaints that I had made of my treatment, reported in favor
of a trial by court-martial of General Gillmore's son, General Dyer's
son, the nephew of the Secretary of War, and some other lesser
lights of America's aristocracy, the secretary decided that a reprimand was sufficient for the offence ; yet ' he did for me what had
never been done for a white boy in like circumstances.' Now, sir,
by consulting my Register of the Academy, issued in 1871, I find that
three cadets of the fourth class were declared ' deficient ' in mathematics—Reid, Boyle, and Walker—and that the first named was
turned back to join the next class, while the other two were dismissed. Now Reid is the Secretary's nephew, so that is the reason
for his doing ' for him what had never been done for a white boy in
like circumstances.'

  " Mr. Editor, I have no objection whatever to any favoritism that
may be shown any member of the Royal Family, so long as it does

not infringe upon any right of my race or myself ; but when any paper tries to show that I have received such impartial treatment at the hands of ' the powers that be,' and even go so far, in their zealous endeavors to shield any one from charges founded upon facts, as to try to make it appear that I was a favorite, a pet lamb, or any other kind of a pet, at West Point, I think it my duty to point out any errors that may accidentally (?) creep into such statements.

" ' The officers also say that Smith was manifestly incompetent, that he had a fair examination,' etc. What officers said that? Those of the War Department, whose attention was attracted by the ' recent attacks on the Board of Visitors,' or those who decided the case at West Point ? In either case, it is not surprising that they should say so, for one party might feel jealous because ' the Secretary of War was extremely liberal in his interpretation of the regulations on behalf of Cadet Smith, and that he did for him what had never been done for a white boy in like circumstances,' while the other party might have been actuated by the desire to prove that ' no colored boy can ever graduate at West Point,' or, as the young gentleman previously referred to said, ' No d—d nigger shall ever graduate at West Point.' As for the unanimous testimony of the Board of Visitors, I can only say that I know not on what ground such testimony is based, for, as I said before, the members of that board were not in the library when I was examined in philosophy ; but perhaps, this is only one of the ' they says ' of the officers. There are some things in this case which are not so manifest as my alleged incompetency, and I would like to bring them to the attention of the *Chronicle*, and of any others who may feel interested in the matter. There has always been a system of re-examinations at the Military Academy for the purpose of giving a second chance to those cadets who failed at the regular examination. This year the re-examinations were abolished ; but for what reason ? It is true that I had never been re-examined, but does it not appear that the officers had concluded ' that Smith was manifestly incompetent,' and that this means was taken to deprive me of the benefit of a re-examination when they decided that I was ' deficient ? ' Or was it done so that the officers might have grounds for saying that ' he did for him what had never been done for a white boy in like circumstances ? ' Again, the examinations used to be public ; but this year two sentinels were posted at the door of the library, where the examinations were held, and when a visitor came he sent in his card by one of the sentinels, while the other remained at the door, and was admitted or not at the discretion of the superintendent. It is said that this precaution was taken because the visitors disturbed the members of the Academic Board by walking across the floor. *Very good excuse, for the floor was covered with a very thick carpet.* We must surely give the Academic Board credit for so much good judgment and foresight, for it would have been a very sad affair, indeed, for those gentlemen to have been made so nervous (especially the Professor of Philosophy) as to be unable to see how ' manifestly incompetent ' Cadet Smith was, and it would have deprived the Secretary of War of the blissful consciousness that ' he did for him what had never been done for a white boy in like circumstances,' besides losing the privilege of handing down to future generations the record of his extreme liberality ' in his interpretation of the regulations on behalf of Cadet Smith.'

" Oh, that this mighty deed might be inscribed on a lasting *leather* medal and adorn the walls of the War Department, that it might act as an incentive to some future occupant of that lofty station ! I advise the use of *leather*, because if we used any metal it might convey to our minds the idea of ' a sounding brass or a tinkling cymbal.'

" Respectfully yours,

" J. W. SMITH,

" *Late Cadet U. S. M. A.*"

THE NEGRO CADETS.

" We publish this morning an account of Cadet Smith's standing at West Point, which should be taken with a few grains of allowance. The embryo colored soldier and all his friends—black, white and tan—believe that the administrationists have used him shamefully, especially in view of their professions and of the chief source of their political strength. Grant went into the White House by means of colored votes, and his shabby treatment of the first member of the dusky army who reached the point of graduation in the country's military school, is a sore disappointment to them.

" Cadet Smith has been a thorn in the side of the Administration from the start. He could not be bullied out or persecuted out of the institution by the insults or menaces of those who, for consistency's sake, should have folded him to their bosoms. He stood his ground bravely, and much against the will of its rulers. West Point was forced to endure his unwelcome presence up to the time of graduation. At that point a crisis was reached. If the odious cadet were allowed to graduate, his commission would entitle him to assignment in our much-officered army, which contains Colonel Fred Grant and a host of other favorites whose only service has been of the Captain Jinks order. The army revolted at the idea. Theoretically they were and are sound on the nigger, but they respectfully and firmly objected to a practical illustration. The Radical General Belknap was easily convinced that the assignment of the unoffending Smith to duty would cause a lack of discipline in any regiment that would be fearful to contemplate.

" Something must be done, and that something was quickly accomplished. They saved the army and the dignity of the horse marines by sacrificing the cadet. To do so, some tangible cause must be alleged, and a deficiency in ' philosophy ' was hit upon.

" In vain did Smith appeal to the Secretary of War for an opportunity to be re-examined ; in vain did he ask permission to go back and join the class below—all appeals were in vain. ' Gentlemen,' says the secretary, ' I don't wish to be misquoted as saying that I can't give Mr. Smith a re-examination, for I say I *won't* do it.' The victim of the army has since published a three-column card in Fred Douglass's paper, in which he says he was dropped for politico-military reasons, and in the course of which he makes an almost unanswerable case for himself, but the Radicals have dropped him in his hour of necessity, and he must submit."

(*From the New York Sun.*)

CADET SMITH'S EXPULSION.

" James W. Smith, the first colored cadet appointed to the Military Academy of West Point, was dismissed after the June examination, having failed to pass an examination in some other studies. Recently the *Sun* received letters from South Carolina charging that the prejudices of the officers of the Academy led to the dismissal ; and to ascertain the truth a *Sun* reporter went to West Point to investigate the matter. He accosted a soldier thus :

" ' Were you here before Smith was dismissed ? '

" ' Yes, sir ; I've been here many years.'

" ' Can you tell me why he was dismissed ? '

" ' Well, I believe he didn't pass in philosophy and some other studies.'

" ' What kind of a fellow was he ? '

" ' The soldiers thought well of him, but the cadets didn't. They used to laugh and poke fun at him in Riding Hall, and in the artillery drill all of them refused to join hands with him when the cannoneers were ordered to mount. This is dangerous once in a while, for sometimes they mount when the horses are on a fast trot. But he used to run on as plucky as you please, and always got into his seat without help. Some of the officers used to try to make them carry out the drill, but it was no use. I never saw one of the young fellows give him a hand to make a mount. He was a proud negro, and had good pluck. I never heard him complain, but his black eyes used to flash when he was insulted, and you could see easy enough that he was in a killin' humor. But after the first year he kept his temper pretty well, though he fought hard to do it.'

"Captain Robert H. Hall, the post adjutant, said : ' Young Smith was a bad boy.'

NATURALLY BAD.

" ' His temper was hot, and his disposition not honorable. I can assure you that the officers at this post did every thing in their power to help him along in his studies, as well as to improve his standing with his comrades. But his temper interfered with their efforts in the latter direction, while his dulness precluded his passing through the course of studies prescribed.

" REPORTER—' He was always spoken of as a very bright lad.'

" CAPTAIN HALL—' He was not bright or ready. He lacked comprehension. In his first year he was very troublesome. First came his assault upon, or affray with, another young gentleman (Cadet Wilson), but the Court of Inquiry deemed it inadvisable to court-martial either of them. Then he was insolent to his superior on drill, and being called upon for an explanation he wrote a deliberate falsehood. For this he was court-martialled and sentenced to dismissal, but subsequently the findings of the committee were reversed, and Cadet Smith was put back one year. This fact accounts for his good standing on the examination next before the last. You see he went over the same studies twice.'

" REPORTER—' What was Cadet Smith found deficient in ? '

" CAPTAIN HALL—' His worst failure was in natural and experimental philosophy, which embraces the higher mathematics, dynamics, optics, mechanics, and other studies. He missed a very simple question in optics, and the examiners, who were extremely lenient with him, chiefly, I believe, because he was colored and not white, tried him with another, which was also missed.'

" REPORTER—' Is optical science deemed an absolutely essential branch of learning for an officer in the army ? '

DEFICIENT IN HIS STUDIES.

"CAPTAIN HALL—' It is useful to engineers, for instance. But that is not the question. In most educational institutions of the grade of West Point, the standing of a student in his studies is decided by a general average of all studies in which he is examined. Here each branch is considered separately, and if the cadet fails in any one he cannot pass. I will assure you once more that in my opinion Cadet Smith received as fair an examination as was ever given to any student. If any thing, he was a little more favored.'

" REPORTER—' What was his conduct in the last year of his stay at the Academy ? '

" CAPTAIN HALL—' Good. He ranked twenty in a class of forty in discipline. Discipline is decided by the number of marks a cadet receives in the term. If he goes beyond a certain number he is expelled.'

" REPORTER—' This record seems hardly consistent with his previous turbulent career.'

" CAPTAIN HALL—' Oh ! in the last years of his service he learned to control his temper, but he never seemed happy unless in some trouble.'

" REPORTER—' Have you any more colored cadets ? '

" CAPTAIN HALL—' Only one—Henry O. Flipper, of Georgia. He is a well-built lad, a mulatto, and is bright, intelligent, and studious.'

" REPORTER—' Do the cadets dislike him as much as they did Smith ? '

" CAPTAIN HALL—' No, sir, I am told that he is more popular. I have heard of no doubt he will get through all right. And here I will say, that had Mr. Smith been white he would not have gone so far as he did.'

" Other officers of the post concur with Captain Hall, but the enlisted men seem to sympathize with Smith. One of them said, ' I don't believe the officers will ever let a negro get through. They don't want them in the army.'

" Cadet Smith's career for the three years of his service was indeed a most unhappy one, but whether that unhappiness arose from

THE INFIRMITIES OF TEMPER

or from the persistent persecutions of his comrades cannot be authoritatively said. One officer attributed much of the pugnacity which Smith exhibited early in his course to the injudicious letters sent him by his friends. In some of these he was advised to ' fight for the honor of his race,' and others urged him to brook no insult at the hands of the white cadets. The menial duties which the ' plebes ' are called upon to do in their first summer encampment were looked upon by Smith as personal insults thrust upon him, al-thought his comrades made no complaint. Then the social ostracism to a lad of his sensitive nature was almost unbearable, and an occa-sional outbreak is not to be wondered at.

" Before he had been in the Academy a week he wrote to a friend complaining of the treatment he received from his fellows, and this letter being published intensified the hostility of the other cadets. Soon after this he had a fight with Cadet Wilson and cut his face with a dipper. Then followed the breach of discipline on drill, the court-martial and sentence, and finally the Congressional investiga-tion, which did not effect any good. Smith says that frequently on squad drill he was detached from the squad by the cadet corporal, and told that he was not to stand side by side with white men.

" WEST POINT, June 19."

THE COLORED CADET.

HIS TRIALS AND PERSECUTIONS—THREE YEARS OF ABUSE—SETTLED AT LAST—" ELI PERKINS" TELLS THE STORY.

To the Editor of the Daily Graphic :

" About the 20th of May, 1870, I saw the colored Cadet, James W. Smith land at the West Point Dock. He was appointed by a personal friend of mine, Judge Hoge, Member of Congress from Columbia, South Carolina. The mulatto boy was about five feet eight inches high, with olive complexion and freckles. Being hungry he tipped his hat to a cadet as he jumped from the ferry-boat and asked him the way to the hotel.

" ' Over there, boy,' replied the cadet, pointing to the Rose Hotel owned by the government.

" On arriving there the colored boy laid down his carpet-bag, registered his name, and asked for something to eat.

" ' What ! A meal of victuals for a nigger ? ' asked the clerk.

" ' Yes, sir, I'm hungry and I should like to buy something to eat.'

" ' Well, you'll have to be hungry a good while if you wait to get something to eat here,' and the clerk of the government hotel pushed the colored boy's carpet-bag off upon the floor.

"Jimmy Smith's father, who fought with General Sherman, and came back to become an alderman in Columbia, had told the boy that when he got to West Point among soldiers he would be treated justly, and you can imagine how the hungry boy felt when he trudged back over the hot *campus* to see Colonel Black and General Schriver, who was then Superintendent of the Academy.

"The black boy came and stood before the commandant and handed him his appointment papers and asked him to read them. Colonel Black, Colonel Boynton, and other officers looked around inquiringly. Then they got up to take a good look at the first colored cadet. The colonel, red in the face, waved the boy away with his hand, and, one by one, the officers departed, speechless with amazement.

"In a few moments the news spread through the Academy. The white cadets seemed paralyzed.

"Several cadets threatened to resign, some advocated maiming him for life, and a Democratic 'pleb' from Illinois exclaimed, 'I'd rather die than drill with the black devil.' But wiser counsels prevailed, and the cadets consented to tolerate Jimmy Smith and not drown or kill him for four weeks, when it was thought the examiners would 'bilge' him.

"On the 16th of June, 1870, I saw Jimmy Smith again at West Point and wrote out my experiences. He was the victim of great annoyance.

"At these insults the colored cadet showed a suppressed emotion. He could not break the ranks to chastise his assaulter. Then if he had fought with every cadet who called him a ' —— black-hearted nigger,' he would have fought with the whole Academy. Not the professors, for they have been as truly gentlemen as they are good officers. If they had feelings against the colored cadet they suppressed them. I say now that the indignities heaped upon Jimmy Smith would have been unbearable to any white boy of spirit. Hundreds of times a day he was publicly called names so mean that I dare not write them.

"Once I met Jimmy Smith after drill. He bore the insulting remarks like a Christian.

"'I expected it,' he said ; 'but it was not so at the Hartford High School. There I had the second honors of my class.' Then he showed me a catalogue of the Hartford High School, and there was the name of James W. Smith as he graduated with the next highest honor.

"On that occasion I asked Jimmy who his father was.

" ' His name is Israel Smith. He used to belong to Sandres Guignard, of Columbia.'

" ' Then he was a slave ? '

" ' Yes, but when Sherman's army freed him he became a Union soldier.'

" ' And your mother ? '

" ' She is Catherine Smith, born free.' Here Jimmy showed his mother's photograph. She looked like a mulatto woman, with straight hair and regular features. She had a serious, Miss-Siddons-looking face.

" ' How did you come to " the Point ?" ' I asked.

" ' Well, Mr. David Clark, of Hartford, promised to educate me, and he got Congressman Hoge to appoint me.'

" ' How came Mr. Clark to become interested in you ? '

" ' Well, a very kind white lady—Miss Loomis—came to Columbia to teach the freedmen. I went to school to her and studied so hard and learned so fast that she told Mr. Clark about me. My father is able to support me, but Mr. Clark is a great philanthropist and he has taken a liking to me and he is going to stand by me.'

" ' What does Mr. Clark say when you write about how the cadets treat you ? '

" The colored boy handed me this letter from his benefactor :

" ' HARTFORD, June 7, 1870.

" ' DEAR JEMMY : Yours, 1st inst., is at hand and noted. I herewith inclose stamps.

" ' Let them call "nigger" as much as they please ; they will laugh out of the other corner of their mouth before the term is over.

" ' Your only way is to maintain your dignity. Go straight ahead. If any personal insult is offered, resist it, and then inform me ; I will then see what I can do. But I think you need have no fear on that score. Have been out to Windham a few days. All well, and send kind regards. Mary sails for Europe Saturday. President Grant is to be here the 2d. He will be my guest or Governor Jewell's.

" ' Yours, etc.,

" ' ,D. CLARK.' "

" ' So Mr. Clark knows the President, does he ? '

" ' Why, yes ; he knows everybody—all the great men. He's a great man himself ; ' and this poor colored boy stood up, I thought, the proudest champion David Clark ever had.

" ' Yes, David Clark is a good man,' I mused, as I saw the grateful tears standing in the colored cadet's eyes.

" When I got back to the hotel I heard a wishy-washy girl, who came up year after year with a party to flirt with the cadets say :

" ' O dear ! it is hawid to have this colod cadet—perfectly dre'fful. I should die to see my George standing next to him.'

" But Miss Schenck, the daughter of General Schenck, our Minister to the Court of St. James, told Jimmy Smith that she hoped he would graduate at the head of his class, and when the colored boy told me about it he said :

" ' Oh, sir, a splendid lady called to see me to-day. I wish I knew her name. I want to tell David Clark.'

" Every white boy at West Point now agreed to cut the colored boy. No one was to say a single word to him, or even answer yes or no. At the same time they would abuse him and swear at him in their own conversation loud enough for him to hear. It is a lamentable fact that every white cadet at the Point swears and chews tobacco like the army in Flanders.

" Again I saw Jimmy Smith on the 9th of July. The officers of the Academy had been changed. Old General Schriver had given place to young General Upton. The young general is a man of feeling and a lover of justice. He sent for the colored boy, and taking his hand he said :

" ' My boy, you say you want to resign, that you can stand this persecution no longer. You must not do it. You are here an officer of the army. You have stood a severe examination. You have passed honorably and you shall not be persecuted into resigning. I am your friend. Come to me and you shall have justice.'

" Then General Upton addressed the cadets on dress parade. He told them personal insults against their brother cadet, whose only crime was color, must cease.

" One day a cadet came to Jimmy and said he would befriend him if he dared to, ' but you know I would be ostracized if I should speak to you.'

" ' What was the cadet's name ? ' I asked.

" ' Oh, I dare not tell ? ' replied the colored boy. ' He would be ruined, too.'

" ' Did your father write to you when you thought of resigning ? '

" ' Yes ; here is his letter,' replied the colored boy :

" ' COLUMBIA, S. C., July 3, 1870. '

" ' MY DEAR SON : I take great pleasure in answering your kind letter received last night. I pray God that my letter may find you in a better state of consolation than when you wrote to me. I told you that you would have trials and difficulties to endure. Do not mind them, for they will go like chaff before the wind, and your enemies will soon be glad to gain your friendship. They do the same to all new-comers in every college. You are elevated to a high position, and you must stand it like a man. Do not let them run you away, for then they will say, the "nigger" won't do. Show your spunk, and let them see that you will fight. That is what you are sent to West Point for. When they find you are determined to stay, they will let you alone. You must not resign on any account, for it is just what the Democrats want. They are betting largely here that you won't get in. The rebels say if you are admitted, they will devil you so much that you can't stay. Be a man ; don't think of leaving, and let me know all about your troubles. The papers say you have not been received. Do write me positively whether you are received or not.

" ' Times are lively here, for everybody is preparing for the Fourth of July. There are five colored companies here, all in uniform, and they are trying to see who shall excel in drill.

" ' Stand your ground ; don't resign, and write me soon.

" ' From your affectionate father,   " ' ISRAEL SMITH.' "

" On the 11th of January I visited West Point again. I found all the cadets still against the colored boy. A system of terrorism reigned supreme. Every one who did not take sides against the colored boy was ostracized.

" At drill one morning Cadet Anderson trod on the colored boy's toes. When Smith expostulated Anderson replied, ' Keep your —— toes away. ' When Smith told about it Anderson got two other white cadets to say he never said so. This brought the colored boy in a fix.

" Last July I saw the colored cadet again. He was still ostracized. No cadet ever spoke to him. He lived a hermit life, isolated and alone.

" When I asked him how he got on with his studies he said : ' As well as I am able, roaming all alone, with no one to help me and no one to clear up the knotty points. If there is an obscure point in my lesson I must go to the class with it. I cannot go to a brother cadet.'

" ' If you should ask them to help you what would they say ? '

" ' They would call me a —— nigger, and tell me to go back to the plantation.'

" Yesterday, after watching the colored cadet for three years, I saw him again. He has grown tall and slender. He talks slowly, as if he had lost the use of language. Indeed many days and weeks he has gone without saying twenty lines a day in a loud voice, and that in the recitation-room.

" When they were examining him the other day he spoke slowly, but his answers were correct. His answers in philosophy were correct. But they say he answered slowly, and they will find him deficient for that. Find him deficient for answering slowly when the boy almost lost the use of language ! When he knew four hundred eyes were on him and two hundred malignant hearts all praying for his failure !

"The colored cadet is now in his third year. The great question at West Point is, Will he pass his examination? No one will know till the 30th of June. It is my impression that the young officers have marked him so low that he will be found deficient. The young officers hate him almost as bad as the cadets, and whenever they could make a bad mark against him they have done it.

" 'Does any one ever speak to you now ?' I asked.

" 'No. I dare not address a cadet. I do not want to provoke them. I simply want to graduate. I am satisfied if they do not strike or harm me ; though if I had a kind word now and then I should be happier, and I could study better.' Then the colored boy drew a long sigh.

"To-day I met General Howard, who was present at the colored cadet's court-martial. I asked him to tell me about it.

" 'Well, Mr. Perkins,' said the General, ' they tried to make out that the colored boy lied.'

" ' Yes,' I interrupted, ' and they all say he did lie at the Point now. How was it ? '

" 'It was this way : They accused him of talking on parade, and, while trying to convict him out of his own mouth, they asked him " If on a certain day he did not speak to a certain cadet while on drill ?" " I did not speak to this cadet while on drill the day you mention," answered Cadet Smith, " for the cadet was not in the parade that day." '

" This answer startled the prosecutors, and, looking over the diary of parade days, they were astonished to find Cadet Smith correct.

" ' What then ? ' I asked.

" ' Why they accuse him of telling a lie in spirit, though not in form, for he had talked on a previous day. Just as if he was obliged to say any thing to assist the prosecutors except to answer their questions.'

" General Howard believes Cadet Smith to be a good, honest boy. I believe the same.

" Eli Perkins."

(From the Savannah (Ga.) Morning News.)

" Lieutenant Flipper seems to have gone back on his Atlanta friends. He came home from West Point with a good Academy record,

14

and behaved himself with becoming dignity. The officers at the barracks treated him—not socially, but as an officer of the army—with due respect, as did the citizens of Atlanta, who felt that he had won credit by his good conduct and success. But in an evil hour the colored friends (?) of Flipper gave him a reception, and in full uniform he made them a speech. Now speech-making is a dangerous thing, and this colored warrior seems to have been made a victim of it. He distorted the official courtesies of the officers at the barracks into social courtesies, and abused the white people of the South because they did not give him and his race social equality. Not only were sensible colored people displeased with his remarks, but many white citizens who went to the meeting friendly to Flipper left disgusted with his sentiments."*

(*From the Savannah (Ga.) Morning News.*)

A COLORED ARMY OFFICER.

" Lieutenant Flipper is his name. He is a living result of the policy of Radicalism which has declared from the first its determination that, under any circumstances, the American citizen of African descent shall enjoy all the privileges of his white brethren. Carrying out this determination, and not dismayed at the fate of colored cadet Smith, who figured so largely in West Point annals a few years ago, cadet Flipper was sent to that institution to try his hand. He has

---

* If a man walks on the streets with me, invites me to his quarters, introduces me to his comrades, and other like acts of courtesy, ought I to consider him treating me socially or officially ? I went to the garrison in Atlanta to pay my respects to the commanding officer. I expected nothing. I met an officer, who, with four others, had introduced himself to me on the cars. My official call had been made. He took me around, introduced me to the officers, and showed me all possible attention. I met another officer in the city several days after this. He offered cigars. We walked up and down the streets together. Many times did we hear and comment upon the remarks we overheard : "Is he walking with that nigger ?" and the like. He invited me into a druggist's to take some soda-water. I went in and got it, although it was never sold there before to a person of color. We rode out to the garrison together, and every attention was shown me by all. Another officer told me that before I came the officers of the garrison assembled to consider whether or not they should recognize me. The unanimous vote was " yes." Was all this official ? No. It is the white people, the disappointed tyrants of Georgia, who try to dis'ort social courtesies in official ones.

The "many white" people were some half-dozen newspaper reporters, whose articles doubtless were partly written when they came. "Old Si" in his spectacles was prominently conspicuous among them.

graduated, and now holds the commission of Second Lieutenant of Cavalry in the United States Army, the first of his race who has ever attained such a position.

" It will be curious to watch young Flipper's career as an officer. Time was when army officers were a very aristocratic and exclusive set of gentlemen, whether they still hold to their old ideas, or not, we do not know. There seems to be enough of the old feeling left, however, to justify the belief that until some other descendants of African parents graduate at the institution, Flipper will have a lonely time. During his cadetship, we learn from no less an authority than the New York *Tribune*, ' the paper founded by Horace Greeley,' that he was let severely alone by his fellow-students. According to that paper, one of the cadets said, ' We have no feeling against him, but we *could not* associate with him. It may have been prejudice but still we *couldn't* do it.' This shows very clearly the animus which will exist in the army against the colored officer. If at West Point, where he had to drill, recite, eat, and perhaps sleep with his white brothers, they couldn't associate with him (notwithstanding the fact that the majority of these whites were Northern men and ardent advocates of Radicalism, with its civil rights and social equality record), how can it be expected that they will overcome their prejudices any more readily after they become officers. The *Tribune* thinks they will, and that in time the army will not hesitate to receive young Flipper, and all of his race who may hereafter graduate at West Point, with open arms ; but the chances are that the *Tribune* is wrong. Your model Yankee is very willing to use the negro as a hobby-horse upon which to ride into place and power, but when it comes to inviting him to his house and embracing him as a brother he is very apt to be found wanting. The only society Lieutenant of Cavalry Flipper can ever hope to enjoy is that which will exist when there are enough of his race in the army to form a *corps d'Afrique*, and by that time he will be too old to delight in social pleasures. Meanwhile he will be doomed to a life of solitude and self-communings, and be subjected to many such snubs as the venerable Frederick Douglass has but recently received at the hands of that champion mourner for the poor African—Rutherford B. Hayes."

The New York *Tribune* is right. The army is officered by men, not by West Point cadets, who are only students and boys.

(*From the Savannah (Ga.) Morning News.*)

CHEERS FOR FLIPPER.

" The miscegenationists and social equality advocates are making a great deal of noise over the facts, first, that a negro has graduated at West Point, and holds to-day a commission in the United States Army ; and second, that when he went up to receive his diploma, he was, alone of all the members of his class, the recipient of a round of applause. Great things are augured from these two circumstances, especially the latter.

" It is reasoned that now, that a negro has at last been able to secure a commission in the military service of the country, the first step towards the recognition of his race on the basis of social equality is accomplished, by degrees prejudice will wear away, and, in course of time, black and white citizens of this republic will mingle freely and without reserve ; and this, it is claimed, is shown by the applause with which the reception into the army of this African pioneer was greeted. For our part we don't see that these negro devotees and miscegenationists have any reason to rejoice. It is just as impossible to establish perfect social equality between the Anglo-Saxon and African races as it is to make oil and water unite. It is against nature, and nowhere in the world is the antipathy to such a mingling shown more than in the North, and by no people so strongly as by the very men who whine so incessantly and so pretentiously about ' men and brethren.' The negro in the South has always found the white man of the South to be his best and truest friend, and such will always be the case, notwithstanding that the Southern white will never consent to social equality with his fellow-citizen of African descent.

" As to the applause which greeted Flipper, that can easily be accounted for. Nothing is more likely than that at West Point there should have been gathered together a lot of old-time South-haters, who were ready to applaud, not so much to flatter Flipper as to show that they were happy over what they felt to be a still further humiliation of the South. That is all there is in that.

" We have no objections to such demonstrations of delight. As far as we are concerned they may be indulged in to the heart's content by those who so desire. But one piece of information we can give to the young colored Georgia lieutenant. If he thinks those who applauded him are going to invite him to their houses he will be greatly disappointed. And if he does not die of overeating until those people invite him to dine with them, he will live to a good old age. Let him take the fate of the recognized leader of his race, Fred Douglass, as an example, and steer clear of his too demonstrative friends. Experience shows that so long as they can use him, they will be very profuse in their professions of friendship ; but when that is done all is done, and he will find himself completely cast aside. If Flipper sees these words, let him mark our prediction."

" And many false prophets shall arise, and deceive many" (Matt. 24 : 11). Amen. That is all that article is worth.

(*From the Monmouth Inquirer, Freehold, N. J.*)

LIEUTENANT FLIPPER.

" When Congress founded West Point, to be a training school for those who were to be paid as public servants and to wear the public livery, we do not think that it was intended that the institution should serve as a hotbed for the fostering of aristocratic prejudices and the assumption of aristocratic airs. Nor do we think that when Lincoln declared the negro a freeman, and entitled to a freeman's rights, either he or the nation designed that the dusky skin of the enfranchised slave should serve as an excuse for ignominy, torture, and disgrace. Yet here, this year, in the graduating class from West Point, steps a young man among his white-skinned fellows, fiftieth in a class of seventy-six members, whose four years of academic life have been one long martyrdom ; who has stood utterly alone, ignored and forsaken among his fellows ; who has had not one helping hand from professors or students to aid him in fighting his hard battle, and whom only his own talents and sturdy pluck have saved from entire oblivion. Yet in spite of all, he was graduated ; he has left twenty-six white students behind him ; he is a second lieutenant in the regular army, and the story of his struggles and his hard-won victory is known from Oregon to Florida. All honor to the first of his race who has stemmed the tide and won the prize.

" We do not think the faculty at West Point have done their duty in this matter. One word, one example from them, would have stopped the persecution, and it is to their disgrace that no such word was spoken and no such example set."

I have not a word to say against any of the professors or instructors who were at West Point during the period of my cadetship. I have every thing to say in their praise, and many things to be thankful for. I have felt perfectly free to go to any officer for assistance, whenever I have wanted it, because their conduct toward me made me feel that I would not be sent away without having received whatever help I may have wanted. All I could say of the professors and officers at the Academy would be unqualifiedly in their favor.

INDEX

IN THE BLACKS IN THE AMERICAN WEST SERIES